WHO'S
WHO

WHO'S WHO

A Book of Mormon Ready Reference

Hoyt W. Brewster Jr.

DESERET
BOOK

Salt Lake City, Utah

To the Who's Who of the
Hoyt W. and Naomi Smith Brewster Family:

Myrle Brewster Stoker
Barbara Brewster Amott
Karen Brewster McMillan
Anne Brewster Neeley
F. Craig Brewster
Judy Thiede Brewster
Donn R. Amott
Stephen E. Neeley
Laurie T. Brewster

Library of Congress Cataloging-in-Publication Data

Brewster, Hoyt W.
    Who's who : a book of Mormon ready reference / Hoyt W. Brewster, Jr.
       p. cm.
    Includes bibliographical references.
    ISBN 978-1-59038-755-9 (pbk.)
    1. Book of Mormon—Encyclopedias. 2. Book of Mormon—Biography. I. Title.
    BX8627.A1B74 2007
    289.3'220922—dc22   2007009327

Printed in the United States of America
Worzalla Publishing Co., Stevens Point, WI

10   9   8   7   6   5   4   3   2   1

— Introduction —

Both the serious and the more casual reader of the Book of Mormon will find this *Who's Who* helpful. The paperback format of this informative and user-friendly *Who's Who* makes it very portable. It can easily be slipped into a purse, backpack, or briefcase. It provides helpful and insightful information on 440 individuals and groups either named or indirectly referred to within the Book of Mormon. Using the system of superscriptions standardized in the Book of Mormon index (Lehi¹ and Lehi², for example), this *Who's Who* easily identifies which Nephi, Helaman, Noah, Shez, or Zoram is being referred to in the text.

This book can be used not only as a quick reference guide, but also as a very readable text that provides interesting insights into the lives of the people of the Book of Mormon. In an effort to "liken all scriptures unto us, that it might be for our profit and learning" (1 Nephi 19:23), life applications and lessons learned from the Book of Mormon people have been included where possible.

Every effort has been made to be accurate and true to the teachings of The Church of Jesus Christ of Latter-day Saints. If inadvertent mistakes have been made, I alone bear the responsibility for such. Although the focus of this *Who's Who* is on becoming acquainted with the identity *and* character of individuals and groups, my overriding purpose in writing this publication could be expressed by echoing the words of Nephi¹:

"For the fulness of mine intent is that I may persuade men to come unto the God of Abraham, and the God of Isaac, and the God of Jacob [Jesus Christ], and be saved" (1 Nephi 6:4).

A

AARON[1]

The brother of Moses is not mentioned by name in the Book of Mormon, but his calling as a "spokesman" for his brother-prophet is (2 Nephi 3:17; cf. Exodus 4:16; JST Genesis 50:35). He was the great priesthood leader after whom the Aaronic Priesthood was named (D&C 84:18; 107:1).

AARON[2]

The genealogy of Aaron[2] is identified by the prophet Ether (Ether 1:16). His grandfather Hearthom was a Jaredite king who was overthrown and imprisoned. While in captivity he begat his son Heth[2], who in turn begat Aaron[2], who lived in captivity his entire life (Ether 10:30–31).

AARON[3]

Aaron[3] was one of the renowned sons of Mosiah[2], who turned his life from one of rebellion and wickedness to one of sacrifice and service to the Lord (Mosiah 27). Aaron's change of heart was precipitated by chastisement from an angel of God, but the mighty change of heart required of one who is truly repentant came because of his desire to forsake evil and to serve the Lord with absolute commitment. Indeed, he and his brothers "could not bear that any human soul should perish" (Mosiah 28:3). Aaron[3] was exemplary in patience and long suffering in his missionary service; he endured severe conditions during imprisonment by those whose lives he was striving to bless through sharing the gospel (Alma 21:13–14; 20:29). He provided a classic model for teaching the gospel in the conversion of the father of the Lamanite King Lamoni (Alma 22). President Ezra Taft Benson (1899–1994) cited this model as an example of how to successfully teach "the 'great plan of the Eternal God'" (*Ensign,* January 2005, 26).

See also Ammon[2]; Himni; Mosiah[2], Sons of; Omner.

AARON[4]

Aaron[4] was a Lamanite king who lived around A.D. 330 and was a nemesis to Mormon[2] and his Nephite armies. In their initial conflict, the Lamanite army of 44,000 was defeated by the Nephite army of 42,000 (Mormon 2:9). About thirty years later, Aaron[4] sent an epistle to Mormon[2] in which he announced his intention to attack the Nephites.

Once more the Nephites were victorious, but they "began to boast" of their victory, which led to Mormon's temporary resignation as their military commander (Mormon 3:4–11). Mormon[2] later reconsidered and once again led the Nephites in their losing battles with the "awful brutality" of Aaron's army (Moroni 9:17).

ABEL

The martyred son of Adam and Eve is mentioned in the context of a description of the rampant growth of the infamous Gadianton band, whose secret oaths had their origin with the devil (Helaman 6:27). Abel's brother Cain entered into the first murderous conspiracy on this planet, depriving Abel not only of his life but of posterity as well (Moses 5:18–33). The Prophet Joseph Smith exclaimed, "Abel was slain for his righteousness" (*Teachings of the Prophet Joseph Smith*, 260).

ABINADI

Although no book within the Book of Mormon bears his name, the prophet Abinadi had a major impact on this ancient scriptural record. About 150 B.C., he appeared on the scene and began to preach repentance to the people in the colony of Zeniff (Mosiah 11:20). At that time they were ruled by the wicked King Noah[3], and the people seemed to have followed their king's example in pursuing wickedness. Abinadi prophesied that great afflictions would come upon them unless they repented.

Upon hearing of Abinadi's boldness, Noah[3] gave a Cain-like ("Who is the Lord that I should know him?" [Moses 5:16]) declaration: "Who is Abinadi," boasted the wicked ruler, "that I and my people should be judged of him, or who is the Lord, that shall bring upon my people such great affliction?" (Mosiah 11:27).

The hard-hearted people's response to the call to repentance was anger and a resolve to capture and kill this man of God (Mosiah 11:26–29). Abinadi was protected by the Lord and remained hidden for two years. He then reappeared, and with his typical boldness he courageously called the people to repentance once again. For His purposes, the Lord allowed Abinadi to be taken prisoner, leading to a series of confrontations between him and the wicked king and his priests. His strong sermon is a classic witness of Jesus Christ (Mosiah 12–16).

Abinadi stood firm in the face of threats, for "he answered them boldly, and withstood all their questions . . . and did confound them in all their words" (Mosiah 12:19). He was totally committed to completing his assignment. "I finish my message," he said, "and then it matters not whither

I go" (Mosiah 13:9). Indeed, when threatened with death unless he recanted his testimony, he declared, "I will suffer even until death, and I will not recall my words" (Mosiah 17:10). True to his testimony, as the flames began to consume his flesh, Abinadi continued to preach until his life was gone.

Abinadi's brief ministry was not fruitless, for he touched the heart of one of Noah's priests, a man named Alma[1] (Mosiah 17:1–5). He became a mighty prophet himself, as did his namesake son, and their posterity became the keepers of the sacred records.

ABINADOM

The son of Chemish, Abinadom is one of five historians who contributed to the small book of Omni (Omni 1:10–11). He provides an insight as to why so little was written at that time (between 279 and 130 B.C.): "I know of no revelation save that which has been written, neither prophecy; wherefore, that which is sufficient is written" (Omni 1:11).

How tragic to declare that the heavens were closed—at least to Abinadom! Perhaps the prophet-recorder Mormon[2] had Abinadom's words in mind when, centuries later, he chided those who deny further revelations of God, who say "they are done away, that there are no revela-tions, nor prophecies" (Mormon 9:7–10).

One thing is clear: revelation is limited by our worthiness and by our desire to receive additional light and knowledge. President Spencer W. Kimball (1895–1985) taught: "Since Adam and Eve were placed in the garden the Lord has been eager—eager to reveal truth and right to His people. There have been many times when man would not listen, and, of course, where there is no ear, there is no voice" (*Ensign,* November 1976, 111).

"It is the sad truth that if prophets and people are unreachable, the Lord generally does nothing for them. . . . The Lord will not force himself upon people, and if they do not believe, they will receive no revelation" (*Ensign,* May 1977, 76–77).

ABISH

Abish was a Lamanite woman who was "converted unto the Lord" (Alma 19:16) through an earlier, unrecorded vision which her unnamed father had. She was a servant of King Lamoni and was present when the king, his wife, other servants, and the missionary Ammon[2] all fell into a spiritual state or trance where they appeared lifeless. Thinking this was a prime opportunity to prompt the people to believe in the power of the true and living God and in the truthfulness of the message being preached by His servant Ammon², Abish enjoined her fellow citizens to gather at the king's residence (Alma 19:12–18).

Rather than being converted by the sight of those who were lying upon the floor, the people began to contend with one another. Some claimed this was evidence that Ammon² had brought evil upon them, while others testified of his spiritual power. One among them even sought to kill Ammon², but he was struck down by the Lord. The contention continued so sharply that Abish stepped forward to change the course of the debate.

Undoubtedly inspired by the Spirit, she took the queen's seemingly lifeless hand in hers and raised her up. The queen expressed her joy in her newfound faith and then took the king by his hand and raised him up. Seeing the contention among his people, the king immediately began to testify of his experience, as did Ammon² and the fallen servants of the king as each rose to his feet (Alma 19:19–33).

Perhaps it might have been said of Abish as it was of the Old Testament Queen Esther, "who knoweth whether thou [wast] come to the kingdom for such a time as this?" (Esther 4:14).

ABRAHAM

The great patriarch known as "the father of the faithful" (D&C 138:41) had his given name of *Abram* changed by the Lord to *Abraham,* signifying "father of many nations" (Genesis 17:5). He is the revered father of two diverse nations of people: the Arab world through his son Ishmael (Genesis 16:15) and the people of Israel, which includes the people of the Book of Mormon, through his son Isaac (Genesis 21:1–3).

While Abraham's life is not recorded in the Book of Mormon, his patriarchal and pivotal position in God's grand plan is an important thread that is intertwined throughout this second witness of Jesus Christ; for "if ye be Christ's, then are ye Abraham's seed, and heirs according to the promise" (Galatians 3:29). Indeed, as Lehi¹ and Nephi¹ both taught, the Lord's covenant with Abraham was that "in [his] seed shall *all* the kindreds of the earth be blessed" (1 Nephi 15:18; 22:9; emphasis added). The resurrected Savior reminded the ancient inhabitants of America of this promise during His visit to them. It is significant that He taught these descendants of Abraham they would be blessed as they turned from their iniquities (3 Nephi 20:25–27). As people turn from sin to Christ, He will gather them safely in His sheepfold.

Father Abraham was among the holy prophets who foresaw the coming of Christ "and was filled with gladness and did rejoice" (Helaman 8:17–18). The prophet Jacob[2] refers to the similitude between Abraham's willingness to offer his covenant son, Isaac, on the altar of sacrifice to that of the great Elohim's sacrifice of His Only Begotten Son in Gethsemane's furnace of affliction and on Golgotha's hill of crucifixion (Jacob 4:5). Abraham is a grand model of faith and obedience under all conditions. "And he believed in the Lord, and he counted it to him for righteousness" (Genesis 15:6). As a result of his faithfulness, Abraham has received his exaltation and now sits on a throne as a god (D&C 132:37).

ADAM

The first man created on earth and father of the human race, Adam was known in the premortal existence as Michael, the archangel (D&C 107:54). President Joseph Fielding Smith (1876–1972) bore testimony of Adam's preeminent position in the plan of salvation: *"Adam was placed here, not a wild, half-civilized savage, but a perfectly-developed man, with wonderful intelligence, for he helped to create this earth. He was chosen in pre-existence to be the first man upon the earth and the father of the human race. . . . The Lord did not choose a being that had just developed from the lower forms of life, to be a prince, an archangel, to preside over the human race forever! Adam, as Michael, was one of the greatest intelligences in the spirit world and he stands next to Jesus Christ"* (Doctrines of Salvation, 1:94–95; emphasis in original).

Father Lehi[1] clearly described Adam and Eve's role in making it possible for Heavenly Father's spirit children to come to earth and receive mortal bodies (2 Nephi 2:18–25). And because of the foreordained Fall, the foreordained Atonement was possible, which opened the way for mortals to repent, to be redeemed from death, and to return to our Father's presence (Helaman 14:15–18; Mormon 9:11–13).

Under the direction of the Savior, Adam presides over the human family and all angels who minister to this earth (Smith, *History of the Church*, 3:385–86; 4:207–8). Prior to the Second Coming, Adam will receive a stewardship accounting of all who have held keys of priesthood authority during the history of this earth (*Teachings of the Prophet Joseph Smith*, 157; D&C 116; Daniel 7:9–14).

In his role as mighty Michael, Adam led the forces of God to victory over the rebellious Lucifer and his forces of perdition in the premortal war in heaven (Revelation 12:7–9). At the end of the Millennium, Adam will once again lead the forces of good to a final victory over the forces of evil (D&C 88:110–15).

AHA

A son of Zoram², who was the chief captain of the Nephite armies around 81 B.C., Aha and his brother Lehi² served under their father's command (Alma 16:5). With the divine intervention provided by the prophet Alma², they were successful in routing their enemies in a battle that freed the Nephite prisoners (Alma 16:6–8).

AHAH

The son of Seth², and the father of Ethem, Ahah was one of the kings who ruled in the ancient Jaredite civilization (Ether 1:9–10). Unfortunately, his reign was marred by much iniquity on his part and "the shedding of much blood" (Ether 11:10).

AHAZ

This king of Judah, the southern kingdom of Israel, lived during the days of the prophet Isaiah¹. He is mentioned in the writings Nephi¹ copied from the plates of brass (2 Nephi 17:1, 3, 10, 12). Isaiah¹ warned King Ahaz about entering into an alliance with another country and counseled him to rely upon the protection of the God of Israel. In a wonderful and well-known Messianic prophecy that was intended to be a sign of His protection for Judah, the Lord foretold the future birth of the Messiah through the house of David (2 Nephi 17:14).

Sadly, Ahaz rejected the divine counsel, and the kingdom of Judah suffered the tragic "consequences that could have been avoided. The people are oppressed, scattered, and taken into slavery. The once-fertile lands are left barren of crops and become useful only for wandering animals" (Brewster, *Isaiah Plain & Simple*, 62).

Ahaz's reign (735–715 B.C.) was marked by wickedness. "He walked in the [wicked] way of the kings of Israel, yea, and made his son to pass through the fire, according to the abominations of the heathen, whom the Lord cast out from before the children of Israel. And he sacrificed and burnt incense in the high places [places of idolatrous worship]" (2 Kings 16:3-4).

AKISH

Among the most evil individuals mentioned in the Book of Mormon is the Jaredite King Akish. His life reached a pivotal point when he was seduced by the wiles of the wicked daughter of Jared². Perhaps he had already started his descent down the dark path prior to being ensnared in her murderous plot to kill her grandfather, King Omer. But when her provocative dancing enticed him to agree to enter into the secret conspiracy, his descent into darkness accelerated (Ether 8:8–11).

To satisfy his carnal lusting, Akish agreed to betray and murder one who had been his friend. Had Akish simply feigned friendship with the Jaredite King Omer for some selfish gain, or had he been a true friend? The answer is not known, for the record simply states that "Omer was a friend to Akish" (Ether 8:11).

Immediately upon agreeing to carry out the murderous deed, "Akish gathered in unto the house of Jared all his kinsfolk. . . . And Akish did administer unto them the oaths which were given by them of old who also sought power, which had been handed down even from Cain" (Ether 8:13, 15). In short, Akish and his co-conspirators entered into a league with the devil.

Because of the Lord's intervention, Akish did not succeed in his plot to behead King Omer. He did, however, marry the daughter of Jared[2], who was anointed king when Omer fled. Akish's lust for power led him to conspire to have his father-in-law beheaded so that he could then occupy the throne (Ether 9:5–6). The cruelty of Akish knew no bounds, for he became "jealous of his son, therefore he shut him up in prison and kept him upon little or no food until he had suffered death" (Ether 9:7).

Akish taught his children "all manner of iniquity," leaving them little opportunity to make right choices (Ether 9:10). Seeking their own position of power, the sons of Akish organized a rebellion against their father and the ensuing war "lasted for the space of many years," leading to "the destruction of nearly all the people" (Ether 9:11–12). Surely this sad story is a classic example of "the sins of the fathers being visited upon the children" (Exodus 20:5).

ALMA[1] (also known as Alma the Elder)

Alma[1] was a Nephite prophet who lived around 173–91 B.C. and who with divine authority (Mosiah 18:13, 18) founded the Church of Christ in his dispensation. Alma[1] the Elder served as one of the priests of the wicked King Noah[3]. He was converted to the gospel of Jesus Christ through the powerful preaching of the prophet-martyr Abinadi (Mosiah 17). Alma[1] knew that it was critically important that he act on his newfound belief (Mosiah 17:2; 18:1). It is not sufficient for one to merely *receive* a witness of truth; it must be *acted upon* and *incorporated* into one's life. Alma[1] believed, exercised faith, and, as a result, experienced a "mighty change" in his heart (Alma 5:11–12).

Following his expulsion from the court of King Noah[3], Alma[1] secretly baptized and organized his followers before they had to flee into the wilderness to escape the king's wrath

(Mosiah 18). The small band of believers established their own righteous community, where they lived a short time in peace before being brought into bondage by a treacherous Lamanite army that had been joined by the wicked priests of King Noah[3]. The priests, led by their leader Amulon, were placed as taskmasters over Alma's colony (Mosiah 23).

When the believers prayed to God for relief, Amulon placed them under a penalty of death if they were caught praying (Mosiah 23:8–11). However, he could not prevent the faithful people from praying in their hearts, and God made their burdens bearable, ultimately delivering them from their bondage (Mosiah 23:12–25).

Prayer proved to be pivotal on another occasion. Alma's son and namesake took the path of rebellion for a time, "causing much dissension among the people" (Mosiah 27:8–9). The father never gave up on his son and "prayed with much faith" that the young man would have a change of heart (Mosiah 27:14). As a result, a messenger from God appeared to Alma[2] the Younger and called him to repentance.

Certainly the prayers of every parent are not answered by angels from heaven. But caring mortals, inspired by the promptings of the Spirit, can *become messengers from God* in reaching out to the wayward, the wandering, and the needy.

"God does notice us, and he watches over us," declared President Spencer W. Kimball (1895–1985). "But it is usually through another person that he meets our needs" (*New Era,* September 1974, 5).

ALMA[2] (Also known as Alma the Younger)

If ever there was an example of an absolute turnabout in one's life, it is found in Alma[2] the Younger. This contrary and rebellious son of the Nephite's chief high priest was "a very wicked and an idolatrous man" who sought to "destroy the church of God" (Mosiah 27:8–10). But like his counterpart on another continent, Paul the Apostle, who also "persecuted the church of God" (1 Corinthians 15:9), Alma[2] the Younger became a powerful preacher of righteousness and a force for good.

Young Alma's life was significantly changed when an angel from the Lord appeared to him and his fellow rebels, calling them to repentance (Mosiah 27:11–17). While the angel's appearance was a highly motivating factor in turning the lives of Alma[2] and his fellow rebels around, it was not sufficient to bring about the "mighty change of heart" that is necessary to true conversion. There have been others throughout history who have been called to repentance by heavenly messengers, most notably Laman[1] and Lemuel, whose repentance was short-lived.

Alma's conversion was permanent because he paid the price. As he later described the strength of his personal testimony, he said: "I do know that these things whereof I have spoken are true. And how do ye suppose that I know of their surety?

"Behold, I say unto you they are made known unto me by the Holy Spirit of God. Behold, *I have fasted and prayed many days that I might know these things of myself*" (Alma 5:45–46; emphasis added).

Alma[1] the Elder selected his namesake son to succeed him as high priest of the Church. The younger Alma[2] was also chosen by the people to be the first chief judge under their new form of government. His qualifications for both positions are suggested in the following description of his performance:

"Alma did walk in the ways of the Lord, and he did keep his commandments, and he did judge righteous judgments" (Mosiah 29:42–43).

During Alma's eight years as chief judge, he successfully kept the government safe against the uprising of rebels who sought to destroy it (Alma 2–3). Unfortunately, in a relatively short time, many of the people began to neglect their covenants and to turn to wickedness. As a result, Alma[2] determined that his time and energy could most effectively be used full-time in his spiritual ministry. Thus, he resigned his political position and selected "a wise man" named Nephihah to take his place as the chief judge, "according to the voice of the people." He did this in order to devote himself fully to his ecclesiastical calling, "seeing no way that he might reclaim [the people] save it were in bearing down in pure testimony against them" (Alma 4:15–20).

The sacrifice in personal popularity which Alma[2] made in resigning his political position was soon very evident in the rude manner in which he was treated by the citizens of the city of Ammonihah. "Behold, we know that thou art Alma; and we know that thou art high priest over the church which thou hast established," they said. "And now we know that because we are not of thy church we know that thou hast no power over us." They then "reviled him, and spit upon him, and caused that he should be cast out of their city" (Alma 8:10–13).

Discouraged and "weighed down with sorrow, wading through much tribulation and anguish of soul, because of the wickedness of the people" and, obviously, because of his rude rejection, he trudged dejectedly down the road. Suddenly, an angel of the

Lord appeared and cheerfully greeted him: "Blessed art thou, Alma" (Alma 8:14–15).

One of lesser faith might have been tempted to say, "Did I hear you correctly? Do you know what I have just been through?" Yet Alma² humbly listened as the angel commended his faithfulness. Then came the test: "Return to the city of Ammonihah, and preach again unto the people," said the angel. Alma² did not waver, but "he returned speedily . . . by another way" and found the man prepared to hear his message—his future missionary companion, Amulek (Alma 8:16–32).

What might have been the consequences to Amulek and his family, and to many others, if Alma² had allowed his discouragement to prevent him from trying one more time? And consider the marvelous teachings of which we would have been deprived had the inspired sermons of Alma² and Amulek not been part of the Book of Mormon!

These missionary companions faced a great trial when they were forced to watch the martyrdoms of the faithful men, women, and children who refused to deny God and His words. Being newer to the ministry, and perhaps less susceptible to the promptings of the Spirit, Amulek asked why they did not step forward with the "power of God" and save the martyrs. Alma's simple response was: "The Spirit constraineth me that I must not stretch forth mine hand; for behold the Lord receiveth them up unto himself" (Alma 14:8–11).

Sometimes inspired men and women of God are called upon to suffer, even severely, for their beliefs. But, as the Lord reminded the Prophet Joseph Smith during a time of suffering, "adversity and . . . afflictions [in mortality] shall be but a small moment; and then, if thou endure it well, God shall exalt thee on high" (D&C 121:7–8).

Another element of Alma's experience at the site of the martyrdoms was his willingness to die for Christ and His gospel. When Amulek expressed the fear that they might also be burned, Alma² expressed both commitment and faith in his classic response: "Be it according to the will of the Lord" (Alma 14:12–13).

His burning desire to share the gospel with everyone was expressed in his wish to have the voice of an angel and "speak with the trump of God, with a voice to shake the earth, and cry repentance unto every people" (Alma 29:1). However, as he pondered this wish he finally concluded: "I ought to be content with the things which the Lord hath allotted unto me" (Alma 29:1–3). This conclusion has great application for any who are in the service of the Lord. Elder

Neal A. Maxwell (1926–2004) taught that the true servant of Christ "will resonate, at times, with the hymnal words, 'More used would I be' (*Hymns*, no. 114), but he realizes that he must 'be content with the things which the Lord hath allotted'" (*Ensign*, May 1975, 102).

Alma's powerful ministry was concluded when "he was taken up by the Spirit, or buried by the hand of the Lord, even as Moses" (Alma 45:19).

AMALEKI[1]

This record keeper was the concluding contributor to the small plates of Nephi, which were kept from 600 B.C. to about 130 B.C. Amaleki[1] was the son of Abinadom and fortunately recorded more than the two verses written by his father (Omni 1:10–12). Amaleki's writings include the only account of the ministry of King Mosiah[1] (Omni 1:12–23). He also recorded the discovery of the people of Zarahemla (commonly referred to as the Mulekites) and their joining with the Nephites under King Mosiah[1] (Omni 1:14–19). Furthermore, Amaleki's record mentions Coriantumr[2], the last survivor of the extinct Jaredite nation (Omni 1:20–21).

Having "no seed," Amaleki[1] passed the small plates to King Benjamin, who then combined the record keeping of the Nephite's secular history, which the kings had kept, with that of the sacred history, which the prophets had generally kept. The resulting record was known as the large plates of Nephi (Omni 1:24–25). Amaleki[1] concluded his record with an appropriate plea for people to "come unto Christ" (Omni 1:26).

AMALEKI[2]

The single mention of Amaleki[2] is in conjunction with an expedition of sixteen men sent to the land of Nephi by King Mosiah[2]. Some years earlier, a "considerable number" of people had left the main body of the Nephites located in Zarahemla to once again inhabit the lands of their forefathers (Omni 1:27–30; Mosiah 7:1–2). King Mosiah's expedition was charged with finding the earlier group. After wandering for forty days, the expedition camped on a hill while their leader, Ammon[1], took Amaleki[2] and two other men to explore further (Mosiah 7:6). They were successful in finding the sought-after colony, which was then led by King Limhi, a grandson of the original founder, Zeniff. After an initial misunderstanding, the foursome was welcomed and eventually led the colony back to the land of Zarahemla (Mosiah 7:5–9; 22:11–14).

See also Ammon[1]; Helem; Hem.

AMALEKITES

The founder of this group of Nephite apostates is not recorded in Mormon's abridgement of the original historical record. However, traditionally the original leader would have been someone named Amaleki. Satan had "great hold on the hearts of the Amalekites" (Alma 27:12). They were consumed with hatred toward those who sought to serve God and live righteously. The Amalekites were foremost in killing the faithful Anti-Nephi-Lehies (Alma 24:28) and "were of a more wicked and murderous disposition than the Lamanites" (Alma 43:6). The efforts of missionaries to reclaim these advocates of evil were nonproductive (Alma 23:14; 24:29).

"And thus we can plainly discern, that after a people have been once enlightened by the Spirit of God, and have had great knowledge of things pertaining to righteousness, and then have fallen away into sin and transgression, they become more hardened, and thus their state becomes worse than though they had never known these things" (Alma 24:30).

Note that the name Amalekites is also found throughout the Old Testament and refers to an Arab tribe that was in constant conflict with the Israelites.

AMALICKIAH

While the names of Gadianton and Kishkumen stand foremost among the nefarious tyrants of Book of Mormon history, certainly the name of Amalickiah must be included among the most wicked of men.

About 73 B.C. there was a great dissension among the Nephites that became so bitter that some sought to kill Helaman[2] and other leaders of the Church of Christ (Alma 45:23–24; 46:1–2). Their leader "was a large and a strong man; and his name was Amalickiah" (Alma 46:3). It is evident from the ensuing tragic events that this man was not just *physically strong,* but he also had an extremely *strong-willed,* but very wicked, spirit.

We do not know the background that brought him to a position of leadership, but certainly his life had been filled with wrong choices that molded his dark disposition. Amalickiah wanted to be king, and he was so adept at deception and flattery that even members of the Church apostatized, turning from light to darkness, in order to follow him (Alma 46:4–7).

His army of rebels was initially defeated by Captain Moroni[1], but Amalickiah escaped and joined forces with the Lamanites, where he succeeded in stirring them up to anger against the Nephites. Through a series of treacherous acts, murdering those in authority over him, he became the king of the Lamanites (Alma 47).

The traitors and dissenters from the Nephites who joined Amalickiah in his wickedness "became more hardened and impenitent, and more wild, wicked and ferocious than the Lamanites . . . , entirely forgetting the Lord their God" (Alma 47:36).

The depth of the darkness into which Amalickiah had plunged is illustrated in his cursing God and vowing to drink the blood of the righteous Captain Moroni[1] (Alma 59:27). Amalickiah was finally slain and went to his reward in hell (Alma 51:33–34; 54:7).

The impact of Amalickiah in placing the people in "exceedingly precarious and dangerous" circumstances (Alma 46:7) is summed up in this classic statement: "We . . . see the great wickedness one very wicked man can cause to take place among the children of men" (Alma 46:9).

AMALICKIAHITES

The followers of the wicked Nephite dissenter Amalickiah took upon themselves the name of Amalickiahites (Alma 46:28). They joined their despot leader in his conspiracy to overthrow the duly elected Nephite government and crown him king (Alma 46:1–10). Captain Moroni[1] was successful in putting down their rebellion (Alma 46:11–35).

AMARON

The son of Omni, Amaron was one of five historians who contributed

to the small book that bears his father's name (Omni 1:1–4). He lived about 279 B.C. at a time when "the more wicked part of the Nephites were destroyed" and the righteous were spared (Omni 1:5–7; cf. Jarom 1:10).

AMGID

Amgid was among the many kings who ruled during the Jaredite civilization. His mention is brief, with a single verse indicating that at the time of his reign the kingdom was divided and he was eventually defeated by his rival Com[2] (Ether 10:32).

AMINADAB

The man Aminadab is introduced as "a Nephite by birth, who had once belonged to the church of God but had dissented from them" (Helaman 5:35). At some earlier point in his life, Aminadab had lost his faith. We are not told whether this loss occurred because of serious transgression, through simple neglect on his part, or by being offended by someone in the Church. We only know that he apostatized.

He joined the Lamanites and was among those who imprisoned the missionary duo of Nephi[2] and Lehi[4] about 30 B.C. Aminadab's group later went to the prison to kill these servants of the Lord, but they were prevented from reaching the missionaries by a circle of fire that protected the marvelous twosome (Helaman 5:20–25).

Following the fire, a "cloud of darkness, and an awful solemn fear came upon [the persecutors]" (Helaman 5:28). A voice from heaven called them to repentance. Aminadab "turned him about" (does this have implications of *repenting* as well as a change in *physical* position?) and saw the glowing faces of Nephi[2] and Lehi[4] as they conversed with heaven (Helaman 5:36).

Aminadab called upon his associates to also turn and look, whereupon they asked him: "What shall we do, that this cloud of darkness may be removed from overshadowing us?" Reaching back into his neglected memory of gospel teachings, this dissenter answered that they must "repent, and cry unto the voice, even until ye shall have faith in Christ" (Helaman 5:37–41).

The cloud of darkness—speaking *physically* and *spiritually*—was dispersed, and the hearts of these would-be murderers and former persecutors of the Lord's servants were changed (Helaman 5:42–50).

The *reconversion* of Aminadab is illustrative of the principle that none should ever be cast aside and forgotten, regardless of how deep their dissent from truth has become. The Atonement of Christ teaches that there is always hope of reclamation.

AMINADI

Aminadi was one of the ancestors of the great missionary Amulek and was himself a descendant of Joseph[1], the great seer who was sold by his brothers into slavery (Alma 10:2–3). Aminadi had a marvelous spiritual experience that is not elaborated on in the current record abridged by the prophet-historian Mormon[2]. This experience consisted of interpreting "the writing which was upon the wall of the temple, which was written by the finger of God" (Alma 10:2). As with other special sacred experiences enjoyed by Saints throughout the ages, the Lord may have restricted the recording of what fully occurred on this special occasion, saving it for some future opportunity when people are spiritually prepared to receive it.

AMLICI

Around 87 B.C., Amlici, described as a "very cunning man" (Alma 2:1), led a contentious rebellion against the newly formed Nephite government of judges. It appears that Amlici was very glib of tongue and perhaps very charismatic, for "by his cunning [he had] drawn away much people after him" and they sought to have him become their king (Alma 2:2). The proposition was put to a vote of the Nephite nation, and Amlici, whom the majority of the people recognized as a "wicked man," was rejected.

Rather than patriotically accepting defeat, he stirred up the feelings of his rabid followers, and they secretly consecrated him to be their king. Not content with his illegally obtained title, he led his traitorous followers in an armed rebellion against the duly elected government. He sought to force all the citizens to live in subjection to him (Alma 2:7–9).

Multiple battles were fought between Amlici's followers (called Amlicites) and the Nephites, who were led by Alma² the Younger. In face-to-face combat between Alma² and Amlici, the prayer of the righteous Alma² prevailed and Amlici was slain (Alma 2:29–31).

Although ultimately defeated, Amlici's treachery caused the deaths of so many people that they "were not numbered, because of the greatness of their number" (Alma 3:1).

The self-centered nature of wicked souls does not allow for concern about the casualties caused by their course of action. Amlici's prideful and rebellious choice not only caused much suffering in mortality, but it has continued its effects upon him and his miscreant followers in the hereafter as they pay the price for their willful wickedness.

AMLICITES

This group of misguided and rebellious people followed the Nephite traitor Amlici in his plot to overthrow the government and become king (Alma 2:1–11). The dissenters were defeated in their initial attack upon the Nephites but then joined forces with a Lamanite army and renewed their assault (Alma 2:14–25). The Nephites were victorious in the ensuing battle, having been "strengthened by the hand of the Lord, having prayed mightily to him that he would deliver them out of the hands of their enemies" (Alma 2:28).

What a lesson for any who are oppressed or who feel overwhelmed by some daunting task! Pray mightily for the help of the Lord, and He will either help you resolve the problem or give you strength to bear up under the burden.

AMMAH

A missionary companion of Aaron³, Ammah was one of three who were imprisoned and "suffered many things" at the hands of those whom they sought to teach (Alma 20:2; 21:11–14). His suffering was such that his skin became "worn exceedingly because of being bound with strong cords" and he "suffered hunger, thirst, and all kinds of afflictions." Nevertheless, he was "patient in all [his] sufferings" (Alma 20:29). He was finally freed through the intervention of the converted Lamanite King Lamoni. While no further mention is made of Ammah in the present record, it is assumed he continued his missionary efforts.

AMMARON

While not considered a major figure in the Book of Mormon, Ammaron certainly made a significant contribution to that sacred record. He was the one who discerned the spiritual capacity of a ten-year-old boy named Mormon[2] and entrusted him with the responsibility of caring for the plates from which this second witness of Jesus Christ was translated (Mormon 1:1–4). Prior to hiding the plates and entrusting them to Mormon's care, Ammaron was the last in a succession of record keepers that had spanned nearly a millennium (4 Nephi 1:47–48).

AMMON[1]

About 121 B.C., Ammon[1] was appointed by King Mosiah[1] to lead an expedition from the land of Zarahemla to the land of Lehi-Nephi in search of a Nephite colony that had previously departed under the leadership of Zeniff (Omni 1:27–30; Mosiah 7:1–3). Ammon[1] is described as "a strong and mighty man."

Upon discovering the colony established by Zeniff and now ruled by King Limhi, Ammon[1] and three companions were temporarily imprisoned until their true identity was discovered. He and his fellow travelers were then warmly welcomed (Mosiah 7:4–16). At the time of their discovery by Ammon[1], the people of the colony of Zeniff were in bondage to the Lamanites. With Ammon's help, they were able to escape and rejoin the people in the land of Zarahemla (Mosiah 22).

See also Amaleki[2]; Helem; Hem.

AMMON[2]

Ammon[2] is first mentioned by name as one of the four sons of Mosiah[2] (Mosiah 27:34). He and his brothers had joined Alma[2] the Younger in a rampage of rebellion against their righteous fathers and the Church of Christ (Mosiah 27:8–9). While engaged in their rebellious activities, they were visited by an angel of the Lord, who rebuked them and called them to repentance (Mosiah 27:10–17). The wake-up call was heard, and Ammon[2] and his brothers joined Alma[2] in turning their lives around and "zealously striving to repair all the injuries which they had done to the church" (Mosiah 27:32–37).

The four sons of Mosiah[2] were so changed that they eschewed their former friends, who "laughed [them] to scorn" (Alma 26:23), and commenced a more than fourteen-year mission among the Lamanites, with Ammon² taking the lead (Alma 17:4, 18).

Like his brothers and fellow missionaries, Ammon² went forth, "trusting in the Lord," among a "wild and a hardened and a ferocious people" (Alma 17:13–14). As soon as he arrived in an area known as the land of Ishmael, he was captured by the Lamanites and taken bound before their king. As was the custom with all captured Nephites, it was then "left to the pleasure of the king to slay them, or to retain them in captivity [presumably as slaves], or to cast them into prison, or to cast them out of his land, according to his will and pleasure" (Alma 17:20). In other words, the captured Nephite's fate rested upon the disposition of the king on that particular day—and none of the options sound very pleasant.

Ammon² undoubtedly impressed the king, whose name was Lamoni, for he asked if Ammon² wanted to stay among the Lamanites. Ammon's affirmative reply so pleased the king that he offered one of his daughters as a wife to this captive Nephite. The missionary refused this offer but instead volunteered to be a servant to the king. It may be that this refusal was displeasing to the king, because he placed Ammon² in an assignment that was life-threatening.

Ammon² joined other servants charged with watching over the king's flocks at the water of Sebus. Unfortunately, if the flocks became scattered and lost (an all-too-common prospect), the king had the assigned shepherds killed. While Ammon² was assisting in caring for the flocks, a trouble-making group did indeed scatter the flocks of King Lamoni. This incident proved providential for this faithful missionary.

Ammon's fellow shepherds immediately "began to murmur, saying: Now the king will slay us, as he has our brethren because their flocks were scattered by the wickedness of these men" (Alma 17:28). In other words, they threw up their hands in despair and resigned themselves to their seeming inevitable fate of death.

Here is where Ammon² displayed his faith, wisdom, and courage. He implemented a plan of action that is a good model for one who seems to be faced with an insurmountable problem. His first action was to try to change the attitude of his distraught companions, encouraging them to cast aside their gloom and to "be of good cheer." He next invited them to take remedial action: "Let us go in search of the flocks, and we will gather them together and bring them back" (Alma 17:31).

After Ammon² and his fellow servants went to gather the flocks, they faced another challenge from the troublemakers, who prepared to once again scatter the flocks. Ammon², the man of action, took charge. He had his companions encircle the flocks, preventing them from being scattered, and then he stood up against those who were intent on scattering the flocks. The end result was that his courage and faith prevailed in the fight and the flocks remained protected (Alma 17:33–39).

Ammon's *humility* is next displayed. He did not march at the head of the servants, who carried the severed arms of the troublemakers to the king. He sought no glory for his faithful service. Rather, he quietly went about the next task which had been assigned to him, which was feeding the king's horses. "Surely," exclaimed the king, "there has not been any servant among all my servants that has been so faithful as this man; for even *he doth remember all my commandments to execute them*" (Alma 18:8–10; emphasis added).

What a wonderful lesson in diligence!

The charitable and pure nature of Ammon's heart continued to be displayed as he later saved King Lamoni from the threatening sword of his angry father. Ammon² turned down an offer of wealth and position for himself in order to provide protection for Lamoni and for his imprisoned fellow missionaries. Lamoni's father

was so impressed that his heart was softened and he desired to learn of Ammon's gospel message (Alma 20:8–27).

While Ammon² was later honored when the converted Lamanites took upon themselves the name "the people of Ammon" (Alma 27:26), his focus was always on serving the Lord and pointing the people's loyalties in that same direction.

"I do not boast in my own strength, nor in my own wisdom," Ammon² declared; "but behold, my joy is full, yea, my heart is brim with joy, and I will rejoice in my God.

"Yea, I know that I am nothing; as to my strength I am weak; therefore I will not boast of myself, but I will boast of my God, for in his strength I can do all things" (Alma 26:11–12).

See also Aaron³; Anti-Nephi-Lehies; Himni; Mosiah², Sons of; Omner.

AMMON, CHILDREN OF

The writings of Isaiah recorded in the Book of Mormon make mention of the children of Ammon (2 Nephi 21:14; Isaiah 11:14). These people were descendants of Abraham's nephew Lot and historically were at odds with the Israelites (Brewster, *Isaiah Plain & Simple*, 117–18).

AMMON², PEOPLE OF

See Anti-Nephi-Lehies.

AMMONIHAH, CITIZENS OF

The citizens of Ammonihah, who are identified as residents of either the *city* or the *land* of Ammonihah, will be discussed as two separate groups: (1) the wicked citizens and (2) the faithful martyrs.

1. *The wicked citizens.* It appears that the vast majority of the citizens of Ammonihah "were of the profession of Nehor, and did not believe in the repentance of their sins" (Alma 15:15). They lived for the pleasure of the moment, and in their wickedness they did not believe any penalty would be extracted for such sins. Indeed, "Satan had gotten great hold upon the hearts of the people of the city of Ammonihah" (Alma 8:9).

The Lord provided the wicked citizens of Ammonihah several chances to repent. However, they rejected each such opportunity and reviled the messengers of God who were sent to call them to repentance (Alma 8:9–13; 9:1–6; 14:6–8). Alma² and Amulek were imprisoned, mocked, and abused. The chief judge, together with the wicked lawyers, priests, and teachers who taunted these holy men, was slain when the Lord destroyed the prison in which the missionaries were held captive (Alma 14:18–29).

When warned of their impending doom if they did not repent, the haughty citizens of Ammonihah replied that their great city could not be destroyed. Yet the words of God and His prophets do not fail, and it was destroyed in one day (Alma 16:9–11).

2. *The faithful martyrs.* Alma² and Amulek did have some success in Ammonihah. Because of the power of their testimonies, those of humble heart believed, repented, and began to search the scriptures (Alma 14:1).

The "more part" of the people of Ammonihah continued in their wickedness. In fact, they were so steeped in sin that they began to persecute those who believed in the testimonies of Alma² and Amulek. Some were cast out and stoned, but a large number were forced into the martyr's fire, along with their scriptural records (Alma 14:2, 7–8).

Alma² provided an answer as to why the Lord did not intervene. He said the Lord received the martyrs into His presence, following their terrible, yet brief, suffering. He allowed the martyrdoms that "the blood of the innocent shall stand as a witness against [their murderers] . . . at the last day" (Alma 14:10–11).

See also Ammonihahites.

AMMONIHAHITES

The single reference to the wicked citizens of the city and land of Ammonihah as Ammonihahites is found in Alma 16:9. The citation tragically states that "every living soul of the Ammonihahites was destroyed, and also their great city, which they said God could not destroy, because of its greatness."

See also Ammonihah, Citizens of.

AMMORON

Following the death of the treacherous Amalickiah, his brother Ammoron became his successor as king and leader of the Lamanite armies (Alma 52:3). Although he is not mentioned in earlier descriptions of the ruthless exploits of his wicked brother, the later record clearly shows that Ammoron walked the same evil path.

One wonders what there was in the nurturing years of these two evil brothers that turned them to their wicked ways. Was there a singular turning point, or did they neglect spiritual sustenance so often that the seduction of sin became overpowering to them? In any event, there is no question that their bad choices continually compounded into more and more wickedness and war.

The lying nature of the hypocritical Ammoron was displayed in his communications to Captain Moroni[1]. He justified his war of aggression on the old lie that the Lamanite people (which now included the apostate Nephites) had been robbed of their "right" to govern all the people (Alma 54:17–18, 23–24). His premise was a lie, for "Ammoron had a perfect knowledge of his fraud" (Alma 55:1). And so it is with all wicked men and women. They seek to justify immoral and unrighteous actions, publicly denying wrongdoing, yet inwardly knowing the truth.

The war waged by Ammoron took a terrible toll in bloodshed, famine, and suffering (Alma 62:35). His mortal life ended on the point of a javelin (Alma 62:36), and most assuredly he joined his ungodly brother where a more severe penalty than mortal death would be paid.

AMNIGADDAH

Identified as a Jaredite king in the Book of Mormon index, Amnigaddah was the son of Aaron[2] and the father of Coriantum[2] (Ether 1:14–15). His great-grandfather King Hearthom was taken into captivity, a captivity that lasted through the next four generations, finally being broken in the fifth when Amnigaddah's grandson Com[2] regained freedom and royal power (Ether 10:30–32).

AMNOR[1]

As distinguished from Amnor[2], which was a Nephite coin (Alma

11:6, 11), Amnor[1] was a spy for the Nephites around 87 B.C. He and three others, together "with their men," were sent to watch the camp of the apostate Amlicites (Alma 2:22). They returned with the alarming news that these dissidents had joined forces with a Lamanite army that was attacking the Nephites (Alma 2:23–25). No other mention is made of him.

AMORON

He was one of the Nephite soldiers, probably an officer, who reported directly to the Nephite commander Mormon[2] on the atrocities committed by Lamanites (Moroni 9:7–8).

AMOS[1]

A Nephite record keeper about A.D. 110–194, who was the son of Nephi[4] and the grandson of Nephi[3] (who was the chief disciple of the resurrected Christ among the people in the Western world; see 4 Nephi 1:19). Amos[1] recorded the sad news that during his lifetime some of the people had already begun to rebel, leaving the Church and taking upon themselves the name of Lamanites (4 Nephi 1:20).

AMOS[2]

The son of Amos[1], Amos[2] became the record keeper following the death of his father (4 Nephi 1:21). The golden years that followed the visit of the resurrected Christ to ancient America came to an end during the eighty-four years he kept the record. Seemingly small things began to creep in among the people, such as "the wearing of costly apparel [did it have to have the right label?], and all manner of fine pearls [could we say expensive or showy jewelry?], and of the fine things of the world." They ceased practicing the law of consecration, which led to their being "divided into classes" and which ultimately led them "to deny the true church of Christ" (4 Nephi 1:24–26).

Their dark descent even led them to unsuccessfully seek to imprison, fetter, muzzle, and try to kill the Three Nephite Disciples who were still among them (4 Nephi 1:30–33). Children were taught to hate those who were different from themselves, and the secret combination of Gadianton robbers rose once again (4 Nephi 1:38–42). How heart wrenching this must have been for both Amos[2] and Mormon[2], who later condensed Amos's record.

AMOZ

Although he was not a Book of Mormon figure, Amoz, the father of the poet-prophet Isaiah, is mentioned twice (2 Nephi 12:1; 23:1). Both instances are quotations from the Old Testament (Isaiah 2:1; 13:1).

AMULEK

The great convert and missionary companion of Alma[2], Amulek gave up a prestigious position in society to become a humble, yet powerful, servant of the Lord. Indeed, he was "a man of no small reputation" with "many kindreds and friends, and . . . much riches" (Alma 10:4). Much of this was lost when he enthusiastically embraced the "treasures in heaven" (3 Nephi 13:20). Amulek's conversion was the end result of being obedient to the charge of an angel of the Lord to open his house to "a holy prophet of God" (Alma 8:20; 10:7). Alma[2] blessed not only Amulek, but his entire house (Alma 8:20; 10:11).

Amulek unhesitatingly responded to his missionary call to serve as Alma's companion, becoming a second witness to the teachings and testimony of Alma[2] (Alma 8:29–32; 10:12). He stood firm in the face of ridicule and even with the threat of martyrdom hanging over his head (Alma 14:9–17). For His purposes, the Lord allowed others to be martyred and Alma[2] and Amulek to be thrown into a dungeon. Yet the power of the Lord was always with the missionary companions, as described in the following verse:

"And they had power given unto them, insomuch that they could not be confined in dungeons; neither was it possible that any man could slay them; nevertheless they did not exercise their power until they were bound in bands and cast into prison. Now, this was done that the Lord might show forth his power in them" (Alma 8:31).

Amulek taught powerfully about the Atonement (Alma 11, 12, 34) and about the importance of prayer and avoiding procrastination (Alma 34). Excerpts from his insightful sermons are frequently quoted in Latter-day Saint meetings.

AMULON

Amulon was the leader of the wicked priests of King Noah[3] after Noah's death. After Noah[3], his priests, and some other members of Zeniff's colony had fled the Lamanites, leaving their wives and children in danger while saving their own lives, a number of those who had fled had a change of heart. They slew Noah[3] and sought to kill his priests, then returned to where their wives and children were. The priests, however, were able to escape from the same fate that befell their wicked king, death by fire (Mosiah 19:21, 23; 23:32). Following their escape, Amulon and his craven companions kidnapped twenty-four of the Lamanite daughters and took them as wives (Mosiah 20:1–5).

The wicked priests later joined a Lamanite army that betrayed a promise to Alma[1] and his colony of believers, placing them in bondage, with Amulon as their chief taskmaster (Mosiah 23:25–39). Obviously, Amulon had a disdain for Alma[1] because of Alma's having turned from wickedness to righteousness. The scriptures remind us that the wicked seek to "persecute the saints" (D&C 121:38). Amulon subsequently laid a heavy burden upon this righteous colony, including the order that they were not to pray, upon penalty of death (Mosiah 24:8–11). As the people of the Lord continued to pray silently in their hearts, the Lord gave His people the strength to bear up under their burdens and eventually guided their escape from their persecutors (Mosiah 24:12–25).

See also Amulon, Children of; Amulonites.

AMULON, CHILDREN OF

These were the forsaken children of Amulon and the other wicked priests of King Noah[3], whose cowardly fathers fled an attacking army, leaving their children and wives at the mercy of the invaders (Mosiah 19:9–12, 23). Being ashamed of their fathers' errant conduct, "they would no longer be called by the names of their fathers, therefore they took upon themselves the name of Nephi" (Mosiah 25:12).

See also Amulon; Amulonites.

AMULONITES

These were the descendants and followers of Amulon and the other wicked priests of King Noah[3], who forsook their first wives and children and later kidnapped and took as wives daughters of the Lamanites (Mosiah 20:1–5). The offspring from these later unions became known as the Amulonites, being joined by others who apostatized from the true faith. The Amulonites were "harder" in their hearts than the Lamanites (Alma 21:3), continually stirring the Lamanites up to wage war against the Nephites and the converted Lamanites (Alma 24:1). The Amulonites were after the "order of the Nehors" (Alma 21:4), an apostate religious sect that followed the false and wicked teachings of Nehor (Alma 1). The tragic history of the Amulonites is that they ended up fulfilling the prophecy of the martyred prophet Abinadi, who had foretold that they would be hunted and slain (Mosiah 17:11–19): "The Lamanites began to hunt the seed of Amulon and his brethren and began to slay them. . . . Thus the words of Abinadi were brought to pass, which he said concerning the seed of the priests who caused that he should suffer death by fire" (Alma 25:8–9).

ANGEL

There are a number of occasions in the Book of Mormon when an unnamed angel appeared to deliver a message from the Lord. The first such angel came to the rescue of Nephi[1] and his brother Sam when they were being beaten with a rod by the rebellious Laman[1] and Lemuel (1 Nephi 3:29–30). An angel showed Nephi[1] the great vision of the birth and mission of the Son of God and a host of other marvelous things (1 Nephi 11:14–14:30).

It was an unnamed angel who revealed to Jacob[2] that the name of the Messiah would be Christ (2 Nephi 10:3). The great sermon of the prophet-king Benjamin was based on knowledge he received from an angel (Mosiah 3:2; 4:1). An angel revealed to the Lamanite prophet Samuel the signs of the coming of Christ and of His later death (Helaman 13:7). Just prior to the mortal birth of the Son of God, "angels did appear unto men, wise men, and did declare unto them glad tidings of great joy" (Helaman 16:14).

The conversion of Alma[2] the Younger and the four sons of Mosiah[2] was precipitated by the rebuke of an angel of God (Mosiah 27:11–17).

Virtually all references to angels refer to heavenly messengers sent from the presence of the Lord with a message to deliver or a mission to perform. The Prophet Joseph Smith referred to them as "ministering servants" of God (*Teachings of the Prophet Joseph Smith*, 312). On occasion, however, the Book of Mormon also refers to fallen angels, meaning the devil and his misled and rebellious followers (2 Nephi 2:17).

Two types of angels were identified in a revelation to the Prophet Joseph: those who once lived on this earth, died, and then were resurrected, such as the Angel Moroni[2]; and those who are still awaiting their resurrection, who are "the spirits of just men made perfect" (D&C 129:1–3).

Angels who appeared to people and prophets prior to the resurrection of Jesus Christ, who was the first to be resurrected, generally appeared as spirit beings. But when Moses and Elijah appeared on the Mount of Transfiguration (Matthew 17:3), they did so as translated beings who were in a terrestrial state where they still had their bodies. Following the resurrection of Christ, they went through an instant death and resurrection and thus appeared as resurrected beings to the Prophet Joseph Smith and Oliver Cowdery in the Kirtland Temple (D&C 110:11, 13).

"The word *angel* is also sometimes used to designate a human messenger, as in JST Genesis 19, and may have some application also in Matt. 13:39–42" (LDS Bible Dictionary, 608).

The Apostle Paul counseled, "Be not forgetful to entertain strangers:

for thereby some have entertained angels unawares" (Hebrews 13:2).

ANGELS OF THE DEVIL

The devil himself is referred to as "an angel of God . . . fallen from heaven" (2 Nephi 2:17), and those spirits who joined him in his rebellion are called *angels of the devil.* They are the "third part of the hosts of heaven" that the devil turned away from God and who followed him in his path to perdition (D&C 29:36–38). That path led these evil spirits to a *temporary* home upon this telestial earth, where they pit their vile powers against the agency of mortals. However, their destiny of eternal damnation cannot be changed. They will "depart into everlasting fire prepared for the devil and his angels" (Mosiah 26:27). Those mortals who willfully sin against the Light will be consigned to that same terrible fate (Mosiah 2:38–39; D&C 29:27–28).

See also Demons; Perdition, Son of.

ANTHON, CHARLES

See Learned, The.

ANTI-CHRIST

The infamous title of *Anti-Christ* is applied *specifically* to Korihor (Alma 30:6, 12), but in theory applies to any who preach against Christ and His divine role in the great plan of salvation.

"In a broader sense it is anyone or anything that counterfeits the true gospel or plan of salvation and that openly or secretly is set up in opposition to Christ. The great anti-Christ is Lucifer, but he has many assistants both as spirit beings and as mortals" (LDS Bible Dictionary, "Antichrist," 609).

See also Korihor; Sherem; Teachers, False.

ANTI-NEPHI-LEHI

The unusual name of Anti-Nephi-Lehi was taken by King Lamoni's brother *after* his father conferred the kingdom on him (Alma 24:3–5). The use of the pronouns in verse three makes it impossible to tell whether Anti-Nephi-Lehi was named by his father or by himself. Evidently Lamoni and his brother ruled over separate kingdoms. Both were involved in the council held under the direction of Ammon[2] to determine how to defend their people from a pending attack.

"The name 'Anti' of 'Anti-Nephi-Lehi' may be a reflex of the Egyptian *nty* 'he of, the one of.' Thus, rather than having the sense 'against,' it has the meaning 'the one of Nephi and Lehi'" (Largey, *Book of Mormon Reference Companion,* 67).

ANTI-NEPHI-LEHIES

The missionary labors of the sons of Mosiah[2] among the Lamanites were so successful that "thousands were brought to the knowledge of the Lord" (Alma 23:5). These new converts turned from their false traditions, laid down their weapons of war, and "were desirous that they might have a name, that thereby they might be distinguished" or recognized as being different from the Lamanites who had not accepted the gospel. Thus, they took upon themselves the name of "Anti-Nephi-Lehies" (Alma 23:16–17).

At the urging of their newly appointed king, who was named Anti-Nephi-Lehi, these new converts determined to never again shed blood, even to defend themselves. They buried all their swords and weapons of war as a sign of their covenant (Alma 24:1–19; 27:28–29).

Their covenant was put to the ultimate test when the apostate Amalekites and Amulonites stirred up the anger of the *unconverted* Lamanites against the Anti-Nephi-Lehies (Alma 24:1–2). They attacked these innocent people and commenced to slaughter the unresisting converts, who simply "prostrated themselves before them to the earth, and began to call on the name of the Lord." In this manner, "a thousand and five" of these innocent people were slain before the invaders stopped the killing (Alma 24:20–24).

In addition to the miracle of faith manifested by the martyrs that day, their example brought about a miracle of repentance on the part of many of the invaders. Stung in their consciences for their murderous actions, many of the attackers threw down their swords and sought spiritual refuge among those whose blood they had just spilt. And "the people of God were joined that day by more than the number who had been slain; . . . thus we see that the Lord worketh in many ways to the salvation of his people" (Alma 24:26–27).

The enmity of the majority of the Lamanites, continually prodded by the apostate Nephites, continued and the Anti-Nephi-Lehies eventually left their lands and took refuge among the Nephites in the land of Jershon. At this point in their history, they became known as "the people of Ammon[2]," in honor of the great missionary who had served among them (Alma 27:26).

Their conversion was bedrock solid, for they "never did fall away" (Alma 23:6). "And they were also distinguished for their zeal towards God, and also towards men; for they were perfectly honest and upright in all things; and they were firm in the faith of Christ, even unto the end" (Alma 27:27).

They set a wonderful example in how to handle false and specious rhetoric. When the anti-Christ Korihor came into their land to preach his false doctrine, "they were more wise than many of the Nephites; for they took him, and bound him, and carried him before Ammon, who was a high priest over that people" (Alma 30:20). In other words, they didn't waste their time listening to Korihor's nonsense. "And [Ammon²] caused that he should be carried out of the land" (Alma 30:21).

The charitable people of Ammon² willingly took in the cast-offs of the more "popular" Zoramites, withstanding the threats made against them, and gave them succor (Alma 35:3–9). Their charity led to their being forced to flee their homes because of the attacking Zoramites and Lamanites (Alma 35:10–13).

This experience is an example that doing the "right" thing does not always bring outward peace. Nevertheless, God will support the righteous. "Whosoever shall put their trust in God shall be supported *in* their trials, and their troubles, and their afflictions, and shall be lifted up at the last day" (Alma 36:3; emphasis added; see also 33:23).

During a time of crisis, when the Nephites who had been their protectors were striving to defend their homes from invading Lamanite armies, the people of Ammon² were tempted to break their oath and take up arms in defense of their country.

However, Helaman² persuaded them to remain true to their covenant "lest by so doing they should lose their souls" (Alma 53:13–15). The Nephites had faith that God would bless them if they refused to allow the people of Ammon² to break their covenant (Alma 56:7–8).

ANTIOMNO

Antiomno was the Lamanite king in the land of Middoni who had jurisdiction over the prison into which the missionaries Aaron³, Muloki, and Ammah were cast (Alma 19:2–4). He was a friend of King Lamoni, who persuaded Antiomno to release the prisoners (Alma 20:28).

ANTIONAH

Antionah was a chief ruler in Ammonihah and thus one of the foremost antagonists in questioning the missionary duo of Alma² and Amulek (Alma 12:20–21). His question led to a lengthy discourse from Alma² on the Fall and Atonement (Alma 12:22–13:31).

ANTIONUM

This Nephite military leader is mentioned as one of the casualties in the final battle at Cumorah around A.D. 385 (Mormon 6:14). He and his ten thousand soldiers were slain in this sad ending to the Nephite civilization.

ANTIPUS

Antipus was appointed by Captain Moroni[1] in about 65 B.C. to be a chief Nephite military commander (Alma 56:9). As a result of heavy casualties in fighting the Lamanites, the troops of Antipus were significantly reduced, but his army was fortified by the arrival of Helaman[2] and his band of stripling warriors (Alma 56:10). Antipus was a clever strategist who decoyed "the most powerful army of the Lamanites" to leave their stronghold and fall into a trap. However, even though the Lamanites were defeated in the battle, the brave Antipus was slain (Alma 56:29–54).

See also People of Antipus.

APOSTLE OF THE LAMB

The particular "apostle of the Lamb" shown to Nephi[1] was identified as John (1 Nephi 14:19–27), one of the twelve special witnesses chosen to accompany the Savior in His mortal ministry (Luke 6:13). He and his brother James were called to leave their fishing nets and to become "fishers of men" (Matthew 4:18–22). These two sons of Zebedee were later elevated to become members of the First Presidency of Christ's Church, along with the Apostle Peter. These three Apostles had a special experience with Christ on the Mount of Transfiguration, when keys of priesthood authority were vested in them (Matthew 17). They were also the only ones invited to accompany Jesus into the Garden of Gethsemane, where the Savior paid the price for our sins and sufferings with His blood (Matthew 26:36–37).

Following the ascension of Christ, John and his fellow Apostles continued to give direction to the Church. John, who is also known as "John the Revelator" (D&C 128:6), was given specific responsibility for recording the great visions shown to him while on the Isle of Patmos (1 Nephi 14:19–27).

So that he could continue his ministry on earth, John was granted the privilege of forgoing death until the time of the Second Coming, when he would be changed to immortality in the "twinkling of an eye" (3 Nephi 28:4–9; D&C 7). Of his continuing ministry, in June of 1831 the Prophet Joseph said that "John the Revelator was then among the ten tribes of Israel . . . to prepare them for their return from their long dispersion" (Smith, *History of the Church,* 1:176, footnote).

Not long before that statement, in May or June 1830, John had joined his fellow Apostles Peter and James in restoring the Melchizedek Priesthood to Joseph Smith and Oliver Cowdery (D&C 27:12).

See also Apostles, Twelve; John the Beloved; John the Revelator.

APOSTLES, TWELVE

The ministry and writings of the "twelve apostles" spoken of in the Book of Mormon refer to those who accompanied Jesus during His mortal ministry (1 Nephi 11:34–36; 12:9; 13:24–41). However, Judas Iscariot is *not* included in these twelve, for he was replaced by Matthias, who "companied with [the Apostles] all the time that the Lord Jesus went in and out among [the Twelve]" (Acts 1:21–26). This reconstituted Quorum of the Twelve will stand at the right hand of Jesus at the Second Coming (D&C 29:12).

ARCHEANTUS

The single mention of Archeantus is as one of the Nephite military officers serving under General Mormon[2] around A.D. 385 (Moroni 9:2). He was one of the "choice men" who were slain in a losing battle with the Lamanites.

B

BENJAMIN, KING

The righteous prophet-king Benjamin was consecrated by his father Mosiah¹ to be the ruler over the combined people of Nephi and Zarahemla (Omni 1:23; Mosiah 2:11). The beginning of his ministry is particularly pivotal because it marked the merging of the record keeping. Prior to this time, the small plates of Nephi had been kept to record the more spiritual aspects of the Nephite history, and the large plates of Nephi had maintained the secular, or detailed historical, record (1 Nephi 9:2–4; Words of Mormon 1:3–11).

Benjamin was a leader who fought boldly at the forefront of battles against both the invading Lamanites and contentious and false teachers among his own people. Indeed, he was described as "a holy man [who] did reign over his people in righteousness" (Words of Mormon 1:12–17). Fortunately, just as righteous leaders today are assisted by others, King Benjamin had "the assistance of the holy prophets" and "many holy men" who were among his people.

"Wherefore, with the help of these, king Benjamin, by laboring with all the might of his body and the faculty of his whole soul, and also the prophets, did once more establish peace in the land" (Words of Mormon 1:16–18).

His effective leadership was demonstrated in his not trying to accomplish difficult tasks without the able assistance of others. This noble leader also set an example in his personal participation in the tasks at hand, laboring alongside his people (Mosiah 2:14). He truly saw the call to *lead* as a call to *serve*.

His oft-quoted sermon to his people (Mosiah 2–5) is not only a powerful witness of Christ—and the need to take His name upon us and follow Him—but it is also a landmark witness of the need for all to regularly provide service to others.

One other point is worth mentioning regarding the effective leadership of King Benjamin. He not only taught the people proper principles, committing them to a covenant of righteousness, but he then set in place a system to continually "stir them up in remembrance of the oath which they had made" (Mosiah 6:1–3).

BROTHER OF JARED²

See Jared², Brother of.

C

CAIN

This infamous son of Adam and Eve is mentioned twice in the Book of Mormon, both times in connection with his evil alliance with Satan that resulted in the martyrdom of Abel (Helaman 6:27; Ether 8:15). There is some conjecture that Cain was rebellious in the premortal life, having a spirit that preceded his rebellion on earth. Elder Bruce R. McConkie (1915–1985) opined: "Though he was a rebel and an associate of Lucifer in pre-existence, and though he was a liar from the beginning whose name was Perdition, Cain managed to attain the privilege of mortal birth" (*Mormon Doctrine*, 108–9).

The incomplete account of Cain's conflict with Abel and with the Lord in the King James Version of the Bible limits an understanding of what led to Cain's downfall in mortality. Fortunately, the Prophet Joseph Smith received additional revelation on the subject. "Cain loved Satan more than God" (Moses 5:18) and he "rejected the greater counsel which was had from God," entering into an unholy alliance with the master of all evil (Moses 5:25–31).

Thus the first of the "secret combinations" that from that time on would continually inflict their tragic consequences of murder, terror, war, and suffering upon the world was formed (2 Nephi 9:9). When Cain killed his brother Abel, he knowingly sinned against the greater light and sealed his fate as a son of perdition. Ironically, because he will have a body, Cain will ultimately rule over Satan in outer darkness (Moses 5:23).

CEZORAM

Cezoram replaced Nephi[2] as chief judge around 30 B.C., when "they who chose evil were more numerous than they who chose good" (Helaman 5:1–2). In the fourth year of his reign, "Cezoram was murdered by an unknown hand as he sat upon the judgment-seat. And it came to pass that in the same year, that his [unnamed] son, who had been appointed by the people in his stead, was also murdered" (Helaman 6:15).

CEZORAM, SON OF

See Cezoram.

CHEMISH

Like his brother Amaron, from whom he received the Nephite record, Chemish was one of five scribes who contributed to the small book that bears his father's name. His total contribution to the record was one verse (Omni 1:9). Perhaps because of the general wickedness of the Nephites at that time (Omni 1:5–7), Chemish felt there was nothing worth recording. On the other hand, this may be a classic example of one receiving a stewardship and failing to magnify the calling. It is reminiscent of the foolish servant whom the Savior chastised for burying the talent which was entrusted to him (Matthew 25:14–30).

CHERUBIM

This plural use of cherub, which is an order of angels, is cited twice in the Book of Mormon in explanations or mini-sermons dealing with the Fall of Adam and Eve (Alma 12:21; 42:2). The Lord placed cherubim to guard the tree of life in order to prevent them from partaking of the tree of life, which at that time would have consigned them to live without the hope of repentance, "forever miserable, having no preparatory state" (Alma 12:26). Thus, God in His mercy ensured that the plan of redemption would come to pass.

As to the identity of the cheru-

bim who were left to guard the tree, President Joseph Fielding Smith (1876–1972) stated: "The simple truth gathered from modern revelation is that these beings that guarded the way to the tree of life were angels. Evidently faithful personages belonging to this world who had not, at the time, received the privilege of partaking of mortality, for the Lord revealed to the Prophet Joseph Smith that 'there are no angels who minister to this earth but those who do belong to it.' (D. & C. 130:5.)" (*Answers to Gospel Questions,* 2:97).

CHILDREN OF CHRIST
See Father, Jesus Christ As.

CHOICE SEER

The ancient prophet Joseph[1] prophesied that at a future day the Lord would raise up a "choice seer" who would be of his posterity (2 Nephi 3:6; JST Genesis 50:26). This seer would be "great" in the eyes of the Lord, and he would be given "power to bring forth [God's] word," the Book of Mormon and other revelation. That which would be written by Joseph's posterity would be combined with that which would be written by his brother Judah's posterity "unto the confounding of false doctrines" (2 Nephi 3:8–12; JST Genesis 50:29–31).

The seer's name would be the

same as the ancient seer Joseph[1] and would be the same as his father's name (2 Nephi 3:15; JST Genesis 50:33).

Joseph Smith Jr., the Prophet of the Restoration, the son of Joseph Smith Sr., was and is that promised seer.

See also Smith, Joseph, Jr.

CHOSEN PEOPLE

The title "chosen people" is used in several different ways in the Book of Mormon. It is first used in a perverted sense. The apostate Zoramites[2] climbed upon their Rameumptom, or elevated place of worship, and proclaimed themselves to be God's "chosen people . . . while others shall perish" (Alma 31:28). This group of false worshipers denied the existence of Christ, prevented the poor from worshiping in their synagogues, preached that God was a spirit, and confined their worship to publicly praying atop their prayer stand once a week. Their religious practices were based on exclusivity. In essence, others were excluded from becoming part of this so-called chosen people.

The second time the title "chosen people" occurs in the Book of Mormon is when the Lamanite prophet Samuel[2] reminded the backsliding Nephites they had been a "chosen people" (Helaman 15:3). His call for them to repent was really a call to return to their special status and act like people called by the Lord to represent Him.

Early in his ministry, the prophet Nephi[1] declared that the Lord chooses people to be His special servants "because of their faith, to make them mighty even unto the power of deliverance" (1 Nephi 1:20). The chosen people are charged with delivering themselves and others from the bondage of sin. Righteous followers of Christ are called to be the chosen people of the Lord in order to show forth good works and *invite all* to "come unto Christ, and be perfected in him, and deny yourselves of all ungodliness" (Moroni 10:32).

In speaking of the responsibility of members of The Church of Jesus Christ of Latter-day Saints to demonstrate gospel principles in their lives, Elder Harold B. Lee (1899–1973) said:

"Clearly it was the intent of our Heavenly Father that this, our day, was to be a *day of demonstration of the power and effectiveness of the gospel of Jesus Christ in the lives of all who are to be members of his Church.* This likewise according to the scriptures, has evidently been his purpose, concerning his chosen people in every dispensation" (in Conference Report, October 1945, 46; emphasis added).

"The Latter-day Saints are the people of God, a chosen people, a royal priesthood, a covenant people, and a covenant-making people," said Elder George F. Richards (1861–1950). "The greatest and most important blessings our Heavenly Father has for his faithful sons and daughters are received by covenant. One of the greatest blessings he has to bestow is membership in his Church and kingdom. This is received by solemn covenant" (in Conference Report, April 1945, 129).

Latter-day Saints do not preach or practice a doctrine of exclusivity. The Church is *inclusive* to all who desire to follow Jesus Christ with all their heart.

Elder David B. Haight (1906–2004) summed up the responsibility of Church members as follows: "Latter-day Saints are a chosen people, so appointed in the premortal world, to be in partnership with the Lord for the salvation of the living and the dead" (*Ensign,* November 1990, 59).

See also Covenant People of the Lord; People of Christ; People of God; People of Jesus; People of the First Covenant; Saints of the Church of the Lamb; Zoramites[2].

CHRIST

This most revered and sacred name appears in the very title of this holy book of scripture: The Book of Mormon: Another Testament of Jesus Christ. It first appears in the text of the book itself on the title page,

where the ancient prophet-scribe Moroni[2] wrote that one of the purposes of this book of scripture is "to the convincing of the Jew and Gentile that JESUS is the CHRIST, the ETERNAL GOD, manifesting himself unto all nations." The divine name of Christ also identifies His "only true and living church upon the face of the whole earth" (D&C 1:30), "even The Church of Jesus Christ of Latter-day Saints" (D&C 115:4; see also 3 Nephi 27:3–11).

Among the Book of Mormon people, the name *Christ* was first revealed to Father Lehi's son Jacob[2] by an angel of God between 559 and 545 B.C. (2 Nephi 10:3). Prior to this time, references to Him in the Book of Mormon included the following: Lord (1 Nephi 1:20); God (1 Nephi 3:21); God of Israel (1 Nephi 5:9); God of Abraham, and the God of Isaac, and the God of Jacob (1 Nephi 6:4); Messiah (1 Nephi 10:4); Savior of the world (1 Nephi 10:4); Redeemer of the world (1 Nephi 10:5); Lamb of God (1 Nephi 10:10); Son of God (1 Nephi 11:18); and Son of the Eternal Father (1 Nephi 11:21).

Elder James E. Talmage (1862–1933) wrote, "*Christ* is a sacred title, and not an ordinary appellation or common name; it is of Greek derivation, and in meaning is identical with its Hebrew equivalent *Messiah* or *Messias,* signifying the *Anointed One.*"

All other scriptural titles applied to Jesus "are expressive of our Lord's divine origin and Godship" (*Jesus the Christ*, 35–36).

The central role of Jesus Christ in the theology of the Latter-day Saints was expressed by the Prophet Joseph: "The fundamental principles of our religion are the testimony of the Apostles and Prophets, concerning Jesus Christ, that He died, was buried, and rose again the third day, and ascended into heaven; and all other things which pertain to our religion are only appendages to it" (Smith, *History of the Church*, 3:30). The Church of Jesus Christ of Latter-day Saints is "Christocentric" said Elder Neal A. Maxwell (1926–2004), who then humbly proclaimed: "I gladly and unashamedly acknowledge Jesus of Nazareth, Savior and King! . . . *I witness that he lives*—with all that those simple words imply. I know I will be held accountable for this testimony; but *as . . . readers, you are now accountable for my witness*—which I give in the very name of Jesus Christ" (*Ensign*, May 1976, 26–27; emphasis added).

The Book of Mormon is filled with marvelous prophecies about and revelations from Jesus Christ. His divine birth was witnessed (1 Nephi 11:13–21; Helaman 14:2–6), including the naming of His mortal mother, Mary (Mosiah 3:8; Alma 7:10).

Additionally, Christ spoke to a Nephite prophet just before His birth, proclaiming, "on this night shall the sign be given, and on the morrow come I into the world" (3 Nephi 1:13).

Prophets in ancient America testified of Christ's mortal ministry and of His Atonement, which gave second witness to the New Testament's implied witness (Luke 24:44) that the Savior would suffer so excruciatingly in Gethsemane that "blood cometh from every pore, so great shall be his anguish for the wickedness and the abominations of his people" (Mosiah 3:7). In fact, the Book of Mormon bears witness that Christ suffered not only for our transgressions, but also for our infirmities, pains, and sicknesses (Alma 7:11–12). Thus, He has absolute and perfect empathy for any suffering we may experience. With full confidence in being heard and understood, we may prayerfully turn to our Father in the name of Christ for relief or strengthening in moments of trial and personal suffering.

Prophecies of Christ's rejection by those whom He lovingly came to teach and of His death by crucifixion are found in the Book of Mormon (1 Nephi 19:9–10; 2 Nephi 6:9; 10:3–5; Mosiah 3:9). On the other hand, prophecies and sermons about His resurrection and its universal implications for all of mankind are comfortingly taught in this second witness of Jesus Christ (2 Nephi 2:8; 9:5–11; Alma 11; 40).

Perhaps most significant of all is the account of the resurrected Christ's visit to ancient America, where He personally taught and ministered among these ancient descendants of Father Lehi[1] and Mother Sariah (3 Nephi 11–28). During this glorious visit, Christ invited the multitude to whom He was speaking to come to Him and to feel the wound in His side and the "prints of the nails in his hands and in his feet" (3 Nephi 11:13–16).

The plea of prophets throughout the Book of Mormon is "come unto Christ, and be perfected in him, and deny yourselves of all ungodliness" (Moroni 10:32; see also Jacob 1:7; Omni 1:26). Indeed, Nephi[1] wrote the following entreaty:

"For we labor diligently to write, to persuade our children, and also our brethren, to believe in Christ, and to be reconciled to God; for we know that it is by grace that we are saved, after all we can do. . . . We are made alive in Christ because of our faith. . . . And we talk of Christ, we rejoice in Christ, we preach of Christ, we prophesy of Christ, and we write according to our prophecies, that our children may know to what source they may look for a remission of their sins . . . ; for the right way is to believe in Christ and deny him not. . . . And now behold, I say unto you that the right way is to believe in Christ, and deny him not; and Christ is the Holy One of Israel; wherefore ye must bow down before him, and worship him with all your might, mind, and strength, and your whole soul; and if ye do this ye shall in nowise be cast out" (2 Nephi 25:23, 25–26, 28–29).

See also Christ, Names of; Father, Jesus Christ As; Father of Heaven and Earth; Immanuel; Jehovah; Jesse, Stem of; Jesus; Lamb of God; Messiah; Only Begotten of the Father; Prince of Peace; Redeemer; Savior; Spirit of the Lord.

CHRIST, NAMES OF

The following names are applied to Jesus Christ in the Book of Mormon: Almighty; Almighty God; Alpha and Omega; Author; Beginning; Beginning and the End; Being; Beloved; Beloved Son; Christ; Christ Jesus; Christ the Lord; Christ the Son; Counselor; Creator; Creator of All Things from the Beginning; End; Eternal Father; Eternal God; Eternal Judge; Everlasting Father; Everlasting God; Father; Father of All Things; Father of Heaven; Father of Heaven and Earth; Father of Heaven and of Earth; Finisher; First; First and the Last; Founder of Peace; Fountain of All Righteousness; God; God of

Abraham; God of Abraham, and Isaac, and Jacob; God of Abraham, and of Isaac, and the God of Jacob; God of Isaac; God of Israel; God of Jacob; God of Miracles; God of Nature; God of the Whole Earth; God of Truth; God over All the Earth; God, the Father of All Things; Good Shepherd; Great and Eternal Head; Great and True God; Great and True Shepherd; Great Creator; Great Light; Great Mediator; Great Spirit; Heavenly King; Holy Child; Holy God; Holy Messiah; Holy One; Holy One of Israel; Holy One of Jacob; Husband; Immanuel; Jehovah; Jesus; Jesus Christ; Keeper of the Gate; King; King of All the Earth; King of Heaven; Lamb; Lamb of God; Last; Life of the World; Life and the Light of the World; Light and the Life of the World; Light of the World; Light That Is Endless; Lord; Lord God; Lord God Almighty; Lord God Omnipotent; Lord God of Hosts; Lord Jehovah; Lord Jesus; Lord Jesus Christ; Lord My God; Lord of Hosts; Lord of the Vineyard; Lord Omnipotent; Lord Our God; Lord the Almighty God; Lord Their God; Lord Thy God; Lord Thy Maker; Maker; Man; Master of the Vineyard; Mediator; Mediator of the Covenant; Messiah; Mighty God; Mighty One of Israel; Mighty One of Jacob; Most High; Most High God; One; Only Begotten of the Father; Only Begotten Son; Prince of Peace; Prophet; Redeemer; Redeemer of All Men; Redeemer of Israel; Redeemer of the World; Rock; Savior; Savior Jesus Christ; Savior of the World; Shepherd; Son; Son of God; Son of Righteousness; Son of the Eternal Father; Son of the Everlasting Father; Son of the Living God; Son of the Most High God; Spirit of the Lord; Stem of Jesse; Stone; Supreme Being; Supreme Creator; True and Living God; True Messiah; True Shepherd; True Vine; Truth of the World; Well Beloved; Wonderful; Word of Truth and Righteousness.

CHRISTIANS

The term *Christians* appears in the Book of Mormon about 73 B.C. (Alma 46:13–16). The inclusion of this word in the record has occasionally been a source of criticism from nonbelievers who cite its use as so-called evidence that the book could not be a translation of plates that predate Christ's birth. The followers of Jesus Christ "were called Christians first in Antioch" (Acts 11:26), the critics argue.

It is of interest to note the origin of the term. President Anthony W. Ivins (1853–1934) noted, "During the earliest history of the Primitive Church its members were not referred to as Christians, but as brethren, disciples or saints. It was . . . about ten years after the crucifixion, that the followers of the Redeemer were first *called Christians, a name applied to them in derision, or contempt"* (in Conference Report, April 1926, 16; emphasis added).

With this in mind, consider that the followers of Christ in the Book of Mormon were *"called by their enemies . . . Christians"* (Alma 48:10; emphasis added).

The Savior Himself taught, "Ye must take upon you the name of Christ, which is my name" (3 Nephi 27:5). It is reasonable to believe that regardless of the age in which one lives, if an individual believes in and embraces Christ as the Son of God, the Redeemer and Savior of the world, he or she would in some form be referred to as a "Christian."

COHOR¹

Cohor¹ was the son of the Jaredite King Corihor¹, who obtained the throne by rebelling against his father. Sadly, Cohor¹ and his brother Noah² followed the bad example of their father and rebelled against the reigning monarch in their day, as well as their father. It appears that Cohor¹, in Lemuel-like fashion, was the follower and not the instigator of the rebellion, for he was drawn into the action by his brother (Ether 7:15).

COHOR²

Cohor² was the son of the Jaredite rebel Noah². Cohor² reigned over half of a divided kingdom until he was slain in a battle with the king of the other half (Ether 7:19–21).

COHOR³

Cohor³ is mentioned incidentally as the father of sons and daughters who did not repent during a period of great wickedness among the Jaredites (Ether 13:16). Judging from the context of the reference to him—that he lived during a time when "mighty men . . . sought to destroy [the king] by their secret plans of wickedness" (Ether 13:15)—it seems likely that Cohor³ was among those wicked men.

COM¹

Com¹ was an early Jaredite king, the son of Coriantum¹ and father of Heth¹ (Ether 1:26–27). The single verse covering his life says only that he "reigned forty and nine years" (Ether 9:25).

COM²

Com² reigned as king in the later period of Jaredite history and was the son of Coriantum² and the father of Shiblon¹ (Ether 1:12–13). He was born while his father was in captivity and was successful in overthrowing half of the kingdom. He was ultimately victorious in a battle with Amgid, the ruler over the other half, thus gaining control of the entire kingdom (Ether 10:31–32). The spread of secret combinations took place during his reign (Ether 10:33–34). To his credit, and for which he was blessed, Com² protected the prophets from the threats of the wicked. He "lived to a good old age" (Ether 11:1–4).

COMBINATIONS, SECRET
See Gadianton.

CORIANTON

This missionary son of Alma² allowed pride to overtake his work, which undoubtedly weakened him in other areas, ultimately leading him to forsake his sacred calling and seek after the harlot Isabel (Alma 39:1–4). Because of Corianton's bad example, many would not believe in the words of his father (Alma 39:11). This is the tragedy of making wrong choices: they *always* have a negative impact on others.

Elder James E. Faust (1920–) taught that "private choices are not private; they all have public consequences. . . . Our society is the sum total of what millions of individuals do in their private lives. That sum total of private behavior has worldwide public consequences of enormous magnitude. There are no completely private choices" (*Ensign,* May 1987, 80). Certainly, Corianton's choice to sin had consequences

beyond what he considered to be his own private life.

Fortunately, Corianton responded to Alma's call to repentance, which included a masterful discourse on the Atonement (Alma 39–42). Satisfied at his son's godly sorrow and complete repentance, Alma called Corianton once again to preach "with truth and soberness" (Alma 42:31; emphasis added).

While Corianton's fall and return should not be looked upon as an excuse for any modern-day missionaries to rationalize bad behavior and broken covenants, it does provide a reminder that the Atonement provides a way back from sin.

"For, behold, the Lord your Redeemer suffered death in the flesh; wherefore he suffered the pain of all men, that all men might repent and come unto him" (D&C 18:11).

"The most wicked of lies," said President Boyd K. Packer (1924–), "is that [transgressors] cannot change and repent and that they will not be forgiven. That cannot be true. They have forgotten the Atonement of Christ" (*Ensign,* May 2006, 28).

Some years later, Corianton sailed to northern lands "to carry forth provisions unto the people who had gone forth into that land" and was not heard from again (Alma 63:10).

CORIANTOR

Coriantor had the unhappy distinction of being born while his father, the Jaredite King Moron, was in captivity, and spent his entire life in that condition (Ether 1:7; 11:18–19). Of particular significance is that Coriantor was the father of the prophet Ether, after whom the record containing the history of the Jaredite civilization is named (Ether 11:23–12:2). The circumstances of Ether's birth are evidence that humble beginnings do not limit one's ability to make a difference for good.

CORIANTUM[1]

This Jaredite king was the son of Emer and the father of Com[1] (Ether 1:27–28). He was a righteous ruler who "did administer that which was good unto his people in all his days" (Ether 9:23). He had no children by his first wife, who lived to the age of 102. Coriantum[1] then married again and "begat sons and daughters," living to an age of 142 (Ether 9:24).

CORIANTUM[2]

This Jaredite was the son of Amnigaddah and the father of Com[2] (Ether 1:13–14). Coriantum[2] was the fifth generation to live in captivity. His son Com[2] was finally successful in breaking free (Ether 10:30–32).

CORIANTUMR[1]

This Jaredite was a son of King Omer, who spent half of his days in captivity (Ether 8:4). Coriantumr[1] was born under these conditions. He and his brother Esrom were successful in restoring their father to his place as head of the kingdom by defeating the army of the king who had deposed him (Ether 8:5–6). Unfortunately, they mercifully spared the life of the ousted king, Jared[3], who soon thereafter plotted once again against King Omer.

CORIANTUMR[2]

Coriantumr[2] was the last king of the Jaredite civilization, and except for the prophet Ether was its last survivor (Ether 15).

The tragic annihilation of the Jaredite civilization might be summed up in two words that apply to Coriantumr[2], "*If only!*"

Coriantumr[2] was the ruling monarch in the days of the prophet Ether (Ether 12:1–2). His reign was marked by constant warfare that was precipitated by the wickedness of the people, including Coriantumr[2] and his family (Ether 13:15–17). The Lord sent Ether to warn the king and his people of the dire consequences of their continued wickedness. Even though the nation was bedeviled by secret combinations, which sought to overthrow Coriantumr[2], Ether gave the king a promise and a warning: the *promise* was that "if he would repent, and all his household, the Lord would give unto him his kingdom and spare the people"; the *warning* was that "otherwise they should be destroyed, and all his household save it were himself. And he should only live to see the fulfilling of the prophecies" (Ether 13:20–21).

If only Coriantumr[2] had turned from his pride and wickedness, how different the history of his household and his people might have been. However, he "repented not, neither his household, neither the people; and the wars ceased not; and they sought to kill Ether" (Ether 13:22).

Coriantumr[2] was first defeated in battle by a man named Shared, who placed Coriantumr[2] in captivity. Coriantumr[2] was later restored to his position, only to reign over a kingdom in which there was "all manner of wickedness" (Ether 13:23–26).

In the continuing warfare, he ultimately faced off with a bloodthirsty man named Shiz. The stubborn, unbending, wicked wills of these two men led to the total destruction of the people of Jared (Ether 14–15).

Ether had prophesied that not only would the unrepentant Coriantumr[2] live to see the annihilation of his people, but also that he would be buried by another people who would inhabit the land (Ether 13:21). This was fulfilled when the people of Zarahemla (generally referred to as the Mulekites) found him and buried him nine months later (Omni 1:21).

CORIANTUMR[3]

The story of this descendant of Zarahemla, who was an apostate Nephite, is found in Helaman 1. He was the leader of an invading army of Lamanites that attacked the Nephite city of Zarahemla, which was the seat of government, around 51 B.C. (v. 15). Because of "so much contention and so much difficulty in the government," the Nephites were not prepared to meet the invading army and fell an easy prey to Coriantumr's forces (vv. 18–22).

Pridefully bolstered by his rapid victory, Coriantumr[3] marched his "large army" through the center of the Nephite land, cutting a swath of slaughter and destruction, sparing neither man, woman, or child (vv. 23–27). However, his vicious march lacked wise military tactics, and he plunged his army into a vulnerable position that led to its defeat and to Coriantumr's death (vv. 28–32).

CORIHOR[1]

Corihor[1] was the son of the Jaredite King Kib (Ether 7:3). At the age of thirty-two, he rebelled against his father and spent some years gathering an army of followers together.

Corihor[1] was successful in defeating his father and placing him in captivity (Ether 7:4–5). Years later, his younger brother Shule succeeded in organizing a revolt against Corihor[1] and restored their father Kib as the rightful ruler (Ether 7:7–9). "Corihor repented of the many evils which he had done," but sadly his own children turned to rebellion (Ether 7:13–15).

CORIHOR[2]

The only mention of Corihor[2] in the Jaredite record is in reference to his children, whom the record states did not repent from their sins (Ether 13:17). What a sad legacy for this father, both from a personal and historical viewpoint. What a different heritage might have been his if he had been able to say, "I have no greater joy than to hear that my children walk in truth" (3 John 1:4).

COROM

A son of the righteous Jaredite King Levi[2], Corom was anointed the successor king by his father. He followed his father's example and "did that which was good in the sight of the Lord all his days" (Ether 10:15–17).

COVENANT PEOPLE OF THE LORD

There are various groups who have been identified as the "covenant people of the Lord." The prophets Nephi[1] and Moroni[2] described scattered Israel as one such group (1 Nephi 14:14; Mormon 8:15). Nephi[1] also identified the Lamanites as the covenant people of the Lord. Nephi[1] further declared that "as many of the Gentiles as will repent are the covenant people of the Lord" (2 Nephi 30:2).

Mormon[2] included the Jews among the covenant people of the Lord (Mormon 3:21), and his son Moroni[2] included the entire house of Israel (Mormon 8:21).

In essence, the covenant people of the Lord are all those who have entered into sacred covenants with Him by receiving the saving and exalting ordinances of the gospel of Jesus Christ through proper priesthood authority.

"According to the terms of the covenant which God made with Abraham, all of the literal seed of that great prophet are entitled to receive the gospel, the priesthood, and all of the ordinances of salvation and exaltation. (Abra. 2:9–11; D. & C. 86:8–11.) When any of those descendants do receive all of these things [or when any are adopted into that lineage by receiving these covenants and ordinances], 'They become the sons of Moses and of Aaron and the seed of Abraham, and the church and kingdom, and the elect of God.'

(D. & C. 84:34.)" (McConkie, *Mormon Doctrine,* 126).

See also Chosen People; People of Christ; People of God; People of Jesus; People of the First Covenant; Saints of the Church of the Lamb.

COWDERY, OLIVER

Oliver Cowdery is not mentioned by name in the text of the Book of Mormon, but he is one of the "three witnesses" of whom Isaiah[1], Nephi[1], and Moroni[2] wrote (2 Nephi 27:12; Ether 5:3).

Furthermore, Oliver Cowdery (1806–1850) was second only to the Prophet Joseph Smith in the bringing forth of the Book of Mormon. While there were others who assisted for a time as scribes, it was Oliver who was to declare: "I wrote, with my own pen, the entire Book of Mormon (save a few pages,) as it fell from the lips of the Prophet Joseph Smith, as he translated it by the gift and power of God. . . . I beheld with my eyes and handled with my hands the gold plates from which it was transcribed" (*Millennial Star* 21 [1859]: 544).

Oliver arrived in Harmony, Pennsylvania on April 5, 1829, and two days later he began his service as the Prophet's scribe in the translation of the Book of Mormon.

It is of interest to note that the Prophet Joseph had a manifestation of the Lord's hand in leading Oliver Cowdery to Harmony to assist in the work. The Prophet recorded the following in his history: The Lord "appeared unto a young man by the name of Oliver Cowdry and shewed unto him the plates in a vision and also the truth of the work and what the Lord was about to do through me his unworthy servant therefore he was desirous to come and write for me and translate" (*The Personal Writings of Joseph Smith,* 8).

During the process of translating the Book of Mormon, Joseph and Oliver came upon numerous passages emphasizing the necessity of baptism. Knowing that true priesthood authority to administer that ordinance of salvation was *not at that time* found upon the earth, the two men made prayerful inquiry on the matter. While they knelt in humble prayer, the veil was parted and "a messenger from heaven descended in a cloud of light" (Joseph Smith—History 1:68).

The two men were visited by the resurrected John the Baptist, who conferred the Aaronic Priesthood upon them, which included the authority to baptize and to administer the "gospel of repentance" (Joseph Smith—History 1:69).

Of this experience, Oliver was later to declare: "*Where was room for doubt? Nowhere; uncertainty had fled, doubt had sunk no more to rise, while fiction and deception had fled forever!*"

(Joseph Smith—History, footnote, page 59; emphasis added.)

Thus began the first of a series of heavenly manifestations Oliver was privileged to share with the Prophet Joseph Smith. "No one except the Prophet Joseph was more honored with the ministering of angels than Oliver Cowdery," observed President James E. Faust (*Ensign,* November 2001, 47).

As the scribe in the translation process, Oliver Cowdery observed firsthand the spiritual power with which Joseph Smith was clothed. Additionally, he was one of three select men, whom we know as the Three Witnesses, who were privileged to have the Angel Moroni[2] personally show them the gold plates from which the Book of Mormon was translated. They heard the voice of God declaring the record to be true and bearing witness that the sacred record was "translated by the gift and power of God" ("The Testimony of Three Witnesses").

Unfortunately, Oliver, who served as the Second Elder of the Church, later succumbed to the disturbing spiritual tremors of disaffection, fault-finding, and pride, which he allowed into his life. Just as earth tremors can shake and cause the fall of once safe and secure buildings, so the spiritual tremors in Oliver's life ultimately led to his total estrangement from the true Church. He was finally excommunicated on April 12, 1838.

Oliver remained away from the faith he had helped found for almost a decade before he expressed a desire to return to his true spiritual roots. President Brigham Young (1801–1877) wrote to Oliver and invited him to "return to our father's house, from whence thou hast wandered, . . . and renew thy testimony to the truth of the Book of Mormon" (Letter from Brigham Young to Oliver Cowdery, 22 Nov. 1847, as quoted in *Ensign,* November 2001, 47).

In contrast to his earlier pride, Oliver came back with deep humility. He appeared before the high priests quorum and said: "Brethren, for a number of years I have been separated from you. I now desire to come back. I wish to come humbly and to be one in your midst. I seek no station. I only wish to be identified with you. I am out of the Church. I am not a member of the Church, but I wish to become a member of it. I wish to come in at the door. I know the door. I have not come here to seek precedence. I come humbly and throw myself upon the decisions of this body, knowing, as I do, that its decisions are right, and should be obeyed" (Smith, *The Restoration of All Things,* 114–15).

Although Oliver reclaimed his membership in the Church, he was unable to reclaim lost blessings that might have been his had he not become disaffected and departed from his faith. Of this loss, President Gordon B. Hinckley said: "He never regained the incomparable promise given him by the Lord that, conditioned upon his faithfulness, he should have glory and be given 'strength such as is not known among men.' (D&C 24:12.)" (*Ensign,* May 1989, 48).

It must be emphasized that in his years away from the Church, even in his bitterness, Oliver Cowdery remained adamant in his declaration of the divine origin of the Book of Mormon and of the heavenly manifestations in which he had been a privileged participant.

Oliver Cowdery was rebaptized and was desirous of joining the main body of The Church of Jesus Christ of Latter-day Saints, which by then was located in the Rocky Mountains, but his health deteriorated and he died before achieving that desire.

True to his testimony of the Book of Mormon, Oliver reiterated his wit-

ness on his deathbed. His half-sister, Lucy C. Young, reported: "Just before he breathed his last he asked to be raised up in bed so he could talk to the family and friends and he told them to live according to the teachings in the book of Mormon and they would meet him in Heaven Then he said lay me down and let me fall asleep in the arms of Jesus and he fell asleep without a struggle" (Letter of Lucy Cowdery Young, 7 March 1887, Archives of The Church of Jesus Christ of Latter-day Saints; quoted in Maxwell, *If Thou Endure It Well,* 61, footnote 11).

Of this momentous and last mortal moment, Elder Neal A. Maxwell (1926–2004) exclaimed: "What an exit endorsement!" (*Ensign,* January 1997, 41).

See also Witnesses, Three.

CUMENIHAH

Cumenihah was among the many military leaders serving under Mormon[2] who was killed with his ten thousand in the Nephites' final battle at Cumorah (Mormon 6:14).

D

DAMASCUS, HEAD OF

See Rezin.

DAVID

This Old Testament king of Israel is referred to twice in the Book of Mormon, once in Isaiah's writings (2 Nephi 19:7; Isaiah 9:7) and once as a bad example (Jacob 1:15).

One of the all-time tragic stories is that of the boy who went from humble shepherd to wearing a king's crown, but in the process lost a crown infinitely more valuable than the golden and jeweled symbol of earthly royalty. David the shepherd boy courageously defended his flock of sheep when they were attacked by a bear and a lion (1 Samuel 17:34–36). With great faith in the Lord, he later defended the flock of Israel against the giant Goliath and his army of Philistines (1 Samuel 17:37–51).

At the time he was anointed king, "David behaved himself wisely in all his ways; and the Lord was with him" (1 Samuel 18:14). That description of young David should serve as both a model and a warning. For while this young hero had clearly set an early course of righteousness, he failed to endure.

David's adulterous affair with another man's wife, and his treacherous act in having the husband killed in a vain effort to cover up his sin, led to David's loss of his exaltation.

David failed to turn away in a moment of weakness, when he allowed lustful thoughts to consume his thinking and then acted on them. Many years later, the Apostle James warned against this very process: "Every man is tempted, when he is drawn away of his own lust, and enticed. Then when lust hath conceived, it bringeth forth sin: and sin, when it is finished, bringeth forth death" (James 1:14–15). Such is the sad story of David!

See also David, House of.

DAVID, HOUSE OF

The house of David is spoken of in the writings of Isaiah[1], which Nephi[1] copied into the Nephite record (2 Nephi 17:2, 13; Isaiah 7:2, 13). In this context, the term has specific reference to prophecies regarding the pending attack upon the southern kingdom of Judah (the house of David) by the kingdoms of Syria and Israel (the northern kingdom). The warnings were directed to Ahaz, king of Judah.

In a more general sense, the house of David has reference to the descendants of him who was once king of united Israel and from whose posterity the Savior was born. In the dedicatory prayer of the Kirtland Temple, the Prophet Joseph Smith prayed that the Lord would extend His mercy to the scattered children of Jacob (Israel) and that "the yoke of bondage may begin to be broken off from the house of David" (D&C 109:62–63).

See also David.

DEMONS

The only mention of demons in all of scripture is in Helaman 13:37, where the Lamanite prophet Samuel states the wicked people are "surrounded by demons." He goes on to identify them as "the angels of him who hath sought to destroy our souls." These evil angels are those rebellious spirits who rejected the greater Light (Christ) and chose to follow the prince of darkness, the devil (D&C 29:36).

See also Angels of the Devil; Perdition, Son of.

DEVIL

The devil is that fallen spirit who in the premortal world unsuccessfully sought to displace Deity and sit on the throne of God, thereby resulting in his being cast out of heaven (2 Nephi 2:17; Moses 4:1–4; Abraham 3:27–28; D&C 76:25–28). He defiantly led away a third of our Heavenly Father's children in the premortal world and continues his war against God and the two-thirds who chose to follow the Father and Christ (D&C 29:36; 76:29). He is described as "the enemy of God" (Mosiah 27:9). The devil's avowed purpose is to make all inhabitants of this earth "miserable like unto himself" (2 Nephi 2:18, 27), for he seeks "to destroy the souls of men" (Helaman 8:28).

Having been cast out of God's presence, the devil continues to wage war on God's plan for the happiness and salvation of His children. In his demented desire to "destroy the world," the devil beguiled Eve to partake of the forbidden fruit, which brought about the Fall. However, as Elder Neal A. Maxwell (1926–2004) observed, "Satan's brilliance is unanchored and contains a *fatal flaw*: now, as then, Satan 'knew not the mind of God' [Moses 4:6]" (*Deposition of a Disciple*, 89; emphasis added). Thus, while the evil one will glory in occasional victories and carnal conquests, his ultimate defeat and banishment are unalterably decreed.

Satan has been described as "multi-talented, but his memories of what might have been gnaw at him constantly. No wonder he is an incurable insomniac" (*Deposition of a Disciple*, 36). He has "great wrath, because he knoweth that he hath but a short time" (Revelation 12:12). "And thus he goeth up and down, to and fro in the earth, seeking to destroy the souls of men" (D&C 10:27).

The devil's treacherous promises of pleasure to those whose hearts and minds he captures lead them down the path of suffering and sorrow. Truly he is "that wicked one who was a liar from the beginning" (D&C 93:25). Those who foolishly follow him and listen to his lies will woefully discover that "the devil will not support his children at the last day, but doth speedily drag them down to hell" (Alma 30:60).

Elder James E. Faust (1920–) noted that the devil "is really a coward, and if we stand firm, he will retreat" (*Ensign,* November 1987, 35). Thus, where righteousness prevails, he has no power (1 Nephi 22:26). However, as the Prophet Joseph Smith warned, "The moment we revolt at anything which comes from God, the devil takes power" (*Teachings of the Prophet Joseph Smith,* 181).

See also Dragon; Evil One; Gadianton; Lucifer; Satan; Son of the Morning.

DEVILS

See Angels of the Devil; Demons; Devil.

DISCIPLES, TWELVE

In vision, Nephi[1] saw the time when the resurrected Redeemer would visit the Nephites and select twelve of them to be His special disciples. Nephi[1] was informed that these twelve disciples were "righteous forever" and would be the judges of his descendants (1 Nephi 12:6–10). The fulfillment of this vision came when the post-crucifixion Christ visited ancient America and gave twelve specially chosen disciples authority to govern His Church among their people (3 Nephi 11:19–22; 12:1; 18:36–37). The twelve were Nephi[3], Timothy, Jonas[1], Mathoni, Mathonihah, Kumen, Kumenonhi, Jeremiah[2], Shemnon, Jonas[2], Zedekiah[2], and Isaiah[2].

While these men are not spoken of as Apostles, perhaps to distinguish them from the twelve who accompanied Jesus in His mortal ministry, their charge to bear witness of Him was the same: "Ye shall testify that ye have seen me, and that ye know that I am" (3 Nephi 12:2). Truly, these ancient twelve disciples were the "special witnesses" of Christ in their day, just as the Apostles of The Church of Jesus Christ of Latter-day Saints are in our day (D&C 107:23, 26).

Before Christ ascended for the final time as He concluded His brief ministry among these ancient people, He invited each of the twelve to express their heartfelt desire to Him. Nine of them asked that, when their ministry was complete, they might "speedily come" to Him in His kingdom. The other three were desirous of remaining on the earth until the Second Coming, and were granted that hope (3 Nephi 28:1–12).

See also Three Nephite Disciples.

DRAGON

The writings of Isaiah[1] recorded in the Book of Mormon speak of one who "wounded the dragon" (2 Nephi 8:9; Isaiah 51:9). Footnote 1ᶜ in Isaiah 27:1 (LDS edition of the Bible) identifies a dragon as "a legendary sea-monster representing the forces of chaos that opposed the Creator."

Who is it that is at war with the Creator, constantly opposing Him? Satan, the devil, the fallen angel Lucifer, the defiant spirit whom Michael defeated in premortal battle (Revelation 12:7–9; 20:2).

E

ELIJAH

Elijah was an Old Testament prophet who held the priesthood keys of sealing. Malachi prophesied that Elijah would return to the earth in order to "turn the heart of the fathers to the children, and the heart of the children to their fathers" (Malachi 4:5–6; 3 Nephi 25:5–6; see also D&C 2:1; Joseph Smith—History 1:36–39). His return to the earth has long been anticipated by the children of Israel. Through the centuries, devout Jews have reserved a vacant seat for him at their annual Passover meal. Unknown to, or presently unaccepted by, these followers of Moses is that while their chairs remained unoccupied, on April 3, 1836, Elijah came to the Kirtland Temple. On that occasion he restored the long-awaited sealing keys of the priesthood to the Prophet Joseph Smith and Oliver Cowdery (D&C 110:13–16).

Elijah's "recorded words are few but forceful, and his deeds are explicit evidences of his strength of will, force of character, and personal courage. He was an example of solid faith in the Lord" (LDS Bible Dictionary, 664).

His life story is full of examples of an undeviating faith that continually showed he was a true servant of Jehovah, the God of Israel. Standing boldly before the wicked ruler Ahab, Elijah declared the heavens would be sealed. No rain fell for three and one-half years. During much of this time Elijah was fed by ravens. He then performed miracles for the widow of Zarephath, who fed him from the last morsels of food she had saved as a final meal for her and her son. In return, Elijah promised that her "barrel of meal shall not waste, neither shall the cruse of oil fail, until the day that the Lord sendeth rain upon the earth." Additionally, he restored the life of her son (1 Kings 17:14).

In a dramatic showdown with 450 priests of Baal, plus 400 idol-worshiping priests of Ashtoreth, this powerful prophet forcefully demonstrated who was following the true and living God. Taunting the priests for their lack of success in having their offering consumed by the lifeless god Baal, Elijah called down fire from heaven, which consumed his offering to Jehovah. He then proceeded to slay all of the false priests (1 Kings 18).

In spite of successfully demonstrating the power of the Lord, Elijah faced a personal point of discouragement because of the continued wickedness of the people. It was on this occasion that, in striking sequence, Elijah experienced the difference between the "still small voice" and wind, earthquake, and fire (1 Kings 19:9–12).

Elijah was dramatically taken from mortality without tasting of death in order that he might continue his ministry (2 Kings 2:11). He appeared on the Mount of Transfiguration to restore the sealing keys to Peter, James, and John (Matthew 17:1–3).

EMER

The son of the Jaredite King Omer and the father of Coriantum[1], Emer was anointed king by his father (Ether 9:14–15). Because of Emer's righteousness, "the Lord began again to take the curse from off the land, and the house of Emer did prosper exceedingly under the reign of Emer" (Ether 9:16). What a different world it would be if all kings, rulers, presidents, and magistrates could have it said of them, as it was of Emer: "And Emer did execute judgment in righteousness all his days" (Ether 9:21).

EMRON

Emron is one of three "choice men" mentioned by Mormon[2] in an epistle to his son Moroni[2] (Moroni 9:2). The men were killed in "a sore battle" with the Lamanites.

ENOS[1]

This son of Seth[1] and grandson of Adam and Eve (Genesis 4:25–26) is not mentioned in the Book of Mormon but is briefly mentioned here in order to clarify why the superscript "2" has been added to the name of Enos[2], the son of Jacob[2]. An account of the ministry of the Old Testament Enos[1] can be found in Moses 6:13–18 and Doctrine and Covenants 107:44, 53.

ENOS[2]

This prophet is distinguished as Enos[2] in the index in the Triple Combination. Enos[1] refers to the Old Testament grandson of Adam who is not mentioned in the Book of Mormon. Enos[2] was the son of Jacob[2] and the grandson of Father Lehi[1] (Jacob 7:27; 1 Nephi 18:7).

Enos[2] became the third of the Nephite record keepers. Lehi's son Nephi[1] was the first, and as he neared the end of his life and ministry he gave the records to his brother Jacob[2], with a charge to write "the things which [Jacob] considered to be most precious" (Jacob 1:1–5). Jacob, in turn, entrusted the record to his son Enos[2], who promised to safeguard the sacred nature of that which should be written on the plates (Jacob 7:27).

It is interesting that Enos[2] is occasionally portrayed in a negative light. The assumption is made that because he admits to a "wrestle which [he] had before God" in seeking a remission of his sins, that he was a wayward man (Enos 1:2). Was Enos[2] really confessing to the life of a prodigal, ready to make a turnabout, *or* was he merely stating his desire to deepen his spirituality?

Consider a similar "confession" of another young man, the Prophet Joseph Smith: "I frequently fell into many foolish errors, and displayed the weakness of youth. . . . In consequence of these things, I often felt condemned for my weakness and imperfections" (Joseph Smith—History 1:28–29). Like Joseph Smith, Enos[2] turned to prayer at a defining moment in his life and received divine direction.

Revelation and forgiveness of sins came to Enos[2] because his "soul hungered" and he "cried . . . in mighty prayer . . . all the day long" and into the night (Enos 1:4). His was not a casual, lip-service approach to heaven's doors, but a deeply felt prayer of faith that came from the depths of his heart.

As a result of his sincere pleadings, the voice from heaven was heard, and the Lord spoke peace to his mind and soul. "Wherefore," Enos[2] recorded, "my guilt was swept away" (Enos 1:6). Enos[2] then experienced an intense feeling of love for both the Nephites and the Lamanites and prayed mightily in their behalf. He followed this epiphany with action, sharing his testimony with others for the rest of his life. It was a path that truly caused him to rejoice (Enos 1:9–19, 26). Before he passed through the veil to see the face of the Redeemer "with pleasure," he passed the records on to his son Jarom (Ether 1:27; Jarom 1:1).

EPHRAIM

Although Ephraim is mentioned in the Book of Mormon, this does *not* refer to an individual who lived in the Nephite-Lamanite or Jaredite period of time in ancient America. Rather, it is a name that appears in the writings of Isaiah[1] found on the plates of brass, and it refers to the *tribe of Ephraim,* named after Ephraim, the son of Joseph[1] (2 Nephi 17:2, 5, 8, 9, 17; 19:8–9, 21; 21:13). Ephraim also represented the dominant tribe of the northern kingdom of Israel, as opposed to Judah, which was the dominant tribe of the southern kingdom.

Elder Erastus Snow (1818–1888) taught that Ishmael[1], whose family joined Father Lehi[1] in their journey into the wilderness, "was of the lineage of Ephraim" (in *Journal of Discourses,* 23:184–85). Most significant to the Book of Mormon, however, is that the Lord Himself called the record "the stick of Ephraim" (D&C 27:5).

There is a hill named Ephraim in the Book of Mormon, which is referenced in the history of the Jaredites (Ether 7:9). The naming of this hill may presuppose it was named after a man named Ephraim. (It could not have been named after the Ephraim in the Old Testament, since the Jaredites departed from the Old World before that Ephraim had been born.)

See also Ephraim, Head of; Manasseh: Pekah.

EPHRAIM, HEAD OF

At a time when the northern kingdom of Israel had joined with the country of Syria in warring against the southern kingdom of Judah, the prophet Isaiah[1] recorded the following: "And the head of Ephraim is Samaria, and the head of Samaria is Remaliah's son" (2 Nephi 17:9; Isaiah 7:9).

At this time the "head" referred to was Pekah, who was the son of Remaliah and the king of the northern kingdom (Ephraim) of Israel, with headquarters in Samaria (2 Nephi 17:1). Pekah was joined in an unholy alliance with the king of Syria (head of Damascus) against the southern kingdom of Judah (2 Nephi 17:1–6).

See also Pekah.

ESROM

This faithful son of the Jaredite King Omer appeared to be born during his father's period of captivity (Ether 8:2–4). Esrom and his brother Coriantumr[1] raised an army and defeated their upstart brother Jared[3], who had placed their father in captivity. Nothing more is recorded of the Jaredite Esrom. The genealogical record of the great patriarch Abraham in the Bible does identify another Esrom (Matthew 1:3; Luke 3:33).

ETHEM

This Jaredite king was the son of Ahah and the father of Moron (Ether 1:8–9). Tragically for the people he ruled, his reign was one of wickedness. His subjects seemed to follow his evil ways, for they rejected the prophets of God who came to save them, "and the prophets mourned and withdrew from among the people" (Ether 11:11–14). Thus, rather than rejoicing in the precious truth offered them, they rejected the Atonement and the Giver of this great gift (D&C 88:33). They chose that which could only bring them ultimate misery.

ETHER

Ether is the prophet who lived to see the destruction of the entire Jaredite civilization and after whom the book containing the account of that people's history is named. He was born during the captivity of his father, Coriantor (Ether 11:23). The record does not reveal how Ether was divinely tutored and called as the Lord's prophet to this doomed people. We are simply told he "came forth in the days of [the Jaredite king] Coriantumr[²], and began to prophesy unto the people, for *he could not be restrained because of the Spirit of the Lord which was in him*" (Ether 12:2; emphasis added).

He was a great example of performing his labors zealously and of magnifying his calling, "For he did *cry from the morning, even until the going down of the sun,* exhorting the people to believe in God unto repentance lest they should be destroyed, saying unto them that by faith all things are fulfilled" (Ether 12:3; emphasis added).

It is conceivable that every time Ether went forth to preach, his courage and his commitment to the calling the Lord had given him were tested. His message of repentance was certainly not one which the remaining inhabitants of a doomed nation wanted to hear. In spite of the "great and marvelous" prophecies of Ether,

the people "esteemed him as naught, and cast him out" (Ether 13:13). In fact, they sought to kill him (Ether 13:22).

He was forced to hide himself in a cave, where he recorded the destruction of the people (Ether 13:13–14). Even then, at the direction of the Lord, Ether made one last effort to call King Coriantumr² and his people to repentance, but to no avail (Ether 13:20–22). Their unquenchable thirst for blood, unbendable pride, and general wickedness destroyed the people just as Ether had prophesied. The obviously saddened prophet "finished his record," of which Moroni² said he had not included "the hundredth part" (Ether 15:33).

Ether's faith and faithfulness are expressed in the "last words" he wrote: "Whether the Lord will that I be translated, or that I suffer the will of the Lord in the flesh, it mattereth not, if it so be that I am saved in the kingdom of God. Amen" (Ether 33:34).

EVE

Eve is mentioned several times in the Book of Mormon in the capacity of her foreordained role to participate in the Fall. Her action put in motion the rest of the plan of salvation, which included bringing Father in Heaven's spirit sons and daughters to earth to gain mortal bodies (1 Nephi 5:11; 2 Nephi 2:15–20; Alma 42:2–15).

While the scriptures are clear that Eve was deceived (1 Timothy 2:14) by the devil, the fact is also clear that her partaking of the forbidden fruit was part of the divine plan. She would be accountable for her actions, but those actions would initiate a key part of God's plan for his children: "Were it not for our transgression," Eve noted, "we never should have had seed, and never should have known good and evil, and the joy of our redemption, and the eternal life which God giveth unto all the obedient" (Moses 5:11). Thus, Satan, who "knew not the mind of God" (Moses 4:6), unwittingly facilitated Eve's making the *right* choice.

Eve was one of the "noble and great ones," male and female, who were chosen in premortality for significant callings on earth (Abraham 3:22). Certainly, "our glorious Mother Eve" (D&C 138:39) was foremost among the "faithful daughters" of the great Elohim.

"For a wise and glorious purpose . . . [God has] withheld the recollection of [our] former friends and birth" ("O My Father," *Hymns*, no. 292). Thus, we know little of our premortal life. There is no question, however, that every human being once dwelt with Heavenly Parents in "royal courts on high," where we were nurtured and taught in the ways of God and His righteousness. Moral agency, the right to choose the course we would pursue, was very much a part of that experience. Using their agency, some excelled in faithfulness. Mother Eve was one who obviously distinguished herself. It would be to her that our Father in Heaven would trust the title of "mother of all living" (Genesis 3:20; Moses 4:26).

The significance of this title, as it applies to all the daughters of Eve, was noted by Patricia T. Holland. Said she, "As I tenderly acknowledge the very real pain that many single women, or married women who have not borne children, feel about any discussion of motherhood, could we consider this one possibility about our eternal female identity—our unity in our diversity? Eve was given the identity of 'the mother of all living'—years, decades, perhaps centuries before she ever bore a child. It would appear that her *motherhood preceded her maternity*, just as surely as the perfection of the Garden preceded the struggles of mortality. I believe *mother* is one of those very carefully chosen words, one of those rich words—with meaning after meaning after meaning. We must not, at all costs, let that word divide us. I believe with all my heart that it is first and foremost a statement about our nature, not a head count of our children" (*Ensign*, October 1987, 33).

EVIL ONE

The evil one clearly refers to the devil, he "who seeketh to destroy the souls of men" (Helaman 8:28). While his followers, both mortals and un-embodied spirits, can be referred to as *an* evil one in seeking to carry out the devil's destructive desires, *the* evil one is one of *his* titles (2 Nephi 4:27; 9:28; Alma 46:8; Helaman 12:4; 16:21; Mormon 1:19). In contrast, the righteous who seek to emulate Christ, embracing "Light and truth[,] forsake the evil one" (D&C 93:37).

EVIL SPIRITS

See Angels of the Devil; Demons; Devil.

EZIAS

This prophet of Old Testament times is mentioned but once in all of scripture (Helaman 8:20). He is cited as one of the ancient prophets who testified of Christ (Helaman 8:13–23). Elder Orson Pratt (1811–1881) suggested that "Ezias may have been identified with Esaias, who lived contemporary with Abraham" (Reynolds, *Dictionary of the Book of Mormon,* 103).

F

FALLEN PEOPLE

As found in the Book of Mormon, the term *fallen people* was specifically applied to the citizens of Ammonihah by the great missionary Alma[2] as he taught the Atonement: "Ye ought to bring forth works which are meet for repentance, seeing that your hearts have been grossly hardened against the word of God, and seeing that ye are a lost and a fallen people" (Alma 9:30). These people had fallen from the Light that could have blessed their lives.

In a *second* and universal sense, Alma[2] taught the doctrine of the Fall and Atonement: "Now we see that Adam did fall by the partaking of the forbidden fruit, according to the word of God; and thus we see, that by his fall, *all* mankind became a lost and fallen people" (Alma 12:22; emphasis added). However, *all* mankind may be redeemed from the effects of the Fall through the Atonement of Christ: "For behold, as in Adam, or by nature, they fall, even so the blood of Christ atoneth for their sins" (Mosiah 3:16).

To be lifted from this fallen state requires not only the grace of Christ, but also obedience to the means whereby the Atonement can become efficacious in our lives: "We believe that through the Atonement of Christ, all mankind may be saved, by obedience to the laws and ordinances of the Gospel" (Articles of Faith 1:3).

In a *third* sense, not specifically mentioned in the Book of Mormon, fallen people refer to the descendants of Father Lehi[1] and Mother Sariah. The Lord identified the Book of Mormon as "a record of a fallen people" (D&C 20:9).

President Ezra Taft Benson (1899–1994) rhetorically asked, "Why did they fall?" In response he replied, "Mormon gives the answer in the closing chapters of the book in these words: 'Behold, the pride of this nation, or the people of the Nephites, hath proven their destruction.' (Moro. 8:27.) And then, lest we miss that momentous Book of Mormon message from that fallen people, the Lord warns us in the Doctrine and Covenants, 'Beware of pride, lest ye become as the Nephites of old.' (D&C 38:39.)" (*Ensign*, May 1989, 4).

FATHER, THE

Just as Adam is the common father of all who have gained a tabernacle of flesh upon this earth, so the Great Elohim is *the* Father of the spirits that inhabit those tabernacles of flesh (Hebrews 12:9; D&C 93:23). President Brigham Young (1801–1877) declared, "Our Father in Heaven begat all the spirits that ever were, or ever will be, upon this earth" (in *Journal of Discourses,* 1:50).

"Of all the titles by which God might have chosen to be known, the fact that he has instructed us to address him as 'Father' should underscore the reverence in which this name should be contemplated and uttered (Matt. 6:9). 'After this manner therefore pray ye: Our *Father* who art in heaven, *hallowed be thy name*' (3 Ne. 13:9; italics added)" (Brewster, *Doctrine & Covenants Encyclopedia,* 176).

FATHER, JESUS CHRIST AS

In speaking to the brother of Jared², the premortal Savior declared: "Behold, I am Jesus Christ. I am the Father and the Son" (Ether 3:14). Centuries later, the Nephite prophet Abinadi taught of Christ's role as Father (Mosiah 15). In an official declaration of doctrine, the First Presidency and the Twelve Apostles wrote: "Jesus Christ is not the Father of the spirits who have taken or yet shall take bodies upon this earth, for He is one of them. He is The Son, as they are sons and daughters of Elohim" (Clark, *Messages of the First Presidency,* 5:34).

Jesus Christ is the "Father" in three very distinct ways. First, as the Creator of this earth, He is appropriately called the Father of heaven and earth (2 Nephi 19:6; Mosiah 15:1–4; Alma 11:38–39; Ether 4:7). Second, through His Atonement, Christ is the Father of those who receive the ordinances and covenants of His gospel and through their obedience qualify for exaltation in the celestial kingdom. "And now, because of the covenant which ye have made ye shall be called the *children of Christ, his sons, and his daughters;* for behold, this day he hath spiritually begotten you; for ye say that your hearts are changed through faith on his name; therefore, ye are born of him and have become his sons and his daughters" (Mosiah 5:7; emphasis added). The third way in which Christ is Father is by divine investiture of authority, granted Him by His holy Father. He is fully empowered to speak and act for the Father. "I and my Father are one," proclaimed this divine Son of God (John 10:30; see also John 17:22; 3 Nephi 20:35; 28:10; D&C 50:43).

See also Father of Heaven and Earth.

FATHER OF HEAVEN AND EARTH

King Benjamin's sermon included the use of a title of the Savior that relates to His premortal earthly role as the Creator: "Jesus Christ, the Son of God, the Father of heaven and earth, the Creator of all things from the beginning" (Mosiah 3:8). Over one hundred years later, Samuel, a Lamanite prophet, also declared the Redeemer to be "Jesus Christ, the Son of God, the Father of heaven and of earth, the Creator of all things from the beginning" (Helaman 14:12).

As directed by His Father, Elohim, Jesus Christ created the heavens and the earth. During the darkness that prevailed upon the lands of America following the crucifixion of the Savior, His voice was heard to declare, "Behold, I am Jesus Christ, the Son of God. I created the heavens and the earth, and all things that in them are" (3 Nephi 9:15).

Moroni², the last scribe of the Book of Mormon record, would later declare Christ to be "a God of miracles, even the God of Abraham, and the God of Isaac, and the God of Jacob; and it is that same God who created the heavens and the earth, and all things that in them are" (Mormon 9:11).

In a doctrinal exposition by the First Presidency and Twelve Apostles in 1916, the meaning of the term *creator* was explained: "The Creator is an Organizer. God created the earth as an organized sphere; but He certainly did not create, in the sense of bringing into primal existence, the ultimate

elements of the materials of which the earth consists, for 'the elements are eternal.' (D&C 93:33). . . . Jesus Christ, whom we also know as Jehovah, was the executive of the Father, Elohim, in the work of creation. . . . He is very properly called the Eternal Father of heaven and earth" (Clark, *Messages of the First Presidency,* 5:26–27).

See also Father, Jesus Christ As.

FREEMEN

About 67 B.C., a group of Nephite patriots arose in response to the efforts of an arrogant portion of the people who took upon themselves the name of king-men. The king-men desired the law to be changed so that a king would replace the chief judge in governing the people. On the other hand, the freemen "covenanted to maintain their rights and the privileges of their religion by a free government" (Alma 51:1–6). The freemen were also called the "people of liberty" (Alma 51:7, 13). The matter was put to a vote of the people, and the king-men were defeated at the polls. However, the matter was not settled in this democratic fashion, for the king-men later rebelled.

The next mention of freemen is several years later in a rebuking epistle of Captain Moroni¹ to Pahoran¹, the chief judge; there the magistrate is wrongly accused of treachery for his lack of support for Moroni's army of freemen, who are battling the Lamanites (Alma 60:25). In the magnanimous response of Pahoran[1], he tells Moroni[1] that he has been deposed by the king-men and the freemen have been prevented through intimidation from coming to Moroni's aid (Alma 61:1–5). The freemen, along with Pahoran[1], had been driven from the city of Zarahemla. In response to the civil uprising, Moroni[1] gathered remnants of freedom-loving people from throughout the land and defeated the king-men in battle, restoring Pahoran[1] to his office and freedom to the people (Alma 62:1–9).

See also King-Men.

G

GADIANTON

Around 51 B.C., Gadianton assumed leadership of the wicked rebels who had formed a secret combination with the intent of killing the chief judge of the Nephites and overthrowing the duly elected government. He "was exceedingly expert in many words, and also in his craft, to carry on the secret work of murder and of robbery." Because of his evil expertise, "he became the leader of the band of Kishkumen" (Helaman 2:2–4).

Gadianton introduced his followers to secret plans of wickedness, enjoining them to engage in acts of terrorism that included murder, robbery, plunder, and whoredoms. They had "secret signs" and "secret words" and entered into evil covenants to protect one another in their diabolical deeds (Helaman 6:22–23).

Although the secret plans of wickedness Gadianton possessed were had anciently by the Jaredite people, he did not obtain his knowledge of the plans from the records of that fallen nation. These records were safeguarded by Helaman[3]. Rather, Gadianton obtained his knowledge of these evil plans from the original

founder of pernicious conspiracy—the devil himself. Gadianton, like Cain before him, joined with the evil one who "spread[s] the works of darkness and abominations over all the face of the land" (Helaman 6:28; see vv. 25–30).

The wicked band of people he led became known as "Gadianton's robbers and murderers" (Helaman 6:18). Their wicked influence and acts of violence continually vexed both the Nephites and the Lamanites, with only temporary interruptions, from the time the secret combination was first organized until the Nephite people were finally destroyed as a nation (Ether 8:21). The Gadiantons prospered in their wickedness because of the iniquity of the general population (Helaman 11:34).

Various forms of Gadianton robbers and murderers are found throughout the earth today, not only in terrorist organizations but also in secret combinations that plot in back rooms to commit fraud, to lie and cheat, and destroy the freedoms of others. The goal of these conspiratorial organizations and groups remains the same as anciently: "to get power and gain" and to "overthrow the freedom of all lands, nations, and countries" (Ether 8:22–25). The ancient prophet-scribe Moroni[2] warned that we should "suffer not that these murderous combinations shall get above you" (Ether 8:23).

GADIANTON ROBBERS

See Gadianton.

GAZELEM

A name given by the Lord to a servant (seer) who would be given a "stone" (Urim and Thummim) whereby he would be enabled to translate ancient records (Alma 37:23; see also Mosiah 8:13). One scholarly source provides the following explanation of the word *gazelem:* "The word appears to have its roots in Gaz—a stone, and Aleim, a name of God as a revelator, or the interposer in the affairs of men. If this suggestion is correct, its roots admirably agree with its apparent meaning—a seer" (Reynolds and Sjodahl, *Commentary on the Book of Mormon,* 4:162).

"In three different revelations, spanning a period of two years (1832–34), Joseph Smith was called 'Gazelam' by the Lord (D&C 78:9; 82:11; 104:26, 43, 45, 46; all in the pre-1981 edition). His name was disguised in order to prevent his enemies from discovering what plans the Lord had in mind at that particular time"

(Brewster, *Doctrine & Covenants Encyclopedia,* 204).

GENTILE

The name *Gentile* is first found on the title page of the Book of Mormon. The ancient prophet Moroni[2] wrote that among the purposes for which the record had been written, safeguarded, and brought forth was "to the convincing of the Jew and Gentile that JESUS is the CHRIST, the ETERNAL GOD."

"The term *Gentiles* is one of the most often used yet least understood words in Mormon culture. Its usage in scripture generally refers to those who are not of the house of Israel (descendants of Abraham through the lineage of Jacob and his twelve sons). However, the principle of adoption applies to all who join The Church of Jesus Christ of Latter-day Saints; they become of Israel regardless of their blood lines (Abr. 2:9–11; Gal. 3:26–29; *TPJS* [1938], 149–50).

"The term *Gentile* has been used in the following ways: (1) to refer to the descendants of Noah's son, Japheth (Gen. 10:1–5); (2) to identify those who have not descended from Abraham; (3) to classify those who have not descended from Jacob; (4) to identify those who have not descended from Judah; and (5) to distinguish the 'non-Mormon.' It is interesting to note that the term *Gentile* has been translated as 'not of Judah' in both the German (*Nichtjuden*) and Dutch (*Niet-Joden*) editions of the Book of Mormon" (Brewster, *Doctrine & Covenants Encyclopedia*, 207).

Additionally, the term *Gentile* has been used "to designate nations that are without the gospel. . . . This latter usage is especially characteristic of the word as used in the Book of Mormon" (LDS Bible Dictionary, 679).

Nephi[1] saw in vision "many nations and kingdoms of the Gentiles" (1 Nephi 13:1–3). He also saw "many multitudes of the Gentiles" coming to the "land of promise," where the "Spirit of the Lord" prospered them, and they "were delivered by the power of God out of the hands of all other nations" (1 Nephi 13:12–19).

This ancient Nephite prophet also saw the "record of the Jews" (the Bible) which proved to be "of great worth unto the Gentiles" (1 Nephi 13:20–23). Although Nephi[1] saw that "many plain and precious things" would be taken from the Bible, he also saw that "other books" containing the "power of the Lamb" (Christ) would clarify and "establish the truth of the first." These records would serve the purpose of convincing both the Gentiles and the house of Israel "that the records of the prophets and of the twelve apostles of the Lamb are true" (2 Nephi 13:24–41).

The Book of Mormon is chief among those "other books" and is the word of the Lord "to the Gentiles" (D&C 19:26–27).

"And it shall come to pass, that if the Gentiles shall hearken unto the Lamb of God in that day that he shall manifest himself unto them in *word*, and also in *power*, in very deed, unto the taking away of their stumbling blocks . . . , they shall be numbered among the house of Israel" (1 Nephi 14:1–2; emphasis added).

GID

A Nephite military officer around 63 B.C., Gid was appointed chief captain of a group of soldiers assigned to guard and escort prisoners to Zarahemla (Alma 57:29). While en route, the Nephites overheard the alarming news that large "armies of the Lamanites" were on their way to attack the Nephite city of Cumeni. Overhearing the news, the Lamanite prisoners took courage and rushed upon Gid and his fellow soldiers, and many were able to escape. Gid led his soldiers to the defense of the city of Cumeni and prevented its loss (Alma 57:30–36). He later was part of a Nephite strategy that enabled them to recapture Nephite cities (Alma 58:16–23). Gid took no personal credit for his successes. "Blessed is the name of our God," he declared, "for behold, it is he that has delivered us;

yea, that has done this great thing for us" (Alma 57:35).

GIDDIANHI

This evil man was the leader of the secret society of Gadiantons around A.D. 16. He sent an epistle to the Nephite governor Lachoneus¹ in which he arrogantly demanded that Lachoneus¹ and his people surrender themselves, their possessions, and their lands to the wicked band of robbers and murderers (3 Nephi 3). In the typical way of the wicked, Giddianhi brazenly accused the righteous of wrongdoing, claiming it was the dissenters who had been wronged (3 Nephi 3:9–10).

Lachoneus¹ responded with the truth, declaring that the dissenters "had received no wrong, save it were they had wronged themselves by dissenting away unto those wicked and abominable robbers" (3 Nephi 3:11). Unable to subsist except through plunder, Giddianhi led the robbers in an attack upon the Nephites in which he was defeated and slain (3 Nephi 4:1–14).

And so it will be with all the wicked who fight against God and His righteous people. They may find temporary power and pleasure through their wickedness and for a time escape the justice of God, but whether in this life or the next, they will ultimately be called to a reckoning.

GIDDONAH¹

Giddonah¹ was the father of the great missionary Amulek and a descendant of Nephi¹ (Alma 10:2–3). The scriptural text indicates that initially Giddonah¹, together with his kinsfolk, were blessed by the visit of Alma² to Amulek's house (Alma 10:11). However, it appears that he later rejected both Alma's message and his son Amulek's conversion (Alma 15:16). Perhaps, like the seeds that fell on "stony places," the seeds of the gospel did not penetrate deeply enough into Giddonah's soul (Matthew 13:2–6).

GIDDONAH²

Giddonah² was a Nephite high priest in the land of Gideon who was challenged by the anti-Christ Korihor around 75 B.C. (Alma 30:21–29). When Giddonah² saw the hardness of Korihor's heart and that he would "revile even against God," neither he nor the chief judge in Gideon would debate the matter with this heretic. They simply bound him and sent him to Alma², the high priest over all the church, and to the chief judge over all the land (Alma 30:29).

Giddonah's handling of the situation is reminiscent of the way in which the Savior later responded to the heretic Herod: "He answered him nothing" (Luke 23:8–9). Both Giddonah and Jesus chose not to degrade the gospel by debating it with an unworthy man. They did not give "that which is holy unto the dogs, neither cast . . . pearls before swine" (3 Nephi 14:6; Matthew 7:6).

GIDEON

This Nephite patriot, who lived around 145 to 191 B.C., was truly one of the great men of the Book of Mormon. He first appeared as a righteous and courageous man who opposed the wicked reign of King Noah[3] (Mosiah 19:4). While he was fighting with the king, the Lamanites invaded the colony and Gideon spared the king's life, only to see the cowardly king and his miscreant priests forsake their families and flee for their own lives (Mosiah 19:5–11). Under Gideon's direction, a search party discovered that the king had been killed and his priests had fled to escape a similar fate (Mosiah 19:18–24).

Gideon then served under Limhi, the successor king, and his wise counsel prevented a massacre from taking place when the Lamanites falsely accused this Nephite colony of wrongs that had actually been done by the fugitive priests of Noah[3] (Mosiah 20:17–26). Gideon eventually proposed a plan that allowed the people to successfully escape the bondage of their captors (Mosiah 22:3–13).

He later became a teacher in "the church of God" and confronted the apostate Nehor, withstanding his false doctrine with "the words of God" (Alma 1:7–8). Angry, Nehor slew Gideon, who at that time was "stricken with many years" (Alma 1:9).

GIDGIDDONAH

The single mention of Gidgiddonah is in Mormon's listing of the Nephite military commanders who were each slain along with the ten thousand troops under their command in the final battle with the Lamanites (Mormon 6:13).

GIDGIDDONI

Appointed as the "chiefest among all the chief captains and the great commander of all the armies of the Nephites," Gidgiddoni came to the forefront of recognition at a critical time (3 Nephi 3:18). His appointment occurred shortly after the arrogant and wicked leader of the Gadianton band demanded the unconditional surrender of the Nephites (3 Nephi 3:1–10). Gidgiddoni's selection to lead the Nephite armies in defending their families was based on a wonderful principle of sound and inspired leadership:

"Now it was the custom among all the Nephites to appoint for their chief captains, (save it were in their times of wickedness) some *one that had the spirit of revelation and also prophecy; therefore, this Gidgiddoni was a great prophet* among them, as also was the chief judge" (3 Nephi 3:19; emphasis added).

The standard for determining a prophet was set long ago by one who understood the principle of prophecy: "The testimony of Jesus is the spirit of prophecy" (Revelation 19:10). How marvelous it would be if all leaders, whether military, political, or ecclesiastical, could meet those qualifications!

Gidgiddoni was successful in preparing the Nephites to defend themselves not only with temporal armor (3 Nephi 3:26) but also with spiritual armor (3 Nephi 4:8–10). The invaders were defeated in battle (3 Nephi 4:12–14; 24–27), and Gidgiddoni and the other righteous leaders restored peace (3 Nephi 6:6).

GILEAD

Gilead was the brother of the Jaredite rebel Shared and a member of the secret combinations of that day (Ether 14:3, 8). His brother had commenced a war against the king, and after his brother's death Gilead followed in his sibling's wicked footsteps in continuing the war and rebellion that had already caused so much bloodshed and suffering.

Gilead was briefly successful in occupying King Coriantumr's throne, but, in the ongoing drama of wickedness begetting wickedness, he was murdered by his own high priest (Ether 14:5–9).

Whether Gilead's actions were motivated by the false philosophy of "getting even" (seeking to avenge his brother's death) or by his own personal lust for power doesn't really matter, for both reasons are faulty. If he was seeking to "get even," he would have profited by following the advice of Elder Neal A. Maxwell (1926–2004), who observed that "we are only falling further behind by insisting on getting even" (*Ensign,* November 1987, 32).

GILGAH

One of four sons of Jared[2], the founder of the Jaredite civilization, Gilgah refused the offer to be a king over the people (Ether 6:14, 22–27). Nothing more is mentioned of him in the present record.

GILGAL

Gilgal was among the dozen military commanders Mormon[2] mentioned by name who were killed, each with his ten thousand soldiers, in the final battle with the Lamanites around A.D. 385 (Mormon 6:14).

GOD

The essence of Latter-day Saints' belief in God is stated in the first of our Articles of Faith: "We believe in God, the Eternal Father, and in His Son, Jesus Christ, and in the Holy

Ghost" (Article of Faith 1:1). These three Holy Beings of the Godhead are separate in form but one in purpose. Indeed, we declare, "The Father has a body of flesh and bones as tangible as man's; the Son also; but the Holy Ghost has not a body of flesh and bones, but is a personage of Spirit. Were it not so, the Holy Ghost could not dwell in us" (D&C 130:22).

The Father (Elohim) and the Son (Jehovah) are perfected and glorified Beings who possess all power, all knowledge, and every godly trait. The "brightness and glory" of their resurrected bodies "defy all description" (Joseph Smith—History 1:17).

We are commanded to humbly and lovingly acknowledge the Great Elohim as our Father and to pray to Him in the name of our Savior and Redeemer, Jesus Christ. "Perfect prayer is addressed to the Father, in the name of the Son (3 Ne. 18:19–21); and it is uttered by the power of the Holy Ghost; and it is answered in whatever way seems proper by him whose ear is attuned to the needs of his children" (McConkie, *Doctrines of the Restoration*, 67).

The names of God, Lord, and Father are among those sacred titles which are used interchangeably to refer to both Heavenly Father and His Beloved Son. However, throughout the Book of Mormon Christ is addressed as the God of the ancient patriarchs, Abraham, Isaac, and Jacob, or the God of Israel. In fact, Nephi[1] declared that his sole purpose in keeping the Book of Mormon record "is that I may persuade men to come unto the God of Abraham, and the God of Isaac, and the God of Jacob and be saved" (1 Nephi 6:4).

See also Christ; Christ, Names of; Father, The; Father, Jesus Christ As; Father of Heaven and Earth; Great Spirit; Holy Ghost; Immanuel; Jehovah; Jesus; Lamb of God; Messiah; Only Begotten of the Father; Prince of Peace; Redeemer; Savior; Spirit of the Lord.

GREAT SPIRIT

This is the term or name which the Lamanite King Lamoni, as well as his people, applied to Deity. The king mistakenly thought that Ammon[2] was the Great Spirit because of Ammon's demonstration of unusual power (Alma 18:1–19). Ammon[2] explained that he was but a servant of the Great Spirit, who was God (Alma 18:24–28). Ammon's brother Aaron[3] later had the opportunity to teach Lamoni's father that the Being he referred to as the Great Spirit was God (Alma 22).

See also God.

H

HAGOTH

This Nephite was "an exceedingly curious man" who around 55 B.C. built and launched many ships to carry adventurous people to lands north of what the Nephites called Bountiful and Desolation (Alma 63:5–8). His first "exceedingly large ship" made one round trip but never returned from a second trip, and it was supposed that the people had been "drowned in the depths of the sea" (Alma 63:5, 8). Alma's son Corianton sailed on one of Hagoth's ships (Alma 63:10). No mention is made of whether Hagoth himself ever embarked on one of his ships.

There is a tradition among Latter-day Saints in Polynesia and New Zealand that the lost ships of Hagoth found their way to the South Seas and that some of the people of that area are therefore descendants of Father Lehi[1] and Mother Sariah. It is alleged that President Joseph F. Smith (1838–1918) said: "You brethren and sisters from New Zealand, I want you to know you are from the people of Hagoth" (*Ensign*, February 1976, 7). However, nothing definitive has been declared as to the fate of Hagoth's ships.

HARRIS, MARTIN

Martin Harris, like his fellow witnesses, is not mentioned by name in the Book of Mormon, but he is one of the "three witnesses" of whom Isaiah[1], Nephi[1], and Moroni[2] wrote (2 Nephi 27:12; Ether 5:3).

Although twenty-two years older than the Prophet Joseph Smith, Martin Harris (1783–1875) was an important friend and colleague to his younger associate in the events that both fulfilled prophecy and brought forth the Book of Mormon. Martin sacrificed personal property and wealth to pay for the printing of this second witness or testament of Jesus Christ. But he also was responsible for the loss of what could have been an additional book or extended account within this sacred volume of ancient scripture. Yet, like his two fellow-witnesses—Oliver Cowdery and David Whitmer—Martin's name has been indelibly etched in the annals of history as one of the significant Three Witnesses to the Book of Mormon.

From April 12 to June 14, 1828, Martin Harris served as the Prophet's scribe. Earlier that year, he unknowingly became a participant in the fulfillment of ancient prophecy. The prophet Isaiah had long before prophesied that at some future time the *words* of a "sealed" book would be "delivered unto a man" (Joseph Smith), who in turn would deliver the words to "another" (Martin Harris), who would show them to the "learned" (Charles Anthon). The "learned" would then request that the entire book be brought to him. The request would be denied because at least a portion of the book was sealed. In response, the "learned" would declare, "I cannot [read it]; for it is sealed" (Isaiah 29:11–12; 2 Nephi 27:6–22; see also Joseph Smith—History 1:63–65).

Martin Harris was the key person in one of the most significant events to occur during the translation and publication of the Book of Mormon. He was responsible for losing 116 pages of translated manuscript that covered a period of history from the time Father Lehi[1] led his family out of Jerusalem in 600 B.C. to the beginning of the reign of the prophet-king Benjamin in about 130 B.C.

Martin had left his home in Palmyra to serve as the Prophet's scribe in Harmony, Pennsylvania. Upon the completion of 116 pages of translated manuscript, Martin persisted in asking Joseph to allow him to take the manuscript back to Palmyra to show his wife and other relatives.

Although the Prophet Joseph's petition of the Lord to permit Martin to take the manuscript was twice denied, at Martin's insistence Joseph asked a third time. This was to prove disastrous, for even though permission was granted, it led to the loss of the precious manuscript.

Martin Harris agreed to a strict promise—a covenant—to show the manuscript only to his wife, Lucy; his father and mother; his brother Preserved Harris; and his wife's sister, Abigail Cobb (Smith, *History of the Church*, 1:21). After arriving home, perhaps in his enthusiasm to share this treasure with others, Martin carelessly broke his covenant and showed the manuscript to others. Through his neglect and broken promise, the manuscript was stolen and never recovered. The Lord reprimanded Martin as "a wicked man" (D&C 3:12; 10:1).

This unfortunate episode in the life of Martin Harris is a firm reminder of how careful one must be in keeping promises and not becoming casual about covenants. The principle is well taught in Alma's counsel to his son Helaman:

"O remember, remember, . . . how strict are the commandments of God. And he said: If ye will keep my commandments ye shall prosper in the land—but if ye keep not his commandments ye shall be cut off from his presence" (Alma 37:13).

In spite of the terrible loss he had caused, Martin Harris was later able to regain the confidence of the Lord and His Prophet. Martin was yet to prove a blessing to the Church.

Of Martin's legacy to the Book of Mormon, Elder Dallin H. Oaks (1932–), of the Quorum of the Twelve Apostles, said:

"One of Martin Harris's greatest contributions to the Church, for which he should be honored for all time, was his financing the publication of the Book of Mormon. In August 1829 he mortgaged his home and farm to Egbert B. Grandin to secure payment on the printer's contract. Seven months later, the 5,000 copies of the first printing of the Book of Mormon were completed. Later, when the mortgage note fell due, the home and a portion of the farm were sold for $3,000. In this way, Martin Harris was obedient to the Lord's revelation:

"'Thou shalt not covet thine own property, but impart it freely to the printing of the Book of Mormon. . . .

"'Pay the debt thou hast contracted with the printer. Release thyself from bondage' (D&C 19:26, 35)" (*Ensign*, May 1999, 36).

One of the reasons Martin had to sell his property was that there was such a "bitter and destructive response" to the publication of the Book of Mormon that it did not sell well enough to pay the debt to the printer (*Ensign*, November 1982, 51).

In fulfillment of the Lord's promise that three special witnesses would be called to view the plates from which the Book of Mormon was translated (D&C 5:11–18), the Prophet Joseph Smith took Martin Harris, Oliver Cowdery, and David Whitmer into the woods near the Peter Whitmer Sr. home in Fayette. Each of the men prayed twice in succession for the promised manifestation, with no results. Finally, Martin suggested that his presence might be the problem, and he withdrew from the other three men. Shortly thereafter, Joseph and the other two men were visited by the Angel Moroni[2], who showed them the plates and other sacred artifacts. As promised, the voice of the Lord was heard from heaven declaring the record of the Book of Mormon to be true.

The Prophet Joseph then went in search of Martin, and found him "fervently engaged in prayer." Joseph joined him and ultimately they succeeded in obtaining the sought-for manifestation. With jubilation—sheer joy—Martin cried out: "'Tis enough; 'tis enough; mine eyes have beheld; mine eyes have beheld" (Smith, *History of the Church*, 1:54–55).

For the next few years, Martin Harris remained true to the Prophet and the Restoration. He was present on the day "the only true and living church upon the face of the whole earth" (D&C 1:30) was restored and was baptized into the Church that very day. He was the first man the Lord later called on by name to consecrate his property to the upbuilding of Zion (D&C 58:35), thus continuing his willingness to sacrifice worldly wealth for the cause of Christ's church.

In 1835, Martin along with the other two who comprised the Three Witnesses, was appointed to "search out the Twelve [Apostles]" (D&C 18:37). The three acted under the direction of the First Presidency (see Roberts, *A Comprehensive History of the Church,* 1:372–75).

Unfortunately, during trying times in the Church in 1837, Martin later confessed that he "lost confidence in Joseph Smith" and "his mind became darkened" (Anderson, *Investigating the Book of Mormon Witnesses,* 110). His faltering faith ultimately led to his departure and excommunication from the Church and from the work in which he had served with such sacrifice.

To one who had been involved in a fraud, this would have been a logical point at which to denounce and deny that which he had previously embraced. However, Martin had not been involved in falsehoods. He stood unwavering in his witness of the truths he had experienced. He would later declare, "It is not a mere belief, but is a matter of knowledge. I saw the plates and the inscriptions thereon. I saw the angel, and he showed them unto me" (*Investigating the Book of Mormon Witnesses,* 116).

With a softened heart, Martin Harris was rebaptized in Kirtland, Ohio, in 1842. Although his family moved to Utah in 1856, Martin remained in Kirtland for some years. During an 1860 census he told the interviewer that he was a "Mormon preacher" (*Improvement Era,* July 1955, 505).

In 1870, at the age of 87, Martin Harris responded to a "warm invitation" from President Brigham Young to join his family and the Saints in Utah. At the age of ninety-two, he died in Clarkston, Utah, true to his testimony of the Book of Mormon and once again enfolded safely in the True Shepherd's flock.

Reiterating his testimony before his death, Martin declared, "I tell you of these things that you may tell others that what I have said is true, and I dare not deny it; I heard the voice of God commanding me to testify to the same" (*Investigating the Book of Mormon Witnesses,* 118).

Elder Dallin H. Oaks taught that there are three specific lessons we can learn from the life of Martin Harris:

"(1) Witnesses are important, and the testimony of the Three Witnesses to the Book of Mormon is impressive and reliable. (2) Happiness and spiritual progress lie in following the leaders of the Church. (3) There is hope for each of us, even if we have sinned and strayed from a favored position" (*Ensign,* May 1999, 37).

See also Learned, The; Witnesses, Three.

HEARTHOM

This early Jaredite king was the son of Lib[1] and the father of Heth[1] (Ether 1:16–17). After reigning for twenty-four years, he was deposed in a rebellion and spent the "remainder of his days" in captivity (Ether 10:30).

HELAM

Helam was among those humble people who responded to the "private" teachings of Alma[1] as he taught the words of the martyred prophet Abinadi. Helam had the distinction of being the first person of record to be baptized by Alma[1] (Mosiah 18:7–14). In a unique fashion, not repeated with subsequent baptisms, Alma[1] buried himself as well as Helam in the baptismal waters. Some have wondered whether Alma[1] was simultaneously baptizing himself. To this query, President Joseph Fielding Smith (1876–1972) responded: "If [Alma[1]] had authority to baptize that is evidence that he had been [previously] baptized. Therefore, when Alma baptized [immersed] himself with Helam that was not a case of Alma baptizing himself, but merely as a token to the Lord of his humility and full repentance" (*Answers to Gospel Questions,* 3:203).

When Alma's small colony of believers had to flee to escape the wrath of the wicked King Noah[3], they went to a land which they named Helam. Perhaps this was in honor of the first convert to Christ's newly formed church (Mosiah 23:1–4, 19).

HELAMAN[1]

The youngest son of the Nephite King Benjamin, Helaman[1] reaped the blessing of having a righteous father who was anxious to have his children properly taught. This prophet-king taught his three sons "in all the language of his fathers, that thereby they might become men of understanding; and that they might know concerning the prophecies which had been spoken by the mouths of their fathers" (Mosiah 1:2). Helaman[1] was taught the importance of searching the scriptures in order to know God and to maintain faith in Him (Mosiah 1:3–8).

HELAMAN[2]

The eldest son of Alma[2] the Younger was given the name of Helaman[2] (Alma 31:7). His trustworthiness and faithfulness is evidenced in the fact that his father passed on to him the responsibility for keeping the records from which the Book of Mormon was translated, as well as entrusting him with safeguarding other sacred resources (Alma 37:1–3, 21–24, 47). Helaman's recording of Nephite history is found in Alma 45 through 62.

The direct counsel of Alma[2] to his son Helaman[2] is found in Alma 36 and 37. This faithful father recounted the story of his conversion and testified, perhaps in anticipation of the trials Helaman[2] would yet face in life, that "whosoever shall put their trust in God shall be supported in their trials" (Alma 36:3). Helaman[2], who was yet in his "youth," was counseled by his father to "keep the commandments of God" and to "let all [his] doings be unto the Lord" (Alma 37:35–36).

Helaman[2] later served as a Church leader, establishing the Church "in all the land" (Alma 45:21–22). He taught "the word of God with much power" (Alma 62:45). In addition to his spiritual ministry, he became a great military leader during a time of widespread warfare. His command consisted of 2,060 of the young sons of the Anti-Nephi-Lehies, or the people of Ammon[2] (Alma 53:18; 57:6). These young men, who were virtually boys, "never had fought, yet they did not fear death; and they did think more upon the liberty of their fathers than they did upon their lives" (Alma 56:47). At critical times, when others' lives were in danger, Helaman[2] and his untested band of young warriors stood the tests and saved the day (see Alma 56–58).

While Captain Moroni's faith and feats received great public acclaim, the compiler of the Book of Mormon wrote the following tribute of Helaman[2] and his associates in the ministry: "Helaman and his brethren were *no less serviceable* unto the people than was Moroni" (Alma 48:19; emphasis added). This is a stirring reminder that one need not occupy the number-one chair, be presented with the gold cup or blue ribbon, receive the citation for being the community's most valuable citizen, have his or her name prominently displayed on public marquees, or even be widely known in order to *make a difference for good* in the world. God needs a "supporting cast" as well as the so-called "headliners."

Following the cessation of warfare, Helaman[2] returned to the ministry and "went forth, and did declare the word of God with much power unto the convincing of many people of their wickedness, which did cause them to repent of their sins and to be baptized unto the Lord their God" (Alma 62:45).

Having accomplished his purpose in life, saving souls as well as lives, this faithful man passed on to continue his work on the other side of the veil (Alma 62:52).

HELAMAN³

This faithful son of Helaman² followed in the footsteps of his righteous father in doing good. He was given responsibility for maintaining the sacred Nephite record (Alma 63:11), and the book of Helaman is named after him. He was elected to fill the position of chief judge and was saved from a murderous plot against him through the intervention of a faithful, yet unnamed servant (Helaman 2:1–9).

The essence of his service is summarized in the following verse: "Helaman did fill the judgment-seat with justice and equity; yea, he did observe to keep the statutes, and the judgments, and the commandments of God; and he did do that which was right in the sight of God continually; and he did walk after the ways of his father, insomuch that he did prosper in the land" (Helaman 3:20).

After the death of Helaman³ (Helaman 3:37), his righteous influence continued through his sons, Nephi² and Lehi⁴. He gave his two

sons meaningful and reminding names—the names of two righteous ancestors, Lehi¹ and Nephi¹. He said he had done this so that they would "remember them; and when ye remember them ye may remember their works; and when ye remember their works ye may know how that it is said, and also written, that they were good.

"Therefore, my sons, I would that ye should do that which is good, that it may be said of you, and also written, even as it has been said and written of them" (Helaman 5:6–7).

HELAMAN², SONS OF

A boy reciting the Scout Oath today pledges on his honor to "do [his] best to do [his] duty to God and to [his] country." Centuries before this oath was even conceived, 2,000 valiant young men known as "stripling soldiers" (Alma 53:22) "entered into a covenant to fight for the liberty of the Nephites, yea, to protect the land unto the laying down of their lives" (Alma 53:17). Having "been taught by their mothers" (Alma 56:47–48; 57:21), they were prepared to act in a time of great need.

These soldiers were sons of the Anti-Nephi-Lehies, or people of Ammon². Their ranks were later enlarged by another sixty of their younger brothers (Alma 57:6). Their military leader, Helaman², referred to them as his "sons" and they affectionately called him "father" (Alma 56:46). Having "put their trust in God continually" (Alma 57:27), their lives were miraculously preserved (Alma 57:24–26).

See also Anti-Nephi-Lehies.

HELEM

The single mention of Helem is his listing as one of three "brethren" of Ammon[1] who accompanied him about 121 B.C. in searching for Zeniff's colony, "the people who went up to dwell in the land of Lehi-Nephi" (Mosiah 7:1; see also Omni 1:27–30). Ammon[1], Helem, Amaleki[2], and Hem were taken prisoner by the guards of King Limhi, who was then reigning among the survivors of Zeniff's colony (Mosiah 7:1–9). Upon discovering that they were not his enemies but instead were searchers sent to find them, the king set them free (Mosiah 7:8–16). Under Ammon's direction, he and his traveling companions led the colony safely back to the main body of the Nephites (Mosiah 22).

See also Amaleki[2]; Ammon[1]; Hem.

HELORUM

Helorum was one of three sons who had the good fortune to be born to the righteous prophet and Nephite King Benjamin (Mosiah 1:2). With his brothers, he was taught to understand and to "diligently" search the scriptures as recorded on the plates of brass and the records of the Nephite prophets (Mosiah 1:2–8). Nothing further is mentioned of him in the record. In keeping with a scriptural declaration, we may suppose that his early training from a righteous father remained with him through the remainder of his life: "Train up a child in the way he should go: and when he is old, he will not depart from it" (Proverbs 22:6).

HEM

Hem was one of "sixteen strong men" who were sent by King Mosiah[2] on an expedition to see if they could locate descendants of the colony of Zeniff that had gone to inhabit the land of Lehi-Nephi (Omni 1:27–30; Mosiah 7:1–2). Hem was selected to join three others in leaving the rest of the group behind at a base camp while the four men explored further (Mosiah 7:3–6). The four men—Ammon[1], the leader; Hem; Amaleki[2]; and Helorum—were taken prisoner by the very people they were trying to find, who had mistakenly thought they were enemies. However, when their true identity was made known, the four captives were released and participated in a plan that freed the remaining inhabitants of the colony of Zeniff from their bondage to the

Lamanites and the wicked priests of King Noah³ (Mosiah 7:7–16; 22).

See also Amaleki²; Ammon¹; Helem.

HETH¹

This early Jaredite was the son of Hearthom and the father of Aaron² (Ether 1:16). He was born during the captivity of his father, a deposed king, and lived his entire life under those conditions (Ether 10:31).

HETH²

Heth lived in the Jaredite civilization and was the son of Com¹ and father of Shez¹ (Ether 1:25–26). Heth² lived during a time of "exceedingly great wickedness," and he himself "began to embrace the secret plans again of old, to destroy his father," who was king at that time (Ether 9:26). The wicked son murdered his father and took his place on the throne (Ether 9:27). Heth's evil acts extended to murdering the prophets, whom he had "cast into pits [leaving] them to perish" (Ether 9:29). The wicked people lost the right to blessings from the Lord and instead suffered from famine, mayhem, and being overrun by poisonous serpents (Ether 9:30–35). The despot king himself, including "all his household save it were Shez," perished in the famine (Ether 10:1).

HIMNI

One of the lesser known of the four sons of King Mosiah², Himni joined his brothers—Ammon², Aaron³, and Omner—in their rebellion against the church around 100–74 B.C. They "were numbered among the unbelievers." Not only did they align themselves with falsehood, but they joined their fellow rebel, Alma², in seeking to destroy the church, "causing much dissension . . . [and] giving a chance for the enemy of God to exercise his power over them" (Mosiah 27:8–10).

Except in individual missionary endeavors, Himni and his brothers are generally referred to as a group—the "sons of Mosiah" (see Mosiah 27:8; 28:1; 29:3; Alma 17:1–2; 36:6). Although raised in the righteous home of King Mosiah², they chose the path of rebellion for a time. Called to repentance by an angel of God, the rebels turned their lives to good (Mosiah 27:11–20).

This incident is illustrative of a gospel truth taught by Elder Dallin H. Oaks (1932–) of the Quorum of the Twelve Apostles: "The power of the Atonement and the principle of repentance show that we should never give up on loved ones who now seem to be making many wrong choices" (*Ensign,* November 2000, 34).

Following this miraculous occurrence, Himni and his brothers ("those who were with Alma at the time the angel appeared unto them") traveled about preaching the "good tidings of good," even though *they* then became the targets of persecution by the unbelievers (Mosiah 27:32–37).

Their former friends now taunted them and "laughed [them] to scorn" (Alma 26:23). Being ridiculed for standing up for righteousness is part of being a committed follower of Christ. Elder Neal A. Maxwell (1926–2004) taught, "Given the perils of popularity, Brigham Young advised that this 'people must *be kept where the finger of scorn can be pointed at them*' (*Discourses of Brigham Young*, sel. John A. Widtsoe [1941], 434)" (*Ensign*, May 1996, 68; emphasis added).

So powerful was the change of heart for Himni and his brothers that these once "very vilest of sinners" now "could not bear that any human soul should perish" (Mosiah 28:3–4). They spent the next fourteen years of their lives preaching the gospel in the most difficult of circumstances.

While the testimonies of the sons of Mosiah[2] may have been initiated by an angelic rebuke, those testimonies were retained and strengthened because of their unwavering commitment to their mission and because they "had searched the scriptures diligently" and "given them-

selves to much prayer, and fasting" (Alma 17:2–3).

See also Aaron[3]; Ammon[2]; Mosiah[2], Sons of; Omner.

HOLE OF THE PIT
See Sarah (Sarai).

HOLY GHOST
This third member of the Godhead is "a personage of Spirit. Were it not so, the Holy Ghost could not dwell in us" (D&C 130:22). President Joseph Fielding Smith (1876–1972) taught that the Holy Ghost "*is a Spirit, in the form of a man*," and "It is a waste of time to speculate" regarding whether or not He will be given a body at some future time (*Doctrines of Salvation*, 1:38, 39).

Based upon the description of Christ's baptism by John the Baptist (1 Nephi 11:27; 2 Nephi 31:8), some have erroneously concluded that the Holy Ghost can assume different forms, even that of a dove. The Prophet Joseph Smith clarified this doctrine: "The sign of the dove was instituted before the creation of the world, a witness for the Holy Ghost, and the devil cannot come in the sign of a dove. The Holy Ghost is a personage, and is in the form of a personage. It does not confine itself to the *form* of the dove, but in [the] *sign* of the dove. The Holy Ghost cannot be transformed into a dove; but the sign of a dove was given to John to signify the truth of the deed, as the dove is an emblem or token of truth and innocence" (*Teachings of the Prophet Joseph Smith,* 276).

Because the Holy Ghost is an individual Personage, He "can no more be omnipresent in person than can the Father or the Son, but by his intelligence, his knowledge, his power and influence, over and through the laws of nature, he is and can be omnipresent throughout all the works of God" (Joseph F. Smith, *Gospel Doctrine,* 61).

A major mission of the Holy Ghost is to testify of the reality of Jesus as the Christ, the Promised Messiah, the Son of God, the Redeemer and Savior of the world. To this end, the truthfulness of the Book of Mormon, which is *Another Testament of Jesus Christ,* can be known "by the power of the Holy Ghost.

"And by the power of the Holy Ghost ye may know the truth of *all* things" (Moroni 10:4–5; emphasis added).

It is by the "power of the Holy Ghost" that truth is carried "unto the hearts of the children of men" (2 Nephi 33:1).

The Holy Ghost is also referred to as the *Holy Spirit.* In addition to testifying of Christ and of all truth,

the Holy Ghost prompts people to make right choices and to eschew evil.

The great missionary Amulek taught that God the Father, Christ the Son, and the Holy Spirit are "one Eternal God" (Alma 11:44), meaning one in purpose, mind, will, power, and godly qualities. Their united goal is to bring about the "immortality and eternal life" of our Father's children (Moses 1:39).

Those who humble themselves, repent, and accept the saving and exalting ordinances of the gospel of Jesus Christ are "sanctified by the Holy Spirit" (Alma 5:54). Such individuals are the recipients of "many revelations," for they "have communion with the Holy Spirit, which maketh manifest unto the children of men, according to their faith" (Jarom 1:4). "For they that are wise and have received the truth, . . . have taken the Holy Spirit for their guide, and have not been deceived" (D&C 45:57).

See also God; Spirit of the Lord.

HOLY MEN

In a specific sense, "holy men" are those priesthood leaders who have been called and received authority to lead Christ's Church upon the earth. In a more general sense, holy men *and* women are they who follow the "Holy One" (2 Nephi 9:41), even Jesus Christ, the Perfect One who thinks and acts in all holiness. Holy men and women are they who "stand . . . in holy places, and [are] not moved" (D&C 87:8).

President Ezra Taft Benson (1899–1994) taught that "these holy places include our temples, our chapels, our homes, and the stakes of Zion, which are, as the Lord declares, 'for a defense, and for a refuge from the storm, and from wrath when it shall be poured out without mixture upon the whole earth' (D&C 115:6)" (*New Era,* May 1982, 50).

To be called a holy man or woman does not imply that one has reached perfection, never again to make a mortal mistake. As a member of the Quorum of the Twelve Apostles, President Lorenzo Snow (1814–1901) provided the following comforting thought for those who are striving to do their best but have occasional missteps:

"And if we could read in detail the life of Abraham, or the lives of other great and holy men, we would doubtless find that their efforts to be righteous were not always crowned with success. Hence we should not be discouraged if we should be overcome in a weak moment; but, on the contrary, straightway repent of the error or the wrong we may have committed, and as far as possible repair it, and then seek to God for renewed strength to go on and do better" (in *Journal of Discourses,* 20:190).

During the righteous reign of King Benjamin, "There were many holy men in the land, and they did speak the word of God with power and with authority; and they did use much sharpness because of the stiff-neckedness of the people" (Words of Mormon 1:17). It is with the help of these holy men that King Benjamin was able to "establish peace in the land" (Words of Mormon 1:18).

Benjamin himself is called a holy man, and other righteous men have also been described with that appellation of honor: Nephi[1], Jacob[2], Joseph[2], and Sam (Alma 3:6); Alma[2] (Alma 10:7–9); and the prophet Elisha (2 Kings 4:9). It is interesting to consider the possibility that the humble shepherds in Bethlehem's fields would be among the "just and holy men" to whom the joyful news of Christ's birth would be announced (Alma 13:25–26). The scriptures were written by "holy men of God [who] spake as they were moved by the Holy Ghost" (2 Peter 1:21).

HOLY SPIRIT
See God; Holy Ghost.

HOUSE OF DAVID
See David, House of.

HOUSE OF ISRAEL
See Israel, House of.

I

IMMANUEL

This name is found twice in the Book of Mormon, both times as quoted from passages from Isaiah found upon the plates of brass (2 Nephi 17:14; 18:8; Isaiah 7:14; 8:8). Immanuel is one of the titles of Christ, who is the Messiah, and it means "God with us." "It signifies that Christ as God will be born into mortality of a virgin and will be among the people to save and redeem them [Matthew 1:23]. This prophecy received its fulfillment in Christ" (LDS Bible Dictionary, 706).

See also Christ.

ISAAC

This Old Testament patriarch is most often mentioned in the Book of Mormon in connection with one of the titles given to Jesus Christ, who is Jehovah, or the God of Abraham, Isaac, and Jacob (1 Nephi 6:4; 19:10; Mosiah 7:19; 23:23; Alma 29:11; 36:2; 3 Nephi 4:32; Mormon 9:11).

Isaac was the miracle child born to 100-year-old Abraham and 90-year-old Sarah (Genesis 17:17). His birth was a similitude of the miracle birth of the Babe of Bethlehem, for, like Jesus, Isaac was born under circumstances that defied usual standards. Isaac was born of an aged woman seemingly not capable of conceiving and bearing children (Genesis 18:11), and Jesus was born of a virgin (Luke 1:34).

Another significant similitude, referred to by the Nephite prophet Jacob[2] (Jacob 4:5), occurred in Isaac's life when his father, Abraham, was commanded by the Lord to offer his covenant son as a sacrifice on Mount Moriah. The covenant Son of the Eternal Father would also be offered as a sacrifice. But while Isaac's life would be spared (Genesis 22:9–13), "there was no voice from heaven to spare the life of Jesus. There was no ram in the thicket to be offered as a substitute sacrifice" (Thomas S. Monson, *Ensign,* December 1990, 4).

While Isaac is often portrayed as being but a young lad at the time of the intended sacrifice, he was more than likely in his thirties. Shortly after the events on Moriah, Sarah, at the age of 127 died, making Isaac 37 at the time of her passing. His age is significant because it indicates that Isaac submitted willingly to Abraham's efforts to offer him as a sacrifice. Certainly, the aged father (probably

137 years old) could not have forcibly bound his much younger son.

Isaac's obedience to, and therefore his faith in, the teachings of his father were very evident in the matter of marriage. While arranged marriages were traditional, it was still an act of obedience and faith on Isaac's part that allowed Abraham to be the broker, as it were, in finding a wife for his son (Genesis 24).

The LDS Bible Dictionary describes Isaac as "a peace-loving shepherd, of great personal piety, full of affection for the members of his own family" (707). His desire for peace was evidenced when the Philistines covered the wells Isaac had dug. Rather than seeking revenge or retribution, Isaac simply moved to another location (Genesis 26:12–17).

Isaac's faithfulness was rewarded with great promises by the Lord (Genesis 26:1–5). We are informed in latter-day revelation that because he was faithful and obedient he has "entered into [his] exaltation" (D&C 132:37).

ISABEL

One of only four women whose names are recorded in the Book of Mormon, Isabel has the dubious distinction of being remembered for her sinfulness. Around 73 B.C. she was a harlot who "did steal away the hearts of many," including that of the mis-

sionary Corianton, Alma's son (Alma 39:3–4). The seduction of this missionary led to nonbelievers rejecting the word of God that Alma[2] and his fellow missionaries had been preaching; "for when they saw [Corianton's] conduct they would not believe" (Alma 39:11).

Isabel's immoral behavior was "most abominable above all sins save it be the shedding of innocent blood or denying the Holy Ghost" (Alma 39:5).

ISAIAH[1]

This Old Testament prophet ministered in Israel from about 740 to 701 B.C. He is responsible for having written a scriptural record containing many Messianic prophecies as well as the history and destiny of the house of Israel. "Tradition states that he was 'sawn asunder' during the reign of [the wicked king] Manasseh; for that reason he is often represented in art holding a saw" (LDS Bible Dictionary, 707).

The name of this Old Testament prophet is found frequently in the Book of Mormon. The prophet Nephi[1] considered Isaiah's writings so important that he copied a number of chapters of Isaiah's writings verbatim onto the plates, which had limited space and on which it was difficult to engrave (see Jacob 4:1). The obvious esteem in which these writings were held by Nephi[1] is found in his declaration, "I shall give commandment unto my seed, that they shall not occupy these plates with things which are not of worth unto the children of men" (1 Nephi 6:6).

"The inclusion of Isaiah in the Book of Mormon is purposeful! Further evidence of this is found in the fact that Jesus Christ Himself quoted the words of this Old Testament prophet during His brief postmortal ministry in the Americas.

"The resurrected Redeemer not only quoted the words of Isaiah, but He commanded that they should be *searched* (3 Nephi 20:11), not just skimmed or, even worse, skipped. Jesus later reemphasized: 'Ye ought to search these things. Yea, a *commandment* I give unto you that ye *search* these things *diligently;* for great are the words of Isaiah' (3 Nephi 23:1; italics added)" (Brewster, *Isaiah Plain & Simple*, xii).

Elder Boyd K. Packer (1924–) astutely observed: "The prophecies of the Old Testament prophet Isaiah . . . loom as a barrier, like a roadblock or a checkpoint beyond which the casual reader, one with idle curiosity, generally will not go. . . . Perhaps only after you read the Book of Mormon and return to the Bible will you notice that the Lord quotes Isaiah seven times in the New Testament; in addition, the Apostles quote Isaiah forty

more times. One day you may revere these prophetic words of Isaiah in both books. The Lord had a purpose in preserving the prophecies of Isaiah in the Book of Mormon, notwithstanding they become a barrier to the casual reader" (*Ensign,* May 1986, 61).

ISAIAH[2]

The only mention of this man is his selection as one of the resurrected Christ's special twelve disciples when He visited the inhabitants of ancient America (3 Nephi 19:4). He obviously was one who was spiritually prepared for this significant calling in which he and eleven others were given priesthood authority to preside over Christ's church in that land. No other specific mention is made of him.

See also Disciples, Twelve.

ISHMAEL[1]

This man of great faith was led by the Spirit around 600 B.C. to forsake his home in Jerusalem and respond to the prophet Lehi's invitation to take his family into the wilderness (1 Nephi 7:1–5). Imagine how Ishmael[1] must have felt when Lehi's sons came with the request that he pack up what was portable and follow these young men to an unknown destination, leaving everything else behind. While "the Lord did soften the heart of Ishmael, and also his household" (1 Nephi 7:5), it nevertheless took great faith on the part of Ishmael[1], his unnamed wife, and his children to make this consecrated sacrifice.

Elder Erastus Snow (1818–1888) provided an insight as to why the family of Ishmael[1] was selected to join with Lehi's family in their journey. Said he, "The Prophet Joseph informed us . . . Ishmael was of the lineage of Ephraim, and . . . his sons, married into Lehi's family" (in *Journal of Discourses,* 23:184–85). Thus, though only the four sons of Lehi[1] and Sariah are mentioned in Nephi's record, there were also daughters in his family.

After the journey from Ishmael's house to the camp of Lehi[1] began, all was not well. Perhaps as a foretaste of tragic events that the future would yet bring to this nomadic group, the ever-murmuring Laman[1] and Lemuel were joined in a rebellion by "two of the daughters of Ishmael, and the two sons of Ishmael and their families" (1 Nephi 7:6). Nephi[1] was successful in quelling this uprising and they continued their journey, joining with Lehi[1] (1 Nephi 7:7–22).

Ishmael[1] and his wife had five unmarried daughters, who soon became the wives of the four sons of Lehi[1] and of Zoram[1], the former servant of Laban (1 Nephi 16:7).

The last mention of Ishmael[1] is of his death at a place in the wilderness they called Nahom (1 Nephi 16:34). Unfortunately, his death became a catalyst for those inclined to a rebellious spirit to once again stir up difficulties in the camp of Lehi[1]. However, "the voice of the Lord came and did speak many words unto them, and did chasten them exceedingly; and after they were chastened by the voice of the Lord they did turn away their anger, and did repent of their sins" (1 Nephi 16:35–39).

ISHMAEL[2]

This man is mentioned only once in the record. The missionary-prophet Amulek, who was the son of Giddonah, identified Ishmael[2] as his grandfather (Alma 10:2). This citation reveals the importance the Nephites placed upon knowing their ancestral lines, for Ishmael[2] is identified as "a descendant of Aminadi; and it was that same Aminadi who interpreted the writing which was upon the wall of the temple, which was written by the finger of God."

ISHMAEL[1], SONS OF

Other than identifying them as sons of Father Ishmael[1], these two men are not identified by name but only by reputation and actions. They, together with their father, mother, and five sisters, were persuaded by the Spirit to join Father Lehi's family in their journey into the wilderness, which eventually led to a "land of promise" (1 Nephi 7:1–5).

The rebellious spirit of these sons of Ishmael[1] was displayed shortly after their journey began, as they joined with Lehi's two rebellious sons, Laman[1] and Lemuel, in challenging the leadership and inspired counsel of Nephi[1]. He was bound by the rebels, and they even sought to kill him (1 Nephi 7:6–16). It is at this point that "one of the sons of Ishmael" joined with his mother and one of his sisters in pleading for the life of Nephi[1] (1 Nephi 7:19). Unfortunately, this is the only recorded occasion when one of these sons of Ishmael[1] tried to do the right thing.

The constant murmuring of these two sons was a hallmark of their character (1 Nephi 16:20; 2 Nephi 4:13). Upon arriving in the land of promise, they remained aligned with Laman[1] and Lemuel and were partakers of the "mark" which the Lord set upon them and their posterity (2 Nephi 5:19–24; Alma 3:6–7; 17:19; 43:13; 47:35).

It is of interest to note that when Nephi[1] was warned by the Lord to take those who would follow him and flee from the murderous intent of Laman[1], Lemuel, and the sons of Ishmael[1] to take his life, among Nephi's followers were his "sisters" (2 Nephi 5:1–6). Were these *sisters* the wives of the sons of Ishmael[1], or were they previously unmentioned sisters? The present record gives no clarification on this matter. Perhaps the answer lies in the 116 pages of the lost manuscript which the Prophet Joseph Smith initially translated (see D&C 3; 10; Smith, *History of the Church,* 1:21–23).

ISHMAELITES

An Ishmaelite in the Book of Mormon is a descendant of Ishmael[1], the father of the two sons who aligned themselves with the rebellious sons of Lehi[1]. Although the term Ishmaelite is occasionally used to refer to them, they essentially lost their distinctive family identity and became known as Lamanites (Jacob 1:13–14; Alma 3:6–7; 47:35). A latter-day revelation promises that the descendants of Ishmael[1], "who dwindled in unbelief because of the iniquity of their fathers," shall yet receive "the knowledge of a Savior" through the Book of Mormon (D&C 3:16–20).

See also Ishmael[1]; Ishmael[1], Sons of.

ISRAEL

This name was given to Isaac's son Jacob[1] by the Lord (Genesis 28:27–28; 35:10), and by extension to his descendants. "Historically, the name *Israel* has been used in the following ways: (1) a personal name for Jacob; (2) a name applied to all of Jacob's descendants; (3) the titular name bestowed on the faithful followers of Christ; (4) the name whereby the northern tribes were known, especially after the division of the United Kingdom (1 Sam. 11:8); (5) the name whereby Judah, the nation of Jews, has been known, whether as a distinct body occupying a land called *Israel,* or as a group of scattered people" (Brewster, *Doctrine & Covenants Encyclopedia,* 270).

See also Israel, House of; Israel, Lost Tribes of; Israel, Tribes of; Jacob[1].

ISRAEL, HOUSE OF

In general, the house of Israel refers to descendants of Jacob[1], whom the Lord renamed Israel (Genesis 32:27–28; 35:10). He had twelve sons that became known as the twelve tribes of Israel. The "house of Israel" is first mentioned on the title page of the Book of Mormon and is found throughout this volume of scripture. In a more limited sense, the house of Israel refers specifically to the *covenant people* of the Lord, those who have made sacred covenants with Him and received priesthood-administered saving ordinances (1 Nephi 13:23; 14:14; 15:14; 3 Nephi 21:22–23).

Latter-day Saints believe that those who accept the restored gospel of Jesus Christ, with its accompanying saving and exalting covenants and ordinances, become the "covenant people" of the Lord, members of the house of Israel (2 Nephi 30:2; Galatians 3:26–29). Thus, the Church is very missionary minded. The Prophet Joseph Smith taught that "one of the most important points in the faith of the Church of the Latter-day Saints, through the fullness of the everlasting Gospel, is the gathering of Israel" (*Teachings of the Prophet Joseph Smith,* 92–93).

Faithful members of The Church of Jesus Christ of Latter-day Saints may receive inspired blessings from an ordained patriarch who declares to them their lineage in one of the tribes of the house of Israel, thereby becoming inheritors of all the blessings promised to the ancient patriarchs, Abraham, Isaac, and Jacob[1]. However, membership in the Lord's Church, or house of Israel, alone does not guarantee salvation. One must remain true to covenants. The Apostle Paul taught, "For they are not all Israel, which are of Israel" (Romans 9:6). Those who remain faithful shall be saved in the kingdom of God (D&C 101:12).

See also Israel; Israel, Lost Tribes of; Israel, Tribes of; Jacob[1].

ISRAEL, LOST TRIBES OF

This body of Jacob's descendants is specifically mentioned twice in the Book of Mormon (2 Nephi 29:13; 3 Nephi 17:4), but it is also identifiable in several other citations (2 Nephi 29:12; 3 Nephi 28:29).

"Who are these ten tribes? An answer to this question is found when one understands the identity of the twelve sons of the Old Testament patriarch Jacob. These sons were Reuben, Simeon, Levi, Judah, Issachar, Zebulun, Joseph, Benjamin, Gad, Asher, Dan, and Naphtali. (See Genesis 35:23–26.)

"God changed Jacob's name to Israel (see Genesis 35:10), and from his twelve sons came the twelve tribes of Israel. However, a tribe is not named for each son. Levi was not numbered among the tribes (see Numbers 1:47–49) because his posterity was given the Levitical Priesthood and they ministered to all the tribes (see Numbers 3:12–13). Joseph was given a double portion through his sons Ephraim and Manasseh. Thus, the twelve tribes include ten of Jacob's sons and two of Joseph's. (See Smith, *Answers to Gospel Questions,* 1:115; see also JST Genesis 48:5–6.)

"The twelve tribes were united under King David and his son Solomon, but ten of the tribes rebelled against Solomon's son Rehoboam and set up their own kingdom, which became known as the Northern Kingdom of Israel. Judah and Benjamin remained in Jerusalem and became known as the Southern Kingdom, or Kingdom of Judah. There were remnants of all the tribes found among the people of Judah. (See 1 Kings 12; Smith, *Answers to Gospel Questions,* 1:115.)

"The tribes of the Northern Kingdom were taken into captivity by the Assyrian king Shalmaneser about 721 B.C. (See 2 Kings 17.) These tribes have come to be known as the lost ten tribes. There appears to be a broader definition of these ten tribes than just limiting them to the ten who originally made up the Northern Kingdom of Israel. An entry in the *Encyclopedia of Mormonism* states: 'For Latter-day Saints, the lost tribes are Israelites other than either the Jewish people or the Lamanites of the Book of Mormon (2 Ne. 29:13).' (2:709, s.v. 'Israel: Lost Tribes of Israel.')" (Brewster, *Behold, I Come Quickly,* 136–37).

When the resurrected Redeemer visited ancient America, He told them He also had a ministry to perform among *yet* other sheep (3 Nephi 16:1–3). These were "the lost tribes of Israel [who] are not lost unto the Father, for he knoweth whither he hath taken them" (3 Nephi 17:4).

Just as the Savior's ministry

among the Nephites is recorded in scripture, so is it reasonable to conclude that His ministry to the lost tribes was also recorded. In this respect, Elder Neal A. Maxwell (1926–2004) spoke of a "third witness for Christ"—that will yet come forth to join with the Bible and the Book of Mormon to "complete a *triad of truth*" (*Ensign,* November 1986, 52; emphasis added). This statement gives latter-day affirmation to the Lord's earlier declaration that He would "speak unto the other tribes of the house of Israel, which I have led away, and they shall write it" (2 Nephi 29:12–14).

While there are varying theories as to the whereabouts of the ten tribes, one inspired utterance is absolutely clear: "We believe in the literal gathering of Israel and in the restoration of the Ten Tribes" (Articles of Faith 1:10). How and when that shall occur we shall leave to the proper jurisdiction and public announcement of the duly ordained prophets, seers, and revelators of The Church of Jesus Christ of Latter-day Saints.

See also Israel; Israel, House of; Israel, Tribes of; Israel; Jacob; Other Sheep.

ISRAEL, TRIBES OF

These twelve tribes are first mentioned in the Book of Mormon by an angel who visited with Nephi[1]. The angel said that the tribes were to be judged by "the twelve apostles of the Lamb," which declaration was repeated centuries later by Mormon[2] (1 Nephi 12:9; Mormon 3:18). The "lost tribes" are referenced twice (2 Nephi 29:13; 3 Nephi 17:4) but are also spoken of as "the other tribes of the house of Israel, which I [the Lord] have led away" (2 Nephi 29:12). The "scattered tribes" are mentioned once (3 Nephi 28:29).

"The 'Tribes of Israel' represent the descendants of Israel (Jacob) through his twelve sons and their posterity. The original twelve tribes were named after each of Israel's sons through his four wives. These sons and their respective mothers were: Reuben, Simeon, Levi, Judah, Isaachar, and Zebulun, sons of Leah; Dan and Naphtali, sons of Bilhah; Gad and Asher, sons of Zilpah; and Joseph and Benjamin, sons of Rachel. (Gen. 29; 30.)

"The Lord, through Jacob, gave Joseph's two sons, Ephraim and Manasseh, an inheritance among the tribes of Israel (JST Gen. 48:5–6). In answer to the question, 'Who was then eliminated from the twelve tribes?' Joseph Fielding Smith said: 'It was Levi and Joseph who were not numbered as tribes in Israel. Joseph received a double portion through his sons, each inheriting through their adoption by their grandfather, and Levi's descendants becoming the ministers to all the other tribes of Israel.' (*AGQ,* 1:115; Num. 3:12–13.)" (Brewster, *Doctrine & Covenants Encyclopedia,* 604).

See also Israel; Israel, House of; Israel, Lost Tribes of; Jacob[1].

J

JACOB[1]

This son of Isaac and grandson of the "father of the faithful"—Abraham—was one of twin sons born to his mother, Rebekah. Jacob's decades-long struggle with his twin brother, Esau, was foreseen while the two were yet in the womb of their mother. The Lord revealed to her that "two nations are in thy womb, and two manner of people shall be separated from thy bowels; and the one people shall be stronger than the other people; and the elder [Esau] shall serve the younger [Jacob[1]]" (Genesis 25:23).

A manifestation of the conflict between the two siblings was seen at their birth, when Jacob[1] had "hold on Esau's heel" as the elder brother emerged from the womb (Genesis 25:25–26). As the first born, Esau had claim to the birthright, but in a moment of weakness he sold it to his younger brother (Genesis 25:29–34).

Jacob[1] had numerous marvelous spiritual experiences, including seeing God "face to face" (Genesis 32:30). One of his most significant experiences was his dream of the ladder that reached from heaven to earth (Genesis 28:12). The Prophet Joseph Smith compared the three degrees of glory described in section 76 of the Doctrine and Covenants to the "three principal rounds of Jacob's ladder," and referred to Jacob[1] as a prophet and seer (*Teachings of the Prophet Joseph Smith*, 12–13, 304–5).

As previously noted under the entry for "Israel," the Lord gave this new name to Jacob[1] (Genesis 35:10). It is by this name that his twelve sons are known—the tribes of Israel. Jacob's faithfulness is attested to by the Lord's latter-day declaration that he has attained the priesthood status of a god (D&C 132:37).

See also Israel; Israel, House of; Israel, Lost Tribes of; Israel, Tribes of.

JACOB[2]

This fifth son of Lehi[1] and Sariah was born during his family's journey in the wilderness, prior to their voyage across the waters to the promised land (1 Nephi 18:7). This was a time referred to by his father as "the days of my tribulation in the wilderness" (2 Nephi 2:1). As a young child, Jacob[2] "suffered afflictions and much sorrow, because of the rudeness" and rebelliousness of his oldest brothers

(2 Nephi 2:1; see also 1 Nephi 18:17–19).

Such afflictions might have turned one of lesser faith and fortitude to murmuring against God for its seeming unfairness. However, Jacob² turned his afflictions to gain because of his steadfast faith (2 Nephi 2:2–4). Jacob's righteousness was affirmed by his brother Nephi¹, who bore testimony that both he and Jacob² had [seen] the Redeemer (2 Nephi 11:2–3). Jacob² himself later spoke of having [heard] the voice of the Lord "from time to time" (Jacob 7:5).

When a divisive split occurred between those who sided with the rebellious brothers Laman¹ and Lemuel and those who followed the righteous Nephi¹, Jacob² chose rightly (2 Nephi 5:6). Recognizing the faith and fortitude of his younger brother, Nephi¹ consecrated Jacob² and the youngest brother, Joseph², to be "priests and teachers" to his followers (2 Nephi 5:26). It is not coincidental that the very next verse states that the people "lived after the manner of happiness" (v. 27).

In an example of how one should *immediately* begin to magnify a calling, shortly after his call to serve, Jacob² was found exhorting the people to righteousness and powerfully testifying of Christ and His gospel (2 Nephi 6–10). Jacob² also provided

other examples of how those called of God to serve Him and preach the gospel of Jesus Christ should function in their callings. Before he went before the people to teach or exhort them, he "first obtained [his] errand from the Lord" (Jacob 1:17). Prayer preceded powerful preaching!

It was also a hallmark of his ministry that Jacob² was unafraid to confront difficult issues. Though often saddened by the words of admonition and chastisement he had to speak, he spoke with courage and boldness (Jacob 2:6–10). In a confrontation with the apostate Sherem, Jacob² remained immovable. Because of his firm faith, he could not be shaken (Jacob 7:5). Furthermore, his steadiness allowed the Spirit to work with him, and he "confounded [the wicked man] in all his words" (Jacob 7:8).

As he approached death at the end of his ministry, Jacob² passed the record-keeping responsibilities to his son Enos², who benefited greatly from the teachings of his exemplary father (see Enos 1:1–3).

JACOB³

Dishonoring the name of the men who so righteously carried that name before him, Jacob³ was a Nephite apostate belonging to the Zoramite sect about 64 B.C. He became the leader of a Lamanite army that captured the Nephite city of

Mulek (Alma 52:20). His pride and lack of the Spirit of God allowed him to be decoyed by Captain Moroni[1] into a trap. Having "an unconquerable spirit," and fighting with "fury," he sought to "cut his way through" the Nephite troops, but his righteous opponents prevailed and Jacob[3] was killed in the battle (Alma 52:21–35).

Being described as having an "unconquerable spirit" appears to be the direct opposite of what is required of one who seeks to follow the Savior's admonition to be like Him (3 Nephi 27:27). While Jacob[3] sought power and position through his unyielding wickedness, *ultimate power*—"thrones and dominions, principalities and powers, shall be revealed and set forth upon all who have endured valiantly for the gospel of Jesus Christ" (D&C 121:29).

These are they who are not haughty, but submissive; not proud, but humble. These are they who offer as a sacrifice to Christ a "broken heart and a contrite spirit" (2 Nephi 2:7; 3 Nephi 9:20).

JACOB[4]

This very wicked man was chosen king by a secret combination of evil doers around 29–30 B.C. (3 Nephi 7:9). Jacob[4] "was one of the chiefest who had given his voice against the prophets who testified of Jesus" (3 Nephi 7:10). He and his band of murderers and robbers established a city they called Jacobugath, named after this infamous leader. Following Jesus' crucifixion, the Lord burned this city, destroying the abominable inhabitants, whose wickedness "was above all the wickedness of the whole earth" (3 Nephi 9:9).

JACOBITES

At the time Nephi[1] died, his brother Jacob[2] said that "the people which were not Lamanites were Nephites, Jacobites, Josephites, Zoramites, Lamanites, Lemuelites, and Ishmaelites," groups being named after their fathers. However, he said from that point on he would call those "Lamanites that seek to destroy the people of Nephi, and those who are friendly to Nephi I shall call Nephites" (Jacob 1:12–14). Centuries later a break-off group referred to the true believers of Christ as "Nephites . . . Jacobites, and Josephites, and Zoramites" (4 Nephi 1:36).

JACOM

Jacom was one of the four sons of Jared[2], the founder of the Jaredite civilization (Ether 6:14). "And they were taught to walk humbly before the Lord; and they were also taught from on high" (Ether 6:17). When the people of Jared[2] desired to be governed by a king, Jacom was among the sons of both Jared[2] and the brother of Jared² who refused to accept the invitation to be the monarch. The position was finally accepted by and bestowed upon the willing youngest son of Jared², Orihah (Ether 6:22–27).

JARED¹

This man who received an ordination under the hands of Father Adam (D&C 107:47) is not mentioned in the Book of Mormon. He is listed here as Jared¹ only to clarify why Jared², the founder of the Jaredite civilization, is identified with a superscript "²" both in this *Who's Who* and in the index to the Triple Combination.

JARED²

This is the first man named Jared mentioned in the Book of Mormon. Jared² is the leader of the people whose history was inscribed on twenty-four gold plates discovered by an expedition sent into the wilderness by the Nephite King Limhi about 121 B.C. (Mosiah 8:7–9; 21:25–27; Ether 1:1–2). The record was later translated and abridged by Moroni², who referred to these people as the "Jaredites" (Moroni 9:23). The original group consisted of the families of Jared², his brother Mahonri Moriancumer, and "some others and their families," who originated at the time of the Tower of Babel (Ether 1:33).

Jared² relied heavily upon his brother for direction, for the brother of Jared² was "a man highly favored of the Lord" (Ether 1:34). Jared² was desirous of keeping his family and friends together at the time the languages were confounded and asked his brother to plead their cause to the Lord. Being successful in this effort, Jared² then asked his brother to beseech the Lord to lead them as a group to a land which he hoped would be "choice above all the earth" (Ether 1:34–38).

Jared², a man of faith and vision, declared: "Let us be faithful unto the Lord, that we may receive [the land of promise] for our inheritance" (Ether 1:38).

The Lord granted this request and, as He did with Noah, commanded them to gather flocks, fowls, fish, bees, and seeds to carry with them in the vessels they would construct to take them to their destination (Ether 1:41–42; 2:1–3).

After arriving at their place of promise and living prosperously for a time, Jared² made an unwise decision. Against the counsel of his brother, Jared² succumbed to pressure by the people to appoint a king as their ruler (Ether 6:22–24). As prophesied by the brother of Jared², this decision ultimately brought the people into captivity as unrighteous kings were placed on the throne (Ether 7:5).

The history of the Jaredite people is evidence of the truth spoken centuries later by a Nephite prophet: "For behold, how much iniquity doth one wicked king cause to be committed, yea, and what great destruction!" (Mosiah 29:17).

The deaths of both Jared² and his brother are recorded without any fanfare (Ether 6:29).

See also Jared², Brother of; Jaredites.

JARED³

Wicked intrigue and treachery filled the life of this Jaredite king. Jared³ was the son of King Omer, against whom the evil son rebelled. After gaining a sufficient following through his flattery and deception, Jared³ was successful in dethroning and imprisoning his father (Ether 8:1–3). Jared³ was later defeated in a battle with his brothers, who placed their righteous father back on the throne, while hearkening to Jared's plea to spare his life (Ether 8:4–6).

Sorrowful about his loss of power, the ever-treacherous Jared³ concocted a murderous plot with his unnamed daughter, who obviously had learned the ways of wickedness from her father. The plan included using "secret plans of old" (those conceived by the devil in his pact with Cain). Through the daughter's dancing, the devilish duo planned to seduce Akish, an al-leged friend of King Omer, into beheading the king and restoring the throne to Jared³. Agreeing to the conspiracy, Akish brought others into the newly formed secret combination (Ether 8:7–18).

The evil scheme failed when the Lord warned King Omer in a dream to flee with his family (Ether 9:1–3). Jared³ resumed his ill-gotten place on the Jaredite throne, but fell victim to his own treacherous ways. His daughter now aligned herself with Akish, who coveted the seat of power and conspired against his father-in-law. Jared³ was beheaded while "giving audience to his people," and Akish ascended to the throne (Ether 9:4–6).

And thus we see "it is by the wicked that the wicked are punished; for it is the wicked that stir up the hearts of the children of men unto bloodshed" (Mormon 4:5).

JARED², BROTHER OF

Perhaps his name was not recorded on the twenty-four gold plates that Moroni² translated and abridged, but it is ironic that a man identified as the first Jaredite prophet would be known only as "the brother of Jared" (Ether 1:34). It is the Prophet Joseph Smith who centuries later would identify this brother's name as *Mahonri Moriancumer* (see George R. Reynolds, *Juvenile Instructor* 27 [May 1, 1892]:

282; see also Reynolds, *Dictionary of the Book of Mormon,* 165).

While Jared[2] appeared to be the leader of the people, Jared's reliance upon, and trust in, his brother was unquestionable. It was Jared[2] who requested that his brother ask the Lord not to confuse the language of their families and the families of their friends when the Lord confounded the languages at the Tower of Babel. Jared[2] also asked his brother to plead with the Lord to send their families and close friends to a separate, even a promised land (Ether 1:33–38).

The brother of Jared[2] was "a man highly favored of the Lord," and the Lord responded favorably to the requests (Ether 1:34–43). In spite of his great spirituality, it appears the brother of Jared[2] became careless and neglected his prayers, for which he was chastened by the Lord (Ether 3:14). The question arises, could one so spiritual cease praying? Or did he allow his prayers to become casual, a mere perfunctory performance with no real intent? Whatever the reason, the Lord's rebuke is a reminder to us all that our approach to heaven should be carefully considered. Our prayers should truly be from the heart, with a sincere desire to communicate with a loving and listening Heavenly Father.

The faith of the brother of Jared[2] was such that he took seemingly unsolvable problems to the Lord for help, such as wondering how to get *light and air* into the barges he was commanded to build. Although the Lord solved the problem of *air,* He required the brother of Jared[2] to find a solution to the *light* problem (Ether 2:18–25; 3:1–6). In response, the brother of Jared[2] "did molten out of a rock sixteen small stones; and they were white and clear, even as transparent glass" (Ether 3:1). He then asked the Lord to touch them with His finger that they might become sources of light.

The absolute faith of the brother of Jared[2] was such that his eyes pierced the veil, and he saw the finger of the Lord as the stones were touched. Furthermore, his faith was so complete that he pledged his willingness to believe things before he had heard them: "Believest thou the words *which I shall speak?*" the Lord asked him (Ether 3:11; emphasis added). Because of this man's faith, Jesus Christ showed him many marvelous manifestations (Ether 3:6–28).

Having followed the inspired instructions received to build the barges, and with the divinely prepared stones to light their way, the travelers set sail towards "the promised land" (Ether 6:2–5). Through prayer, the voyagers were kept safe for the "three hundred and forty and four days upon the water" (Ether 6:6–12). Why was the voyage so long? A simple and correct answer is: "Because that is how the Lord planned it to give the seafarers whatever experiences He wanted them to have!"

The brother of Jared[2] died several years after his arrival in the promised land (Ether 6:29).

See also Jared[2]; Jaredites; Spirit of the Lord.

JARED[3], DAUGHTER OF

She is not identified by personal name, but is referred to only as the daughter of Jared[3] (Ether 8:8–9:4). Perchance her anonymity is a blessing to some modern-day girl or woman whose name might have been besmirched because of its similarity or association with the name of one who was so wicked. She plotted with her villainous father to have her kindly grandfather, King Omer, beheaded. She instigated the searching out and renewed use of the ancient oaths and secret combinations whose purpose is to promote murder, plunder, ill-gotten power, and "all manner of wickedness and whoredoms" (Ether 8:9, 15–18).

This wicked woman failed in her plot to murder her grandfather, who, being warned of the Lord, escaped the intended assassination. However, she married Akish, the designated assassin, and he later beheaded his father-in-law Jared[3] as he sat upon his royal throne. Nothing more is recorded of the infamous daughter of Jared[3].

JAREDITES

The Jaredites made one of the three separate migrations to ancient America that are recorded in the Book of Mormon. The history of these people is found in the book of Ether. The other two migrations were (1) the colony of Father Lehi[1] and Mother Sariah, which arrived in their land of promise about 590 B.C. and then split into two major groups, the Nephites and the Lamanites (2 Nephi 5); and (2) the people of Zarahemla (often referred to by the nonscriptural term of "Mulekites"), who left Jerusalem at the time of its prophesied destruction by the Babylonians and were led to ancient America by the hand of the Lord (Mosiah 25:2; Omni 1:14–17).

Elder George Reynolds (1842–1909) provided the following succinct summary of the Jaredites: "[They were] the descendants of *Jared* and his associates, who were led by the power of God from the Tower of Babel to this [the American] continent. Here they became one of the mightiest of nations, and flourished in a manner unsurpassed in the history of the post-diluvian races, until they fell into decay through corruption and iniquity and were ultimately destroyed in a desolating internecine war, at the end of which but one man, *Coriantumr*[2], remained as the representative of this once mighty people. The destruction of the Jaredites took place, as nearly as can be gleaned from the record, about the same time as the Nephites reached this land (say B.C. 590.)" (*Dictionary of the Book of Mormon,* 147.)

See Jared[2]; Jared[2], Brother of.

JAROM

The son of Enos[2] and grandson of Jacob[2], Jarom was given responsibility for keeping the sacred history of the Nephites on the small plates about 420 B.C. (Jarom 1:1). He must have received the plates at a relatively young age, for he had them for fifty-nine years (Enos 1:25; Jarom 1:13). Unfortunately, Jarom recorded very little in those years, virtually one-fourth of a verse each year they were in his possession!

Why?

Jarom's explanation is that "it must needs be that I write a little; but I shall not write the things of my prophesying, nor of my revelations. For *what could I write more than my fathers have written?* For have not they revealed the plan of salvation? I say unto you, Yea; and this sufficeth me" (Jarom 1:2; emphasis added).

Was Jarom so self-effacing or shy that he did not consider his "prophesying" or his "revelations" significant enough to record? Or was the "diffi-culty of engraving" (Jacob 4:1) too much of a task for him? We simply do not have an answer. From the little he did write, it seems clear that Jarom was a righteous man, so the lack of the written record does not seem to be a result of willful iniquity on his part. Surely Jarom was among the "prophets, and the priests, and the teachers" who persuaded the people "to look forward unto the Messiah, and believe in him to come as though he already was" (Jarom 1:11).

JEBERECHIAH

This man's name is mentioned in the writings of Isaiah[1] that Nephi[1] recorded on the Book of Mormon plates. He was the father of Zechariah, one of two witnesses Isaiah[1] used to verify the truthfulness of the recording containing his son's name (2 Nephi 18:1–2; Isaiah 8:1–2).

JEHOVAH

This very sacred and revered name of Jesus Christ is generally used when referring to Him as the God of the Old Testament and in His pre-mortal stewardship, although He has also been addressed as Jehovah in His postmortal ministry. The name Jehovah appears twice in the Book of Mormon (2 Nephi 22:2; Moroni 10:34), and is found in three sections of the Doctrine and Covenants (109:34, 42, 56, 68; 110:3; 128:9).

The name Jehovah is "the covenant or proper name of the God of Israel. It denotes the 'Unchangeable One,' 'the eternal I AM' (Ex. 6:3; Ps. 83:18; Isa. 12:2; 26:4). The original pronunciation of this name has possibly been lost, as the Jews, in reading, never mentioned it, but substituted one of the other names of God, usually Adonai. Probably it was pronounced Jahveh, or Yahveh. In the KJV, the Jewish custom has been followed, and the name is generally denoted by LORD or GOD, printed in small capitals" (LDS Bible Dictionary, 710–11).

A mistranslation in the King James Version of the Bible leads people to believe that the Lord was not known by his title of Jehovah. However, as corrected by prophetic inspiration, the text now reads: "And I appeared unto Abraham, unto Isaac, and unto Jacob. I am the Lord God Almighty, the Lord JEHOVAH. And was not my name known unto them?" (JST Exodus 6:3).

See also Christ; Christ, Names of; Father, Jesus Christ As; God; Immanuel; Jesus; Lamb of God; Messiah; Only Begotten of the Father; Prince of Peace; Redeemer; Savior.

JENEAM

One of the Nephite military commanders who perished along with his ten thousand troops around A.D. 385 during the final battle of that doomed civilization (Mormon 6:14).

JEREMIAH[1]

This Old Testament prophet was a contemporary of Father Lehi[1]. Many of his prophecies were contained on the plates of brass that Lehi[1] was commanded of the Lord to take with him when he and his family fled Jerusalem (1 Nephi 5:13). Jeremiah[1], like Lehi[1], testified of the impending destruction of Jerusalem (Helaman 8:20).

The ministry of the prophet Jeremiah[1] covered a span of forty years, from 626 to 586 B.C. He was initially unsure of his ability to be the mouthpiece of the Lord, "But the Lord said unto me, . . . thou shalt go to all that I shall send thee, and whatsoever I command thee thou shalt speak" (Jeremiah 1:7). Such a reassuring promise is given to any individual who is called to service in the Lord's vineyard: "For he whom God hath sent speaketh the words of God" (John 3:34).

Jeremiah[1] is a great example of a servant of the Lord who unhesitatingly carried out his responsibilities in the face of formidable and dangerous opposition. In fact, his ministry was one continual round of defining moments where he had to choose between having physical comfort and safety or placing himself in jeopardy by steadfastly carrying out the Lord's will.

He was mocked and had his writings destroyed. He was physically assaulted, tried in courts, placed in stocks, confined in dungeons, thrown into miry pits, and had his life threatened (Jeremiah 11:19; 20:1–3; 26:8, 36; 38; 1 Nephi 7:14).

Yet he stood firm. Tradition holds that Jeremiah[1] concluded his ministry as a martyr, being stoned to death by those who rejected the truths he sought to teach them.

JEREMIAH[2]

One of the twelve specially selected disciples chosen by the resurrected Redeemer to lead His church in ancient America (3 Nephi 19:4).

See also Disciples, Twelve.

JESSE

The father of the Old Testament King David is mentioned in the writings of Isaiah[1] that are recorded in the Book of Mormon (2 Nephi 21:1, 10). He is an ancestor of all the kings of Judah that followed David and also of Jesus Christ (Ruth 4:17, 22; 1 Chronicles 2:5–12; Matthew 1:5–6).

JESSE, ROD OUT OF THE STEM OF

Isaiah[1] prophesied that "there shall come forth a rod out of the stem of Jesse" (2 Nephi 21:1; Isaiah 11:1). "An 1838 revelation identified this as 'a servant in the hands of Christ, who is partly a descendant of Jesse as well as of Ephraim, or of the house of Joseph, on whom there is laid much power.' (D&C 113:3–4.) Certainly the priesthood power bestowed on Joseph Smith, the Prophet of the Restoration, qualifies him to be this servant. Consider also the Angel Moroni's proclamation, following a recitation of the eleventh chapter of Isaiah to young Joseph, that 'it was about to be fulfilled.' (Joseph Smith—History 1:40.) Furthermore, the ancient seer Joseph, he who rose to such power in ancient Egypt, prophesied that one of his descendants—bearing the name of Joseph—would be raised up to do a great work for the Lord. (2 Nephi 3:6–15; JST Genesis 50:26–33.)

"With respect to Joseph's lineage, Brigham Young declared he was 'a pure Ephraimite.' . . . However, as Joseph Fielding Smith pointed out, 'No one can lay claim to a perfect descent from father to son through just one lineage.' . . . Therefore, though Joseph's lineage may be traceable directly back to Ephraim through a given line, of necessity there were intermarriages that took place, making it possible for his descent to have also come from Jesse through his forefather, Judah" (Brewster, *Isaiah Plain & Simple,* 109).

JESSE, ROOT OF

Speaking of the recovery of the remnant of Israel that will take place prior to the Second Coming, Isaiah[1] prophesied, "And in that day there shall be a root of Jesse, which shall stand for an ensign of the people; to it shall the Gentiles seek; and his rest shall be glorious" (2 Nephi 21:10; Isaiah 11:10). A latter-day revelation identifies "root of Jesse" as "a descendant of Jesse, as well as of Joseph, unto whom rightly belongs the priesthood, and the keys of the kingdom, for an ensign, and for the gathering of my people in the last days" (D&C 113:5–6).

"It appears that the Prophet Joseph Smith is both the 'rod' and the 'root' that will come from Jesse. . . . He is the one upon whom the keys of the kingdom were bestowed, including the keys of the gathering of Israel. (See D&C 13:1; 27:12–13; 90:2–3; 110:11–16.) However, [Professor] Victor Ludlow suggested that 'Joseph Smith might not be the only "root of Jesse" in these last days. Many presidents of the Church have been related to him by blood, and all have held the priesthood and the keys of the kingdom that he held. . . . The "root of Jesse" could also be that particular prophet who will hold the keys when

Christ returns to preside personally over his kingdom. The term could even represent the office of the president of the Church. In any case, the "root of Jesse" designates a great leader in the Church of Jesus Christ in this dispensation'" (Brewster, *Isaiah Plain & Simple,* 112–13).

JESSE, STEM OF

Isaiah[1] prophesied that "there shall come forth a rod out of the stem of Jesse, and a branch shall grow out of his roots" (2 Nephi 21:1–5; Isaiah 11:1–5). Jesus Christ was a descendant of Jesse, the father of King David, through His mortal mother Mary and is the "Stem of Jesse" mentioned in verse one (D&C 113:1–2). Some of His attributes are enumerated in verses two through five. Christ is also the "Branch," the messianic King David, who was prophesied to come forth in the last days (see Brewster, *Isaiah Plain & Simple,* 108–9).

JESUS

This given name of the Savior of the world first appears in the writings of the prophet-scribe Nephi[1] (2 Nephi 25:19–20) in his powerful chapter declaring his testimony of Jesus Christ, in which he passionately pleads for people to believe in "the right way" to live, "for the right way is to believe in Christ" (2 Nephi

25:28–29). The name *Christ* was first revealed to Father Lehi's son Jacob[2] by an angel of God between 559 and 545 B.C. (2 Nephi 10:3).

Prior to this time, Book of Mormon references to Him included: One (1 Nephi 1:9); Lord (1 Nephi 1:20); God (1 Nephi 1:22); God of Israel (1 Nephi 5:9); God of Abraham, and the God of Isaac, and the God of Jacob (1 Nephi 6:4); Messiah (1 Nephi 10:4); Savior of the world (1 Nephi 10:4); Redeemer of the world (1 Nephi 10:5); Lamb of God (1 Nephi 10:10); Son of God (1 Nephi 10:17); Son of the most high God (1 Nephi 11:6); Son of the Eternal Father (1 Nephi 11:21); Son of the everlasting God (1 Nephi 11:32); Lamb (1 Nephi 13:35); Shepherd (1 Nephi 13:41); everlasting God (1 Nephi 15:15); rock (1 Nephi 15:15); true vine (1 Nephi 15:15); true and living God (1 Nephi 17:30); God of nature (1 Nephi 19:12); Holy One of Israel (1 Nephi 19:14); Lord of Hosts (1 Nephi 20:2); the first, and . . . the last (1 Nephi 20:12); Redeemer of Israel (1 Nephi 21:7); Mighty One of Jacob (1 Nephi 21:26); Father of heaven (1 Nephi 22:9); Mighty One of Israel (1 Nephi 22:12); prophet (1 Nephi 22:20); Lord God (2 Nephi 1:5); true Messiah (2 Nephi 1:10); Holy Messiah (2 Nephi 2:6); Holy One (2 Nephi 2:10); Mediator (2 Nephi 2:28); Lord my God (2 Nephi 5:1); Mighty God (2 Nephi 6:17); Lord thy maker (2 Nephi 8:13); Creator (2 Nephi 9:5); Holy God (2 Nephi 9:39); Maker (2 Nephi 9:40); keeper of the gate (2 Nephi 9:41); Lord God Almighty (2 Nephi 9:46).

The name *Jesus* was given to the Son of God in accordance with the direction given by the angel Gabriel in a vision to Joseph, the husband of Christ's mother, Mary (JST Matthew 2:3–4; Matthew 1:21; Luke 2:21). The name is the Greek form of *Joshua* or *Jeshua,* meaning "God is help or Savior."

Because the name Jesus is His common or given name, one should always close a testimony or a prayer by including the appellation "Christ." Thus the witness becomes a true testimony in which one declares, "I say this in the name of Jesus [Who is the] Christ!" Such a witness is in keeping with the declared purpose of the Book of Mormon as found on the title page of that sacred volume of scripture: "to the convincing of the Jew and Gentile that JESUS is the CHRIST."

"The solemn testimonies of millions dead and of millions living unite in proclaiming Him as divine, the Son of the Living God, the Redeemer and Savior of the human race, the Eternal Judge of the souls of men, the Chosen and Anointed of the Father—

in short, the Christ" (James E. Talmage, *Jesus the Christ*, 1–2).

See also Christ; Christ, Names of; Father, Jesus Christ As; Father of Heaven and Earth; God; Immanuel; Jehovah; Jesse, Stem of; Lamb of God; Messiah; Only Begotten of the Father; Prince of Peace; Redeemer; Savior.

JEW

This term is found on the title page of the Book of Mormon, and in its singular form is found exclusively in 1 and 2 Nephi (1 Nephi 13:23–24, 38; 14:23; 2 Nephi 10:16; 26:33; 33:8, 10). Its plural form, *Jews,* is abundantly used.

"The name indicated first of all a man of the kingdom of Judah, as distinguished from persons belonging to the northern kingdom of Israel. Its first chronological occurrence in the Bible is in 2 Kgs. 16:6, about 740 B.C. It has become customary to use the word Jew to refer to all the descendants of Jacob, but this is a mistake. It should be limited to those of the kingdom of Judah or, more especially today, those of the tribe of Judah and his associates. Thus all Jews are Israelites, but not all Israelites are Jews, because there are descendants of the other tribes of Israel also upon the earth" (LDS Bible Dictionary, 713).

In 2 Nephi 30:4, the descendants of the Nephites are referred to as "de-scendants of the Jews," and modern revelation also identifies the Lamanites as remnants of the Jews (D&C 19:27; see also D&C 57:4). "Since Lehi and Ishmael, the fathers of the Nephite and Lamanite nations, were descendants of Joseph through Manasseh and Ephraim, respectively (1 Ne. 5:14; Alma 10:3; *Journal of Discourses*, 23:184–85), an explanation is in order. President Joseph Fielding Smith said: '*Lehi was a citizen of Jerusalem, in the kingdom of Judah . . . and all of the inhabitants of the kingdom of Judah, no matter which tribe they had descended through, were known as Jews.*' . . . It should also be remembered that the Nephites and Lamanites intermixed with the descendants of Mulek, who was a son of the king who ruled Judah at the time it was destroyed by the Babylonians. . . . Thus, the literal blood of Judah was mixed with that of Joseph" (Brewster, *Doctrine & Covenants Encyclopedia*, 280).

JOHN THE BAPTIST

He is not mentioned by name in the Book of Mormon, but John the Baptist is clearly identified as the prophet who "should baptize the Messiah" and "prepare the way before him" (1 Nephi 10:7–10; 11:27; 2 Nephi 31:4). He was, in a sense, a miracle child, for he was born to Elisabeth and Zacharias at a time when they were "well stricken in years" (Luke 1:7). Furthermore, John's life was spared through the sacrifice of his martyred father. The date of the infant's birth was such that he fell under the death edict for all male children under the age of two issued by the heinous King Herod.

"Zacharias hid his infant son from the executioners and refused to disclose the child's whereabouts. As a result, the wicked Herod decreed that the father should forfeit his life. . . .

"Over thirty years later, Christ referred to the death of this faithful father as He spoke of the blood shed by martyrs from Abel to Zacharias (Matthew 23:35)" (Brewster, *Martyrs of the Kingdom*, 19).

John's birth was foretold by angelic announcement (Luke 1:13), and his mission was also preceded by prophetic pronouncements on two separate continents (Isaiah 40:3; 1 Nephi 10:7–10). When only eight days old, he received an ordination from "the angel of God" which empowered him "to overthrow the kingdom of the Jews, and to make straight the way of the Lord before the face of his people, to prepare them for the coming of the Lord" (D&C 84:28).

This "ordination" was not to the priesthood, for that would come at a later time, but it was to his divine calling as a forerunner to Jesus Christ—the long-awaited Messiah. Both the Savior and the Apostle John identified John the Baptist as *an* Elias, or as one who prepares the way for something greater (John 1:20–28; Matthew 17:12–13; D&C 27:7). John understood his secondary position to the One whose path he was preparing. "He that cometh after me is mightier than I" (Matthew 3:11), declared the Baptist. "He must increase, but I must decrease" (John 3:30).

John the Baptist, like his father, Zacharias, before him, suffered a martyr's death. He was beheaded at the instigation of the wicked Herodias, who wanted to see the Baptist's head on a platter (Matthew 14:3–11). His disembodied spirit did not linger long in the spirit world, for following the resurrection of Christ, the bodies of John and other worthy Saints back to the time of Adam and Eve, who had died prior to the Savior's rising from the grave, also experienced a reuniting of their spirits with their glorified, resurrected bodies (Matthew 27:52–53; 3 Nephi 23:9).

As a resurrected being, John the Baptist has helped prepare the way for the Second Coming of Christ. On May 15, 1829, he appeared to the Prophet Joseph Smith and Oliver Cowdery and bestowed upon them the Aaronic Priesthood, with authority to once again administer the saving ordinance of baptism (D&C 13).

JOHN THE BELOVED

In addition to his title of John the Revelator, this special witness chosen by Christ to be one of His inner circle of twelve is also known in gospel literature as "John the Beloved." It is interesting that it is in his own writings, in the current King James Version of the Bible, that John refers to himself as the disciple "whom Jesus loved" (John 13:23; 19:26; 20:2; 21:7, 20). But also the resurrected Christ spoke of the Apostle John as "John, my beloved" (3 Nephi 28:6). Furthermore, in an inspired rendition of a conversation between Christ and His Apostle John that is currently missing in the Bible, the Lord addressed him as "John, my beloved" (D&C 7:1).

John is the person to whom Christ delegated the responsibility for looking after his mother, Mary, at the time He was dying on the cross. "And from that hour that disciple took her unto his own home" (John 19:25–27).

See also Apostle of the Lamb; John the Revelator.

JOHN THE REVELATOR

While the Apostle John is often referred to as "John the Revelator," the only scriptural use of this title is by the Prophet Joseph Smith in the Doctrine and Covenants (128:6). However, it is a fitting title for one who recorded the visions in the book of Revelation and whom an angel of the Lord identified as being "ordained" by the Lord to write the visions not only shown to him but to others (1 Nephi 14:19–27; Ether 4:16).

See also Apostle of the Lamb; John the Beloved.

JONAS[1]

A son of the great prophet Nephi[3], he was selected to join his father to serve among the twelve special disciples the resurrected Christ chose to preside over and lead His church in ancient America (3 Nephi 19:4).

See also Disciples, Twelve.

JONAS[2]

One of two men named Jonas who were selected by Jesus Christ to be one of His twelve special disciples at the time of His post-resurrection ministry to ancient America (3 Nephi 19:4).

See also Disciples, Twelve.

JOSEPH[1]

Joseph[1], one of the great heroes of the Old Testament, was the firstborn son of Jacob[1] (Israel) and his second wife, Rachel (Genesis 30:22–24). He became the ancient seer whose spiritual insight not only allowed him to interpret dreams for both servant and king, but also to foresee the coming forth of the latter-day Prophet of the Restoration, whose name would also be *Joseph* (2 Nephi 3:6–15; JST Genesis 50:26–33).

Father Lehi[1] was a descendant of Joseph[1] through his son Manasseh (1 Nephi 5:14; Alma 10:3), and Father Ishmael[1] was a descendant of Joseph[1] through his son Ephraim (in *Journal of Discourses,* 23:184–85). Through their posterity, the prophecy of Jacob[1] that Joseph[1] would be a "fruitful bough . . . whose branches run over the wall" (Genesis 49:22; see also chapter heading) came to fruition.

Because of the transgression of Reuben, the firstborn son of Jacob's first wife, Leah, the birthright blessings were given to Joseph[1] as firstborn son of the second wife, granting him the leadership role among his brothers. Joseph's wisdom was a hallmark of his character, although as a young teenager he was probably insensitive to the feelings of his brothers when he told them about his dreams, which symbolically depicted the brothers being subservient to their younger sibling (Genesis 37). The animosity was further aggravated when Jacob gave Joseph[1] a special "coat of many colours" (one representing preeminent or royal status). The brothers "could not speak peaceably to him" (Genesis 37:3–4).

The brothers' anger towards Joseph[1] led them to sell him as a slave; he was ultimately purchased by "Potiphar, an officer of Pharaoh's and captain of the guard" (Genesis 37:36; 39:1). This led to a series of defining moments in which the depth of Joseph's spiritual strength was shown on numerous occasions. His work ethic and trustworthiness led to his being appointed overseer in Potiphar's house. It was here that his moral character was severely tested by the constant enticing of Potiphar's unfaithful wife for Joseph[1] to commit adultery. His classic response was, "How then can I do this great wickedness, and sin against God?" (Genesis 39:9). Angered by his rejection, the wicked woman falsely accused Joseph[1], which led to his being put in prison for somewhere between three and twelve years.

Joseph[1] had the fortitude and faith to make the best of every situation, and he was eventually appointed the overseer of the other prisoners (JST Genesis 39:22). His spiritual gifts were recognized by the prisoners, and his fame in interpreting dreams led to his interpreting the famous dream of Pharaoh in which a forthcoming famine was revealed. Pharaoh saw Joseph[1] as "a man in whom the Spirit of God" (Genesis 41:43) resided and appointed him a ruler over all of Egypt (Genesis 41).

It was in this capacity that

Joseph[1] was reunited with his brothers and his father, Jacob[1]. At a time when he might have sought retribution, he instead forgave his brothers (Genesis 42–45). "The story of Joseph is . . . an illustration of the way in which God works in history, preserving his people" (LDS Bible Dictionary, 716).

JOSEPH[2]

The youngest son of Lehi[1] (1 Nephi 18:7), Joseph[2] was born in what his father called "the wilderness of mine afflictions; yea, in the days of my greatest sorrow did thy mother bear thee" (2 Nephi 3:1; see also 1 Nephi 18:17–18). Young Joseph[2] suffered himself because of the difficult conditions, including the grief of his mother, frequently brought about by the murmuring and rebellious actions of his older brothers (1 Nephi 18:19). However, Joseph's life proved that being born in the furnace of affliction can serve as a refining process that enables one to better handle adversity and remain true and faithful.

Joseph[2] was promised by his father that he and his posterity would be blessed according to covenants God had made with ancient prophets (2 Nephi 3:23). He was admonished to "hearken unto the words of thy brother, Nephi" (2 Nephi 3:25). His father also related to him the wondrous prophecy of Joseph[1] of old, who foretold the coming forth of the Prophet Joseph Smith in the latter days (2 Nephi 3:6–24).

Joseph[2] followed the counsel of his father and pursued the course of righteousness set forth by his prophet-brother Nephi[1]. When the followers of Nephi[1] parted from the followers of the rebels Laman[1] and Lemuel, Joseph[2] was with Nephi[1] (2 Nephi 5:5–6). He was later consecrated by Nephi[1] to be a priest and teacher over the people (2 Nephi 5:26). The only other mention of Joseph[2], who perhaps was overshadowed by his older brother Jacob[2], is his later being described as a just and holy man (Alma 3:6). What better epitaph could one want?

JOSEPH[3]

Although he is not identified in the triple combination index as such, for the purposes of this *Who's Who* Joseph Smith Sr. is given the identifying superscript of "[3]." He is mentioned in the prophecy found in 2 Nephi 3:6, 15.

See also Choice Seer; Smith, Joseph, Sr.

JOSEPH[4]

Although neither he nor his father are identified in the triple combination index with a superscript, for the purposes of this *Who's Who*, Joseph Smith Jr., the Prophet of the Restoration, is given the identifying superscript of "4." He is mentioned in the prophecy found in 2 Nephi 3:6–24. He also, of course, is featured prominently in the introductory pages to the Book of Mormon.

See also Choice Seer; Smith, Joseph, Jr.

JOSEPHITES

These descendants of Father Lehi's youngest son, Joseph², are mentioned only three times by the name Josephites (Jacob 1:13; 4 Nephi 1:36–37; Mormon 1:8). As the prophet-scribe Jacob² explained, they usually identified themselves as Nephites (Jacob 1:13–14).

See also Joseph².

JOSH

One of the score of Nephite military commanders who, together with their ten thousand respective troops, were slain in the last battle of their doomed nation about A.D. 385 (Mormon 6:14).

JOTHAM

This king of the southern kingdom of Judah and the son of Uzziah is mentioned in the writings of Isaiah¹ copied by Nephi¹ onto the record he kept (2 Nephi 17:1). He reigned from 758 to 742 B.C. and was the father of Ahaz, who succeeded him as king.

Jotham was a righteous ruler, for "he did that which was right in the sight of the Lord" (2 Kings 15:34).

JUDAH

As used in the Book of Mormon, Judah generally refers to the southern kingdom of Israelites that inhabited the area around Jerusalem (1 Nephi 1:4). Following the death of King Solomon, his successor, Rehoboam, was unable to keep the Israelites united under one monarch, and ten of the twelve tribes broke away to form the northern kingdom of Israel. The kingdom of Judah consisted of the tribe of Judah and the greater part of the tribe of Benjamin, although because the temple was located in Jerusalem there were some people from every tribe that lived in that area.

Judah as an individual, and after whom the tribe and kingdom of Judah is named, was the fourth-born of Jacob's twelve sons (Genesis 29:35). It was Judah who interceded to save his brother Joseph's life by selling him into slavery rather than to leave him in a pit to die (Genesis 37:23–28). It is from Judah that the Jews are descended, and he is also the forefather of the Divine Son of Mary, even Jesus Christ.

The Book of Mormon gives second witness to Ezekiel's prophecy about the "fruit of the loins of Judah" or the "stick of Judah" (the Bible) being joined with the "fruit" of Joseph's loins or "stick of Joseph" (the Book of Mormon) to confound false doctrine (2 Nephi 3:11–12; Ezekiel 37:15–20).

See also Israel; Jew.

K

KIB

Kib was the grandson of Jared[2], who was the founder of the Jaredite civilization; the son of Orihah, the first king of the Jaredites; and the father of Corihor[1] and Shule (Ether 1:31–32; 7:3). Kib became the second Jaredite king, succeeding his father, but was dethroned by his rebel son, Corihor[1]. This proved to be the sad beginning of a tragic pattern that would continue to plague the Jaredites throughout their history, in fulfillment of the warning of the brother of Jared[1] (Ether 7:3–5). Shule succeeded in overthrowing his rebel brother and restoring the kingdom to their father, Kib (Ether 7:7–9).

KIM

This Jaredite king was the son of Morianton[1] and the father of Levi[2] (Ether 1:21–22). It appears that Kim did not have the best example in his father's personal behavior, for Morianton[1] "did do justice unto the people, but not unto himself because of his many whoredoms" (Ether 10:11). Following his father's bad example, "Kim did not reign in righteousness, wherefore he was not favored of the Lord" (Ether 10:13).

After an eight-year reign, Kim was overthrown by his unnamed brother, and he then spent the remainder of his life in captivity (Ether 10:14).

KIMNOR

The description of Kimnor is limited to a single verse, which simply identifies him as the father of the wicked Akish, who brought the destructive secret combinations into the Jaredite civilization (Ether 8:10).

See also Akish.

KING-MEN

This name aptly describes the haughty Nephite citizens "of high birth . . . who sought power and authority over the people" by changing the form of government from one of judges to having a king (Alma 51:5–8). Their arrogance even led to their refusing to take up arms in defending their country against invading armies (Alma 51:13). As a result of their defiance, Captain Moroni[1] went against them in battle, slaying four thousand of the dissenters who lifted their swords against the forces of freedom before they finally surrendered. Their leaders were put in prison, and the others agreed to join in defending their country at that critical time (around 67 B.C.) (Alma 51:14–20).

Moroni[1] later recounted the fact that had it not been for the rebellion of the king-men, the Nephites would not have had such difficulties in defending their freedom and much bloodshed could have been avoided. He lamented that the Nephites' failure to unite, because of the conflict created by those who desired power and unrighteous authority over others, caused them to suffer unnecessarily (Alma 60:16). Surely there is a message in this verse to all who participate in partisan politics. Following a legitimate vote by the people in a democratic process, there must be a uniting of purpose in the cause of freedom if the blessings of the Lord are to be received.

The king-men overthrew the legitimate government for a time, but fortunately Moroni[1] led the forces of freedom in defeating them. The dissenters were properly tried and "executed according to the law" (Alma 62:9).

See also Freemen.

KING OF ASSYRIA

The king of Assyria who reigned from 747 to 734 B.C. is mentioned in the writings of Isaiah[1] that Nephi[1] copied onto the Nephite record (2 Nephi 17:17, 20; 18:7). This king's name was Tiglath-pileser (2 Kings 16:7), also spelled "Tilgath-pilneser" (1 Chronicles 5:26). He was hired by Ahaz, king of the southern kingdom of Judah, to come to the aid of the beleaguered southern kingdom and fight its oppressors Syria and the northern kingdom of Israel (2 Kings 16:7–9). Although Tiglath-pileser earned his bounty by conquering the Syrians, he later turned on Ahaz and "distressed him" (2 Chronicles 28:20).

KISH

Kish was one of the Jaredite kings. He was the son of Corom and the father of Lib[1] (Ether 1:18–19). It is interesting that praise is given to Kish's father ("he did that which was good in the sight of the Lord all his days"), and to Kish's son (he "also did that which was good in the sight of the Lord"), but there is no mention of Kish's character or behavior (Ether 10:17–19).

KISHKUMEN

This infamous Nephite lived around 51 B.C. Kishkumen appeared on the scene as one of the leaders of a group of dissenters who sought to "destroy the liberty of the people." Kishkumen was selected to assassinate the chief judge Pahoran[2] (Helaman 1:7–9). He and his murderous band entered into secret covenants to uphold one another in their wickedness

(Helaman 1:11–12; 2:3). Kishkumen joined forces with Gadianton, who became the leader of the secret combination, whose object was "to murder, and to rob, and to gain power" (Helaman 2:8). These two evil men were cofounders of the conspiratorial band that ultimately led to the destruction of the Nephite nation (Helaman 6:18, 24).

When Helaman[3] was appointed as the new chief judge, the secret combination sent Kishkumen to kill him. However, one of Helaman's servants discovered the plot and killed Kishkumen before he could carry out his planned assassination (Helaman 2:2–9).

See also Gadianton.

KORIHOR

Korihor is among the more recognized, yet infamous, names in the Book of Mormon. Korihor was an anti-Christ, meaning he openly rebelled against Christ and all that He represents. Korihor appeared on the Nephite scene about 74 B.C. and preached against the prophecies concerning Christ. Because the Nephites enjoyed freedom of speech, "the law could have no hold upon him" (Alma 30:12).

Korihor had great success among the Nephites in preaching his false philosophy that "whatsoever a man did was no crime" (Alma 30:17). His teaching was the same old satanic lie that has existed from the beginning and is so prevalent in the world today: "There is no ultimate, divinely declared moral standard. So, if anything has the potential to bring you pleasure, then experience it. Do it! Live for the moment!"

As noted in the entry on the Anti-Nephi-Lehies, or the people of Ammon[2], Korihor's teachings were immediately rejected by these faithful followers of Christ, and he was "carried out of [their] land" (Alma 30:19–21).

While Korihor's demented course included a series of points where he might have repented and changed direction, perhaps the major moment was when he was confronted by the high priest of the Church and chief judge of the land, Alma[2]. Point by point, Alma refuted the false rhetoric of the anti-Christ. It finally came down to Korihor's demand that he be shown a sign. Alma's classic response was that Korihor had seen "signs enough; . . . and all things denote there is a God" (Alma 30:44).

Korihor persisted in seeking a sign and Alma[2] replied, "This will I give unto thee for a sign, that thou shalt be struck dumb . . . that ye shall no more have utterance" (Alma 30:48–49). The die was cast and the dumbstruck anti-Christ confessed in writing that he had really known all along that his teachings were false. He admitted to being caught up in the maze of popularity and pride, preaching blasphemy with "much success, insomuch that [he] verily believed that [his false teachings] were true; and for this cause [he] withstood the truth" (Alma 30:50–53).

Alma² refused Korihor's plea to remove the curse, noting that the wicked man would return to his old ways and continue to preach false doctrine (Alma 30:54–55). The anti-Christ ended up as a beggar, going door to door for food. He was ultimately killed by the Zoramites (Alma 30:56–60).

The epitaph of his misused and tragic life, which should serve as a reminder to all that sin leads to misery, is found in these words: "And thus we see that the devil will not support his children at the last day, but doth speedily drag them down to hell" (Alma 30:6).

See also Anti-Christ; Teachers, False.

KUMEN

The only mention of Kumen is when he was selected as one of the resurrected Christ's special twelve disciples during His visit to the inhabitants of ancient America (3 Nephi 19:4). As with his associates in the Twelve, Kumen was obviously spiritually prepared for this significant priesthood calling.

See also Disciples, Twelve.

KUMENONHI

As with at least ten of the others selected by the resurrected Redeemer to be His twelve special-witness disciples in ancient America, Kumenonhi is mentioned by name in only one citation (3 Nephi 19:4). The exception to this general anonymity was Nephi³, who was the chief among them and is mentioned a number of times before and after Christ's visit.

See also Disciples, Twelve.

L

LABAN

This custodian of the brass plates was aptly described by Elder George Reynolds (1842–1909) as "a rich, unscrupulous and powerful Israelite of the tribe of Joseph, though a dweller in Jerusalem. . . . He was a robber and, at heart, a murderer" *(Dictionary of the Book of Mormon,* 171, 173).

The plates of brass which Laban had in his possession contained "the five books of Moses, which gave an account of the creation of the world, and also of Adam and Eve, who were our first parents; and also a record of the Jews from the beginning, even down to the commencement of the reign of Zedekiah, king of Judah; and also the prophecies of the holy prophets, from the beginning, even down to the commencement of the reign of Zedekiah; and also many prophecies which have been spoken by the mouth of Jeremiah. And . . . a genealogy of [Lehi's] fathers" (1 Nephi 5:11–14).

After fleeing Jerusalem with his family, Lehi[1] had been commanded by the Lord to send his sons back to the city to obtain these plates of brass from Laban who, like the prophet Lehi[1], was a descendant of Joseph[1] (1 Nephi 5:14–16). The four drew lots to see who would go to request the record from Laban, and the assignment fell to Laman[1]. His request for the plates was angrily rejected by Laban, who threatened to kill him (1 Nephi 3:1–14).

Unsuccessful in this first attempt, Nephi[1] proposed that they purchase the plates with the wealth they had left behind in their abandoned Jerusalem home. Lusting after their property, Laban refused the exchange, kept their property, and had his servants try to murder the four sons of Lehi[1] (1 Nephi 3:15–27). It was then the Lord took over. Finding Laban unconscious, Nephi[1] received a commandment from the Lord to slay the evil man. "Behold the Lord slayeth the wicked to bring forth his righteous purposes. It is better that one man should perish than that a nation should dwindle and perish in unbelief" (1 Nephi 4:13). Obedient to the direction of the Lord, Nephi[1] slew Laban and was able to obtain the plates (1 Nephi 4:14–38).

LACHONEUS[1]

This righteous chief judge and governor of the Nephites lived in the ancient Americas at the time the Babe of Bethlehem was born in the Old World (3 Nephi 1:1). This was a difficult time for the Nephites because the unbelievers were so numerous that they had threatened to kill those who believed in the prophecies of Christ's birth if the promised signs did not occur by a deadline date the wicked had presumptuously set (3 Nephi 1:4–9). However, the signs were given and mass murder was avoided.

About fifteen years after he became chief judge, Lachoneus[1] received an epistle from the leader of the wicked band of Gadianton robbers demanding that the Nephites surrender themselves, their properties, and lands to this horde of evil doers (3 Nephi 3:1–10). Lachoneus[1] "was a just man, and could not be frightened by the demands and the threatenings of a robber . . . but he did cause that his people should cry unto the Lord for strength" (3 Nephi 3:12). He called the people to repentance and spoke "marvelous . . . words and prophecies" (3 Nephi 3:15–16). Furthermore, he appointed as the chief captain of the defending armies a man who "had the spirit of revelation and also prophecy . . . a great prophet among them, as also was the chief judge" (3 Nephi 3:19).

Lachoneus[1] gathered all the people into one safe location with all their provisions, and the people fortified themselves against the pending attack of the robbers. The great chief judge and governor not only prepared them with temporal provisions but he also prepared them spiritually, "insomuch that they did repent of all their sins; and they did put up their prayers unto the Lord their God" (3 Nephi 3:22–25).

He was successful in defeating the invaders and was honored for establishing peace in the land (3 Nephi 6:6).

LACHONEUS[2]

This son of the powerful Nephite prophet-leader Lachoneus[1] succeeded his father as the chief judge and governor of the Nephites (3 Nephi 6:19). In spite of the peace and prosperity that followed the successful conclusion of a war against the wicked (3 Nephi 3–4), pride once again raised its ugly head and the Nephites fell into transgression in a very short period of time (3 Nephi 6:10–19). Murderous alliances were formed, which led to the slaying of "the chief judge of the land," whom we may conjecture was Lachoneus[2] (3 Nephi 7:1). Following his murder, the people divided into tribes with no central form of government (3 Nephi 7:2–3).

LAMAH

Lamah was among the many Nephite military commanders who,

together with their ten thousand soldiers, were killed in the final struggle of the doomed Nephite nation (Mormon 6:14).

LAMAN[1]

This oldest son of Father Lehi[1] and Mother Sariah was the source of much sorrow and suffering for his parents (1 Nephi 18:17–18). In fact, Laman's constant murmuring and disobedience caused much heartache and suffering for many.

Like conjoined twins, Laman[1] and his brother Lemuel were together in their rebellion. While Laman[1] was the obvious spokesman and initiator of their wayward actions, Lemuel was inseparably connected to his rebellious brother in word and deed.

Very early in the Book of Mormon record they are described as stiffnecked, hard-hearted, nonbelieving, murmurers (1 Nephi 2:11–18). They smarted under the righteous leadership of their younger brother Nephi[1], saying, "We will not that our younger brother shall be a ruler over us" (1 Nephi 18:10). Their anger against Nephi[1] often led to their physically assaulting him or seeking his life (1 Nephi 3:28–29; 7:16; 16:36–38; 18:11; 2 Nephi 5:2–3).

Neither the chastening words of Father Lehi[1] nor their brother Nephi[1] had a lasting effect on changing their behavior from rebellion to obedience.

Even miraculous experiences such as being personally chastised by an angel (1 Nephi 3:29–31), or hearing the chastening voice of the Lord (1 Nephi 16:29), had a life-changing effect on them.

On one occasion, they experienced the power of God that was with Nephi[1] as he reached out and shocked them with his touch, causing them to shake. This experience led them to fall down and seek to "worship" their younger brother, who rebuked them with the admonition that it is God who should be worshiped (1 Nephi 17:48–55).

These experiences are reminders that miraculous manifestations do not form the foundation of lasting faith and true conversion. A mighty change of heart must follow such experiences, not just a *temporary* altering of behavior.

One of the major failings of Laman[1] and Lemuel was their unwillingness to *personally* seek direction from the Lord. In response to Nephi's question, "Have ye inquired of the Lord?" the two disbelieving brothers replied, "We have not" (1 Nephi 15:8–9). Their lack of faith deprived them of revelation that could have grounded them in the gospel and changed the course of their lives. One is reminded of an observation by President Spencer W. Kimball

(1895–1985) regarding personal revelation:

"Since Adam and Eve were placed in the garden the Lord has been eager—eager to reveal truth and right to His people. There have been many times when man would not listen, and, of course, where there is no ear, there is no voice" (*Ensign,* November 1976, 111).

The lives of Laman[1] and Lemuel were filled with opportunities to change for the better; however, they constantly chose wrongly. A sad summary statement about these two miscreant brothers was uttered by Nephi[1], who warned them that they "were swift to do iniquity but slow to remember the Lord" (1 Nephi 17:45).

The anger of Laman[1] and Lemuel continued to the point where they plotted to take Nephi's life, and the Lord warned Nephi[1] to flee with his followers. Thus emerged the two separate nations, the Nephites and the Lamanites (2 Nephi 5).

As a result of Laman's and Lemuel's wrong choices, generations of their posterity were deprived of blessings that might have been theirs. In the words of Elder Spencer W. Kimball, the posterity of Laman and Lemuel have been "a people who have had visited upon their heads the sins of their fathers not unto the third and fourth generation but through a hundred generations" (*Improvement Era,* June 1954, 425).

See also Lamanites; Lemuel.

LAMAN[2]

Around B.C. 200, this Lamanite king ruled in the land originally occupied by the forefathers of the Nephites. The adventurer Zeniff, "being over-zealous to inherit the land of his fathers [was] deceived by the cunning and craftiness of king Laman" and entered into what he perceived was a peaceful and generous treaty which allowed him and his followers to settle on the land (Mosiah 7:21; 9:10; 10:18). However, once established, the colony of Zeniff found itself captive to Laman[2], who then demanded a tax of 50 percent of everything they produced (Mosiah 7:22).

Observing the Nephite's prosperity, and fearful that they could no longer be held in bondage, King Laman[2] stirred his people up to create wars and contentions with the colony (Mosiah 9:11–13). Relying upon the Lord through fervent prayer, for a time the Nephites were successful in driving the Lamanites out of their land. However, when King Laman[2] died, his namesake son followed the same pattern of his father and stirred his followers up to contend with the Nephites (Mosiah 10:8).

LAMAN³

As noted in the previous entry, this namesake son of the Lamanite king Laman² (Mosiah 24:3) succeeded his father as king and immediately began to stir his people up to contend against the Nephites (Mosiah 10:8). Once again the small colony prevailed in its battle with the larger force because they "did go up in the strength of the Lord to battle" (Mosiah 10:10).

Several years later, after being discovered by the expedition of Ammon¹, the descendants of those who established the original colony were able to escape the bondage of King Laman³. Fleeing the land of Lehi-Nephi, they traveled to the land of Zarahemla, where they were united with the people of King Mosiah² (Mosiah 22). King Laman³ was unsuccessful in recapturing those who fled his land, but his pursuing army did discover the colony Alma¹ established in the land of Helam. Treacherously breaking a promise to Alma¹, King Laman³ placed this righteous colony under subjection. The king then appointed Amulon, the leader of the wicked priests of King Noah³, as the overlord of their new captives (Mosiah 23:36–39).

Alma¹ and his people were able to escape the land of Helam and join with the main body of Nephites in the land of Zarahemla. Nothing more is mentioned of Laman³ (Mosiah 24).

LAMAN⁴

A Lamanite by birth but a Nephite citizen by choice, Laman⁴ was selected by Captain Moroni¹ for a special military mission (Alma 55:4). He had been one of the servants of the Lamanite king who was treacherously slain by the power-hungry Nephite dissenter Amalickiah, who had then falsely accused Laman⁴ and his fellow servants of the brutal murder (Alma 47:12–35).

A plan was devised whereby Laman⁴ would lead a small group of soldiers to feign friendship with some Lamanites guarding Nephite prisoners. After gaining the trust of the guards, Laman's group was able to incapacitate them and allow the prisoners to escape. This resulted in turning the tide of the battle in the Nephites' favor (Alma 55:6–24). Nothing more is recorded of Laman⁴. He is one of those heroes who stands center stage in a moment of need and then quietly steps back into the shadows of anonymity, while presumably continuing faithful.

LAMANITES

This term generally describes a descendant of Laman¹ *or* one of those who originally followed him in his rebellion against his prophet-brother Nephi¹.

A dark skin was originally placed upon the Lamanites to distinguish them from the Nephites and to keep the two people from mixing (2 Nephi 5:21; Alma 3:7–8) President Joseph Fielding Smith (1876–1972) has written that "the dark skin was the *sign* of the curse. The *curse was the withdrawal of the Spirit of the Lord*" (*Answers to Gospel Questions,* 3:122; emphasis added). Thus, when the Lamanites or any other people accept the light of the gospel, "their *scales of darkness shall begin to fall from their eyes*" (2 Nephi 30:6; emphasis added).

The name *Lamanite* also describes later dissenters who apostatized from the Nephites, particularly those who rejected the gospel of Jesus Christ and joined with the Lamanites. The prophet-scribe Jacob[2] wrote that "I shall call them Lamanites that seek to destroy the people of Nephi" (Jacob 1:14).

The book of Alma provides the following inclusive definition of a Lamanite: they "were a compound of Laman and Lemuel, and the sons of Ishmael, and all those who had dissented from the Nephites, who were Amalekites and Zoramites, and the descendants of the priests of Noah" (Alma 43:13).

It should be remembered that not all people whose ancestry traced back to the original Lamanite rebels continued in the wicked traditions of their forefathers. For example, the Anti-Nephi-Lehies, or people of Ammon[2], were marvelous examples of righteousness (Alma 23:6–7).

In the great apostasy that took place following the golden era of peace among the Nephites (around 84 A.D.), the term *Lamanite* was applied to those who forsook their faith and "revolted from the church" (4 Nephi 1:20). Thus, *these apostate dissenters were not distinguished by ancestry or skin color, but by their slide into spiritual darkness.* In terms of ancestry, they were a mixture of those who descended from three of the tribes of Israel: from Manasseh through Father Lehi[1], from Ephraim through Ishmael[1], and from Judah through Mulek.

Ultimately the Lamanites destroyed the Nephites and became the forefathers of what the Prophet Joseph Smith identified as the western tribe of Indians (*Teachings of the Prophet Joseph Smith,* 17, 92–93).

An interesting phrase is used in latter-day revelation that is associated with the Lamanites. The Doctrine and Covenants mentions "the line running directly between Jew and Gentile" in reference to a boundary of land the Saints were commanded to purchase (57:4). "This expression," said President Joseph Fielding Smith (1876–1972), "has reference to the line separating the Lamanites from the settlers in Jackson County. At this time the United States Government had given to the Indians the lands west of the Missouri. . . . The Lamanites who are Israelites, were referred to as Jews, and the Gentiles were the people, many of whom were the lawless element living east of the river" (*Church History and Modern Revelation*, 189).

As Mormon[2] prepared to close his history, he wrote the following insightful comments regarding the future of the people called Lamanites: "This people shall be scattered, and shall become a dark, a filthy, and a loathsome people, beyond the description of that which ever hath been amongst us, yea, even that which hath been among the Lamanites, and this because of their unbelief and idolatry. . . . They were once a delightsome people, and they had Christ for their shepherd; yea, they were led even by God the Father. . . . But . . . *the Lord [will] remember the covenant which he made unto Abraham and unto all the house of Israel*" (Mormon 5:15-20; emphasis added.)

"Today, because of this promise to the Lamanites, the skin color of the modern Lamanites has a new significance. That is, it does not signify either a people descended from Laman and Lemuel, or a people in rebellion against God. Rather, that bronze color persists today to identify and set apart the modern remnant of the seed of Joseph for whom wonderful blessings have been reserved, that same group that Joseph of Egypt and all the prophets of the Book of Mormon prayed and sacrificed for, and whose ultimate triumph over darkness they foresaw. Mormon spoke to today's Lamanites: 'I speak unto you, ye remnant of the house of Israel. . . . Know ye that ye are of the house of Israel. . . . Know ye that ye must come to the knowledge of your fathers . . . ye are a remnant of the seed of Jacob; therefore ye are numbered among the people of the first covenant.' (Morm. 7:1-2, 5, 10.)" (Jackson, *Studies in Scripture, Volume 7: 1 Nephi to Alma 29*, 112).

President Joseph Fielding Smith reaffirmed that in our day "the dark skin of those who have come into the Church is no longer considered a sign of the curse" (*Answers to Gospel Questions*, 3:123).

See also Amalekites; Amalickiahites; Amlicites; Amulonites; Ishmaelites; Laman[1]; Lemuelites; People of the First Covenant.

LAMB OF GOD

This title of Jesus Christ, as presently recorded in the Bible, was first used by John the Baptist prior to administering the ordinance of baptism to the Savior (John 1:29). It is interesting that the name *Lamb of God* is first found in the Book of

Mormon in a text referring to John's baptism of Jesus (1 Nephi 10:10). The sacred title is found frequently in this second witness of Jesus Christ; and He is also referred to as *the Lamb* (1 Nephi 12:11).

This significantly symbolic title has reference to the Savior's role as the Sacrificial Lamb whose blood was shed to take away the stains of our sins. Indeed, we are "healed by the power of the Lamb of God" (1 Nephi 11:31). Because of faith in the Lamb of God, the *righteous* have their garments washed clean in His atoning blood (1 Nephi 12:10).

Elder Jeffrey R. Holland (1940–) provided the following insight on the significance of lambs in sacrifice:

"Long ago the troubled and enslaved Israelites had been 'passed over,' spared, finally made free by the blood of a lamb sprinkled on the lintel and doorposts of their Egyptian homes (see Ex. 12:21–24). That, in turn, had been only a symbolic reiteration of what Adam and all succeeding prophets were taught from the beginning—that the pure and unblemished lambs offered from the firstlings of Israel's flocks were a similitude, a token, a prefiguration of the great and last sacrifice of Christ which was to come (see Moses 5:5–8)" (*Ensign,* November 1995, 67).

Elder Dallin H. Oaks (1932–) observed the symbolism between the Lamb of God shedding His blood for us and our partaking of the sacrament. He said: "At the beginning of the Savior's ministry, John the Baptist exclaimed, 'Behold the Lamb of God, which taketh away the sin of the world' (John 1:29).

"At the end of his ministry, as Jesus blessed the cup and gave it to his disciples, he said, 'For this is my blood of the new testament, which is shed for many for the remission of sins.' (Matt. 26:28.) As Latter-day Saints partake of the sacrament of the Lord's Supper, we drink water in remembrance of his blood, which was shed for us. (See D&C 20:79)" (*Ensign,* November 1988, 66).

See also Christ; Christ, Names of; Father, Jesus Christ As; God; Immanuel; Jehovah; Jesse, Stem of; Jesus; Messiah; Only Begotten of the Father; Prince of Peace; Redeemer; Savior.

LAMONI

Lamoni was the Lamanite king over the land of Ishmael who was converted by the missionary Ammon[2]. His father and brother Anti-Nephi-Lehi were also later converted. When Ammon[2] arrived in the Lamanite-occupied land of Ishmael, he was taken prisoner by the servants of King Lamoni and brought before the ruler. His fate was dependent on "the pleasure of the king" (Alma 17:19–21).

Evidently Ammon's physical bearing was impressive, for Lamoni offered to give him one of his daughters as a wife. Ammon[2] refused, preferring to be a servant rather than a son-in-law. Perhaps offended by the refusal, the king set Ammon[2] in the precarious service of watching over the flocks at the water of Sebus. This was a dangerous task because if any of the flocks were lost, the attending servants were put to death by the king (Alma 17:22–29; 18:5–7).

When Ammon[2] successfully defended the king's flock, Lamoni was so impressed with his power that he mistakenly thought this Nephite servant to be "the Great Spirit" (Alma 18:1–4, 11). Ammon[2] sought to dispel the king's notion by declaring himself to be but "a man" and the king's "servant" (Alma 18:17).

After discerning that Ammon[2] could perceive his thoughts, the king agreed to listen to Ammon's testimony, declaring: "I will believe all thy words" (Alma 18:23). The "plan of redemption" was then expounded and "the king believed all [Ammon's] words" (Alma 18:40). As a result of his conversion, Lamoni experienced a miraculous outpouring of the Spirit, and the way was opened for Ammon[2] to teach many of the king's subjects (Alma 19).

The depth of Lamoni's conversion was shown when he desired to have Ammon[2] go with him to the land of Nephi and teach his father. However, the Lord warned Ammon[2] that Lamoni's father would attempt to kill him and he should instead go to Middoni and free his imprisoned brothers. Lamoni insisted on accompanying his mentor to Middoni; during their journey, Lamoni and Ammon[2] were met by Lamoni's father, who was "king over all the land" (Alma 20:8).

Lamoni's father was angry with his son because he had not attended a birthday celebration and because he was in the company of a hated Nephite. The father commanded Lamoni to kill Ammon[2] and forgo his announced intention to travel to Middoni and free the imprisoned brothers. At this point, Lamoni bore his testimony that Ammon[2] and his imprisoned brothers were "just men and holy prophets of the true God" (Alma 20:9–15).

As a result of this response, the angry father sought to slay his son, but he was prevented by Ammon's intervention. Lamoni was then able to continue to Middoni and secure the release of the imprisoned missionaries (Alma 20:16–28).

Lamoni and Ammon[2] returned to the land of Ishmael, where the king built synagogues in which he taught his people. He also had Ammon[2] teach his subjects "and they gave heed unto his word, and they were zealous for keeping the commandments of God" (Alma 21:18–23).

Lamoni and his brother Anti-Nephi-Lehi were part of a council held with Ammon[2] in which they discussed how the newly converted Lamanites could be protected against the hatred of their former neighbors. Lamoni and his people covenanted that they would never take up weapons of war again, even in defending themselves. As a result of their resolve, many were slaughtered by the angry invaders, who were their former friends and neighbors. However, remorse struck many of the attackers, and "the people of God were joined that day by more than the number who had been slain" (Alma 24:26).

See also Lamoni, Father of; Lamoni, Wife of.

LAMONI, FATHER OF

The unnamed father of the Lamanite King Lamoni, who was the king over all the land, is first mentioned as having planned a "great feast" to which Lamoni had been invited (Alma 18:9). Because of the events surrounding his conversion, Lamoni did not attend the feast (Alma 18–20). When Lamoni proposed to take his missionary mentor Ammon[2] with him to visit his father in the land of Nephi, the Lord warned Ammon[2] not to go, "for behold, the king will seek thy life" (Alma 20:1–2). He was instructed to go instead to the land of Middoni and obtain the release of missionaries who were in prison.

Lamoni accompanied Ammon[2] on his journey, and on the way they met Lamoni's father, who was very angry for two reasons: first, because his son had missed the "great feast," and second, because he was in the company of "this Nephite, who is one of the children of a liar" (Alma 20:7–10). The father was further angered when Lamoni told him he was on his way to secure the release of Nephites being held in prison. The angry father demanded that his son kill Ammon[2] and refrain from trying to help the imprisoned Nephites. When Lamoni refused, the hot-tempered father drew his sword to slay his son. Ammon[2] interceded and disarmed the father, who pleaded for his life by offering the defender "even to half of the kingdom" (Alma 20:23).

Ammon's response astonished the king, for he sought nothing for himself but only the release of the imprisoned missionaries and that Lamoni would be able to retain his kingdom. This led to the father's not only granting the requests, but expressing a desire to learn the teachings

Ammon² had taught to Lamoni (Alma 20:24–27).

Following his release from prison, Ammon's brother Aaron³ went to the land of Nephi and taught Lamoni's father. The father's heart had been so softened by his experience with Ammon² and by the workings of the Spirit that he expressed almost a childlike faith in his willingness to accept the teachings of Aaron³: "If now thou sayest there is a God, behold I will believe," and "tell me concerning all these things, and I will believe thy words" (Alma 22:7, 11). These responses are reminders of the Lord's promise: "And who receiveth you receiveth me. . . . And who receiveth you as a little child, receiveth my kingdom; and blessed are they, for they shall obtain mercy" (D&C 99:2–3).

The king experienced a marvelous outpouring of the Spirit as he accepted the truths taught by the missionary Aaron³. The power of the conversion that came upon the father of Lamoni, and of his absolute commitment to the cause of Christ which he had embraced, is illustrated in his declaration that "I will give up *all* that I possess, yea, I will forsake my kingdom, that I may receive this great joy" (Alma 22:15; emphasis added). Note the difference between this response and his earlier offer to give up "half of the kingdom" just to save his life

(Alma 20:23). Furthermore, he was willing to "give away *all* my sins to know [God]" (Alma 22:18; emphasis added).

What an exemplary model this declaration is for all who declare their desire to follow Christ with *all* their heart. Elder Neal A. Maxwell (1926–2004) has provided us with the following keen insight regarding our need to fully change our lives:

"Indeed, one of the most cruel games anyone can play with self is the 'not yet' game—hoping to sin just a bit more before ceasing; to enjoy the praise of the world a little longer before turning away from the applause; to win just once more in the wearying sweepstakes of materialism; to be chaste, but not yet; to be good neighbors, but not now. One can play upon the harpstrings of hesitations and reservations just so long, and then one faces that special moment—a moment when what has been sensed, mutely, suddenly finds voice and cries out with tears, 'Lord, I believe; help thou mine unbelief.' (Mark 9:24.)"

"The truth is that 'not yet' usually means 'never'" (*Ensign,* November 1974, 13).

The king's conversion led to thousands of his subjects accepting the gospel message and changing their name from Lamanites to Anti-Nephi-Lehies (Alma 23:17). The king died after conferring his kingdom on his son Anti-Nephi-Lehi (Alma 24:2–3).

See also Lamoni.

LAMONI, WIFE OF

The wife of Lamoni is another of the unnamed but truly wonderful women of the Book of Mormon. Her husband King Lamoni had fallen into a deathlike trance as a result of his responding favorably to the gospel message taught to him by the missionary Ammon². He was carried to his wife and laid on a bed "as if he were dead for the space of two days and two nights" (Alma 18:40–43).

Since the people thought he was dead, they were about to lay him "in a sepulchre, which they had made for the purpose of burying their dead." It was at this point that the unnamed queen sent for Ammon². She explained she had heard he was a prophet with "power to do many mighty works" in the name of God. In a magnificent declaration of love for her husband, which is reminiscent of a wife or husband who is willing to overlook the shortcomings of a spouse, she declared that some "say that he is dead and that he stinketh . . . *but as for myself, to me he doth not stink*" (Alma 19:5; emphasis added).

Ammon² knew the king was not dead, that he was simply going through a transformation of dispelling darkness and replacing it with light. Ammon² promised her that the king would arise from his bed the following day (Alma 19:6–8). Her simple faith was demonstrated when she replied: "I believe that it shall be according as thou hast said" (Alma 19:9).

"And Ammon said unto her: Blessed art thou because of thy exceeding faith; I say unto thee, woman, there has not been such great faith among all the people of the Nephites" (Alma 19:10).

When King Lamoni arose the following day, he bore powerful testimony of the Redeemer, then once more was overcome with the Spirit, and both he and the queen "sunk down, being overpowered by the Spirit." In the course of pouring out his heart in joyful gratitude for the conversion of these people, Ammon² also fell into a spiritual sleep (Alma 19:11–14). The three of them were soon joined by some of the king's servants who were also overpowered by the Spirit. As the king's subjects gathered to observe the sight of the king, queen, servants, and Nephite lying seemingly lifeless on the floor, a contention arose as to the meaning of this miraculous event. One observer was struck dead as he attempted to kill Ammon², which led to an "exceedingly sharp" contention among the onlookers. It was at this point that Abish, a convert woman, touched the queen, who arose and declared her testimony of Jesus and asked for His mercy to be on the people. Immediately the king and the others also arose, "and they did all declare unto the people the self-same thing—that their hearts had been changed; that they had no more desire to do evil. . . . And thus the work of the Lord did commence among the Lamanites; thus the Lord did begin to pour out his Spirit upon them; and we see that his arm is extended to all people who will repent and believe on his name" (Alma 19:29–36).

See also Lamoni.

LEARNED, HIM THAT IS NOT

See Learned, The; Harris, Martin; Smith, Joseph, Jr.

LEARNED, THE

This individual is mentioned in a prophecy of Isaiah[1] recorded in both the Bible and the Book of Mormon (Isaiah 29:11–12; 2 Nephi 27:6–22). This "learned" man was to be shown the "words which are not sealed" (2 Nephi 27:15) from the Book of Mormon, and he would declare "I cannot read it" (2 Nephi 27:18).

Latter-day Saints believe "the learned" to be Professor Charles Anthon. He taught classical studies at Columbia College (now Columbia University) in New York from 1820

until his death in 1867. He had published a *Classical Dictionary* in 1825, which was an update of an earlier work published in 1788. He was a respected scholar of ancient languages and, according to one historian, "was probably as well equipped as anyone in America" to respond to Martin Harris' inquiry regarding the authenticity of the characters that had been copied from the gold plates" (Bushman, *Joseph Smith: Rough Stone Rolling*, 64).

Martin Harris had taken copies of the characters from which the Book of Mormon was translated, together with a brief extract of the translation, to New York to seek professional opinion regarding the authenticity of their ancient origin. He eventually ended up in the office of Professor Anthon. The official version of the visit is found in Joseph Smith's history (Joseph Smith—History 1:63–65), in which Martin affirms that Professor Anthon initially verified the ancient origin of the characters and the correctness of the translation. However, when the professor was informed that the record from which the characters came had come into Joseph Smith's hands by a heavenly messenger, he tore up the affidavit and requested that the plates be brought to him to translate. When informed by Martin that he could not bring them because a portion was sealed, the professor declared, "I cannot read a sealed book!" That declaration by a *learned* man was what Isaiah[1] had prophetically penned centuries earlier (Isaiah 29:11–12; 2 Nephi 27:6–22).

"Anthon and Harris differed substantially in their accounts of their encounter. Anthon wrote letters in 1834 and 1841 to critics of the Mormons, denying that he had verified Joseph's translation or the authenticity of the characters. Anthon claimed he saw through the hoax at once, feared that Harris was about to be cheated of his money, and warned the 'simple-hearted farmer' to beware of rogues. Anthon, however, contradicts himself in an important detail. In the first letter Anthon said he refused to give Harris a written opinion; according to the second, the opinion was written 'without any hesitation,' in an attempt to expose the fraud.

"There is also confusion about what he actually saw. Anthon said that on the paper Harris showed him was a 'singular medley' of Greek and Hebrew letters with other strange marks, with 'sundry delineations of half moons, stars, and other natural objects, and the whole ended in a rude representation of the Mexican zodiac.' Inexplicably, no moons, stars, or natural objects appear on the surviving copy of the 'Anthon Transcript,' as it was published in 1844.

The characters are identifiably Egyptian, though not formed into Egyptian sentences. One scholar has argued there were two separate transcripts, one with a translation and one without. Harris said he showed Anthon both Joseph's translation and the untranslated characters and received confirmation of both. According to Harris, Anthon then said that the characters were Egyptian, Chaldaic, Assyriac, and Arabic, and gave Harris 'a certificate certifying to the people of Palmyra that they were true characters, and that the translation of such of them as had been translated was also correct.' Satisfied with the professor's observations, Harris was leaving when Anthon inquired about the origins of the plates. When he was told that an angel had revealed their location, he asked for the certificate and tore it up. Anthon wanted to see the plates themselves, but Harris said they could not be shown because part was sealed. 'I cannot read a sealed book,' Harris reported Anthon saying. With that they parted. Whatever happened, Martin Harris came back more convinced than before. He went right to translating and later funded publication of the Book of Mormon" (*Joseph Smith: Rough Stone Rolling*, 64–65).

An interesting facet of the pivotal exchange between Martin Harris and Charles Anthon is the question of how truly skilled the professor was at that point in reading and verifying ancient languages, particularly the unknown "Reformed Egyptian" in which the Book of Mormon was written. It must be remembered that the ancient Nephite scribes had "altered" their language and that it was unknown by any other people (Mormon 9:32–34).

"Just how much Anthon knew about the Egyptian or Reformed Egyptian languages is highly debatable," wrote Professor Stanley B. Kimball. "*Anthon most likely was showing off* to Harris and later destroyed the certificate he had offered [for fear of being scoffed at by his fellow scholars]. The real importance of Anthon is not how much he knew of the Egyptian language but that Harris returned home convinced of the truth of the Book of Mormon, supporting Joseph Smith financially and as a scribe" (in Garr, *Encyclopedia of Latter-day Saint History,* 30; emphasis added).

The most significant point in this matter is not whether or not Charles Anthon could actually read the translation or verify the authenticity of the characters, but the fact that his declaration "I cannot read a sealed book" *was* a fulfillment of prophecy.

See also Harris, Martin.

LEHI[1]

This grand patriarch of the people of the Book of Mormon was a contemporary of the prophet Jeremiah[1]. Father Lehi[1] was among the "many prophets" sent by the Lord about the year 600 B.C. to the inhabitants of Jerusalem, "prophesying . . . that they must repent, or the great city Jerusalem must be destroyed" (1 Nephi 1:4).

Lehi[1] and his wife Sariah were the parents of Laman[1], Lemuel, Sam, Nephi[1], Jacob[2], Joseph[2], and several unnamed daughters (1 Nephi 2:5; 1 Nephi 18:7; 2 Nephi 5:6).

There were numerous defining moments in Father Lehi's life and ministry, and much can be learned from the way he responded at such junctures. As a father and a leader, he not only taught but he also "prayed . . . with all his heart, in behalf of his people" (1 Nephi 1:5). Such an approach to ministering opened his mind and eyes to inspiring "visions and . . . dreams" (1 Nephi 1:6–16). Additional inspiration also came because he searched the scriptures (1 Nephi 1:12).

In spite of being mocked, Lehi[1] was relentless in preaching, warning the people of their impending destruction if they did not repent. Disdaining the prophet's words, and in angry reaction, the unrepentant people turned from simply mocking

Lehi[1] to seeking his life (1 Nephi 1:19–20).

The Lord commended His prophet for his faithfulness and commanded him to take his family and leave Jerusalem. Perhaps one of the finest tributes that could be given to any person is the simple description of Lehi's response: "And it came to pass that *he was obedient* unto the word of the Lord, wherefore he did as the Lord commanded him" (1 Nephi 2:3; emphasis added). His obedience also included his willingness to sacrifice, leaving "his house, and the land of his inheritance, and his gold, and his silver, and his precious things" as he faithfully followed the Lord's will (1 Nephi 2:4).

This pivotal response not only spared Lehi's life, but set in motion a chain of events that would ultimately lead to the publication of the book that would alter the eternal destiny of untold millions—The Book of Mormon: Another Testament of Jesus Christ!

While the magnitude of the sacrifice may not be the same, there is a parallel in Lehi's example of obedience and sacrifice to men and women who accept mission calls that require them to "leave their house and precious things" to travel in the wilderness of the world to preach the gospel.

Lehi's life taught the importance of living in such a way that the Spirit can be a constant influence. He was enabled to teach and speak "with power, being filled with the Spirit," because of his faithfulness (1 Nephi 2:14). He remained steadfast in the face of the complaints of his family that he was "a visionary man" (1 Nephi 2:11; 5:1–3). Yet, like two future servants of God who would affirm the truthfulness of their visions, even the Apostle Paul and the Prophet Joseph Smith (Joseph Smith—History 1:24–25), Lehi[1] was unwavering in his witness of the divine direction given to him (1 Nephi 5:4).

In addition to his eagerness to do the will of the Lord, Father Lehi[1] also had great desires for the welfare of his family (2 Nephi 1:16; 2:30). In partaking of the fruit of the tree of life, which "filled [his] soul with exceedingly great joy," this faithful father was immediately desirous that his "family should partake of it also" (1 Nephi 8:11–12).

While several rebellious children refused their father's imploring invitation to join the rest of the family in partaking of the fruit, to his dying day this father-patriarch did all within his power to continue to teach and testify of gospel truths to his posterity (2 Nephi 4).

LEHI[2]

According to the index in the Triple Combination, this son of Zoram[2], who was a chief captain of the Nephite armies, was "possibly the same as Lehi[3]." Around 81 B.C. Lehi[2] and his brother Aha accompanied their father on a visit to the prophet Alma[2]. The men sought Alma's inspiration on military matters, which led to their victory in battle (Alma 16:5–8).

What a different world we would have if all leaders righteously sought counsel from men of God who "had the spirit of prophecy," or even better, if they themselves were living in such a way that they were possessed of that same spirit.

LEHI[3]

The index to the Book of Mormon suggests the possibility that Lehi[2], who was the son of Zoram[2], and Lehi[3] could be the same individual. However, for the purposes of this entry, we will presume them to be two different men.

Lehi[3] was one of the chief Nephite military leaders acting under Captain Moroni[1] during the long war described in Alma 43 through 62. Throughout this conflict, Lehi[3] faced many occasions where his courage and faith combined to inspire his troops in their battle for freedom. His inspired leadership of the Nephite warriors was legendary among their enemies, "for they feared Lehi exceedingly" (Alma 49:17).

More important than his military prowess, however, was the fact that Lehi[3] was a man of righteousness. Indeed, it was said of him that "he was a man *like unto Moroni,* and . . . [was] beloved by all the people of Nephi" (Alma 53:2; emphasis added). And of Captain Moroni[1] it was said, "If all men had been, and were, and ever would be, *like unto Moroni,* behold, the very powers of hell would have been shaken forever; yea, the devil would never have power over the hearts of the children of men" (Alma 48:17; emphasis added).

How different our world would be today if every Latter-day Saint, every Christian, and every person were "like unto Moroni" *and* Lehi[3]!

LEHI[4]

This son of Helaman[3] and brother of the great prophet Nephi[2] was equally as valiant as his father and brother. While he did not get the "headlines" accorded to his brother, he was an important member of the team the Lord had assembled at that time to move His work forward. Lehi[4] "was not a whit behind [Nephi[2]] as to things pertaining to righteousness" (Helaman 11:19).

The importance for parents to prayerfully and carefully select names for their children is exemplified in how Lehi's father, Helaman[3], named his two sons. They were given the names of their "first parents [Lehi[1] and Nephi[1]] who came out of the land of Jerusalem; . . . that when you remember your names ye may remember them; and when ye remember them ye may remember their works; and when ye remember their works ye may know how that it is said, and also written, that they were good" (Helaman 5:6).

This is not to suggest that all children should be named after scriptural or famous people. But they should be given names that are approved by the Spirit and that will be a source of joy and a motivation to do good throughout their lives.

Lehi[4] was a powerful missionary, at one point converting eight thousand Lamanites (Helaman 5:18–19). He and his brother were cast into a prison for "many days without food" and were saved from the swords of their captors by a protecting circle that appeared as fire (Helaman 5:20–24). This manifestation was followed by "a cloud of darkness" and "a voice as if it were above the cloud of darkness, saying: Repent ye, repent ye, and seek no more to destroy my servants whom I have sent unto you to declare good tidings" (Helaman 5:28–29). In the midst of all this, the faces of the two brothers "did shine exceedingly, even as the faces of angels" (Helaman 5:36). As the captors now had their hearts turned toward becoming converts, they themselves became "encircled about, yea every soul, by a pillar of fire" (Helaman 5:43). As a result of their change of heart, these new converts became a righteous people, and "their righteousness did exceed that of the Nephites, because of their firmness and their steadiness in the faith" (Helaman 6:1). The mighty change of heart of these converts was later mentioned by the prophet-historian Mormon[2] (Ether 12:14).

A lesson for priesthood leaders, parents, and all who are faced with situations of contention is found in the way in which Lehi[4] and his righteous brethren handled such occasions. "Nephi and Lehi, and many of their brethren who knew concerning the true points of doctrine [they knew the scriptures], having many revelations daily [were worthy to be directed by the Holy Ghost], therefore they did preach unto the people, insomuch that they did put an end to their strife" (Helaman 11:23).

LEHONTI

This Lamanite military leader led a group of soldiers who refused their king's orders to attack the Nephites without provocation. They secluded themselves on a mount called Antipas (Alma 47:1–7). The treacherous Amalickiah was sent to bring Lehonti and his soldiers back. At first, Lehonti was wary of Amalickiah's overtures, refusing to leave his place of safety to meet with him. However, as the cunning Amalickiah persisted in luring him out of his safe place, Lehonti was put in a position where he ultimately was murdered as he ingested "poison by degrees" (Alma 47:10–18).

What a lesson about the importance of always keeping one's guard up against the forces of evil! We are reminded that Amalickiah's poisonous strategy was the same which the devil uses in all his evil plots. He will seek to "pacify, and lull [us] away into carnal security, that [we] will say: All is well in Zion; yea, Zion prospereth, all is well—and thus the devil cheateth [our] souls, and leadeth [us] away *carefully down to hell*" (2 Nephi 28:21; emphasis added). In other words, he administers "poison by degrees."

LEMUEL

The history of this rebel son of Lehi[1] and Sariah was inexorably connected to his older brother Laman[1]. As noted in the entry on Laman[1], these two brothers were like conjoined twins; it is essentially impossible to separate Laman[1] and Lemuel in a discussion of their lives and character. While Laman[1] was the obvious spokesman and initiator of their wayward actions, Lemuel was the easily persuaded sibling who readily followed the bad example of his older brother.

Their parents "suffered much grief because of their children" (1 Nephi 18:17). Lemuel was admonished by his prophet-father to be like a valley later referred to as the "valley of Lemuel" (1 Nephi 2:14), "firm and steadfast, and immovable in keeping the commandments of the Lord" (1 Nephi 2:10).

Neither the admonishing words of Father Lehi[1] nor the chastening words of his brother Nephi[1] had a lasting effect in changing Lemuel's behavior from rebellion to obedience. Even miraculous experiences such as being personally chastised by an angel (1 Nephi 3:29–31), or hearing the chastening voice of the Lord (1 Nephi 16:29), had a life-changing effect on Lemuel and his brother Laman[1]. The troublesome duo "were swift to do iniquity but slow to remember the Lord" (1 Nephi 17:45).

Father Lehi[1] "feared for Laman and Lemuel; yea, he feared lest they should be cast off from the presence of the Lord" (1 Nephi 8:36). Their continuing rebellion brought fulfillment of Lehi's concerns, for later they were "cut off from the presence of the Lord" (2 Nephi 5:19–20).

Lemuel and his posterity took upon themselves the name of Lamanites. His younger prophet-brother later wrote, "I, Jacob, shall not hereafter distinguish [Lemuel's descendants] by [the name Lemuelites], but I shall call them Lamanites that seek to destroy the people of Nephi" (Jacob 1:13–14).

See also Laman; Lamanites; Lemuelites.

LEMUELITES

A general term applied to descendants of Lemuel, son of Lehi[1] and Sariah. However, the designation was rarely used inasmuch as the Lemuelites were assimilated into the Lamanites, as were all others who descended from dissenters who rejected the leadership and teachings of Nephi[1] and his successors. Jacob[2] records that he amalgamated all such groups under the single heading of Lamanites (Jacob 1:13–14).

Some of Lemuel's descendants later rejected the false traditions taught by their forefathers and embraced the true gospel (Alma 24:29). The name Lemuelite surfaced again when people began rejecting Christ's teachings a number of years after His historic visit to ancient America: "They who rejected the gospel were called Lamanites, and Lemuelites, and Ishmaelites; and they did not dwindle in unbelief, but they did wilfully rebel against the gospel of Christ; and they did teach their children that they should not believe, even as their fathers, from the beginning, did dwindle" (4 Nephi 1:38).

LEVI[1]

This son of Jacob[1] (Israel) by his wife Leah (Genesis 29:34) is mentioned once in the Book of Mormon (3 Nephi 24:3). Levi[1] and his sons were charged with the responsibility of ministering the priesthood to the other tribes (Genesis 29:34; Numbers 3:12; 8:14–26). Specifically, the sons of Levi[1] represent holders of the priesthood in our day.

When the resurrected Savior visited the inhabitants of ancient America, He told them His Father had instructed Him to provide the people with several chapters from the Old Testament which they did not possess (3 Nephi 26:2). Included was Malachi 3, in which the prophet speaks of a future time when the Savior will come as a "refiner" and "*purify* the sons of Levi, and *purge* them as gold and silver, that they may offer unto the Lord an offering in righteousness" (Malachi 3:3; 3 Nephi 24:3; emphasis added). To purify and refine or purge is to remove all impurities. Thus, *priesthood holders who live worthy may then offer the Lord their offerings in righteousness.*

The following verse of Malachi states that in conjunction with this purifying, "Then shall the offering of Judah and Jerusalem be *pleasant* unto the Lord" (Malachi 3:4; 3 Nephi 24:4; emphasis added).

Commenting on these verses,

Elder Joseph Fielding Smith (1876–1972) said: "Now we understand, and the whole world could understand, that the offering of Judah in the days of Christ's ministry, was not pleasant. Levi was not at that time cleansed, but Judah and Levi turned away from the Lord. It is in the Dispensation of the Fulness of Times that these things are to be fulfilled" (in Conference Report, April 1948, 131).

LEVI²

This Jaredite king was the son of Kim and the father of Corom (Ether 1:20–21). His father was placed in captivity by Levi's unnamed uncle, and Levi² lived in captivity for forty-two years following his father's death (Ether 10:15). Levi² eventually overthrew his captor and was crowned as king himself. "And after he had obtained unto himself the kingdom he did that which was right in the sight of the Lord; and the people did prosper in the land; and he did live to a good old age" (Ether 10:16).

Levi² is an example that one need not be trapped in following the bad behavior of one's upbringing, for his father Kim "did not reign in righteousness" (Ether 10:13).

LEVI¹, SONS OF

See Levi¹.

LIB¹

Another of the many Jaredite kings, Lib¹ was the son of Kish and the father of Hearthom (Ether 1:17–18). While nothing is said of the character of his father, his grandfather Corom set a proper example for his family as well as for his subjects, for he "did that which was good in the sight of the Lord all his days" (Ether 10:17).

Lib¹ followed that example, for he "also did that which was good in the sight of the Lord" (Ether 10:19). It was during his reign that the plague of the poisonous serpents ceased, which opened areas for hunting that were previously unavailable. We are told that Lib¹ "became a great hunter" (Ether 10:19).

Under his leadership the people prospered. They were "exceedingly industrious" (Ether 10:22). "And never could be a people more blessed than were they, and more prospered by the hand of the Lord. And they were in a land that was choice above all lands, for the Lord had spoken it" (Ether 10:28).

LIB²

This murderous man was among the Jaredites who embraced the dark plans of the secret combinations. Lib² had an imposing physical presence, for he "was a man of great stature, more than any other man among all the people" (Ether 14:10).

His brief recorded history focuses on the war that raged between him and his rival Coriantumr², in which Lib² was finally killed (Ether 14:11–16). His brother Shiz then took his place in the ongoing conflict (Ether 14:16–17).

LIMHAH

Limhah was one of the many Nephite military commanders who was killed along with his ten thousand soldiers in the Nephites' final battle with the Lamanites around 385 A.D. (Mormon 6:14).

LIMHER

Limher was one of several spies whom Alma² sent to search out the plans and plots of the traitorous Amlicites (Alma 2:21–22). Limher and his fellow soldiers discovered that the Amlicites had joined forces with an invading Lamanite army and were attacking the people in the land of Nephi (Alma 2:23–25). As a result of this information, Alma's forces were able to repel the invaders, for they were "strengthened by the hand of the Lord, having prayed mightily to him that he would deliver them out of the hands of their enemies" (Alma 2:26–28).

LIMHI

The son of the wicked King Noah³, who had killed the prophet Abinadi, Limhi succeeded his father as king over the Nephite colony of Zeniff around 121 B.C. The colony had been established by Limhi's grandfather Zeniff, who was "over-zealous to inherit the land of his fathers" (Mosiah 7:21) and had entered into an ill-conceived agreement with a Lamanite king in the land of Nephi that eventually brought his people into bondage (Mosiah 9). The record of Zeniff's colony is found in chapters 9 through 22 of Mosiah, with additional portions being added in chapters 7 and 8.

Limhi became the leader of the colony following his father's cowardly actions in deserting his people; Noah³ had left them to fend for themselves while fleeing for his own safety when an invading army of Lamanites attacked (Mosiah 19). Limhi did not follow in the wayward steps of his wicked father, for he was a "just man" (Mosiah 19:17).

Limhi's people were under severe persecution from their overseers at the time they were discovered by the search expedition headed by Ammon¹. Prior to this, Limhi had sent his own expedition out to try to find the way back to the land of Zarahemla from whence Zeniff and his followers had originally come. Although Limhi's expedition was unsuccessful in their objective, they did find the remains of the extinct

Jaredite civilization, including twenty-four gold plates (Mosiah 8:5–14; 21:25–28). These plates were later given by Limhi to Mosiah[2] and were passed down from succeeding record keepers into the hands of Moroni[2], who translated the record.

Following the arrival of the expedition of Ammon[1], Limhi "entered into a covenant with God, and also many of his people, to serve him and keep his commandments" (Mosiah 21:32–35). After their successful escape from their captors, when they became the subjects of King Mosiah[2], Limhi and his people were baptized by Alma[2] (Mosiah 25:16–18).

LUCIFER

The single usage of the name Lucifer in the Book of Mormon is in a quotation from the plates of brass containing the writings of the prophet Isaiah[1] (2 Nephi 24:12; Isaiah 14:12).

It is also found once in the Doctrine and Covenants (76:26).

"Lucifer is the name whereby the devil was known in our premortal existence. In Hebrew the title means morning star or son of dawn. It may have some implication to the timing of his birth as a spirit child in the premortal life or reference to his once-held position of prominence before his fateful fall" (Brewster, *Doctrine and Covenants Encyclopedia,* 332).

See also Antichrist; Devil; Evil One; Perdition, Son of; Satan; Son of the Morning.

LURAM

The only mention of Luram in the Book of Mormon is in an epistle of Mormon[2] to his son Moroni[2]. Luram was one of three Nephite men mentioned by name who had "fallen by the sword," along with "a great number of our choice men," during a battle with the Lamanites (Moroni 9:2).

M

MAHAH

Mahah was one of four sons of Jared[2] (Ether 6:14). This is the single reference to Mahah by name, but we do know that he was among the children who "were taught to walk humbly before the Lord; and they were also taught from on high" (Ether 6:17). We also know that he and his two older brothers turned down the offer to be the king of the newly formed nation of Jaredites (Ether 6:22–27).

MAHER-SHALAL-HASH-BAZ

This unusual name is found in the writings of Isaiah[1] recorded in the Book of Mormon (2 Nephi 18:1, 3; Isaiah 8:1, 3).

"Isaiah is told to write the name of his newborn son, Maher-shalal-hash-baz, on a large scroll or tablet. The child's name, which incidentally is the longest word in the Bible, means 'to speed to the spoil, he hasteneth the prey' ('quick to the plunder, swift to the spoil'). The name was symbolic of the pending fall of Damascus (capital of Syria) and Samaria (capital of the northern king-dom) to the invading Assyrian armies" (Brewster, *Isaiah Plain & Simple,* 75).

MALACHI

At the behest of His Father (3 Nephi 26:2), the resurrected Christ quoted passages from the writings of this Old Testament prophet when He visited the ancient inhabitants of America (2 Nephi 24; 25; Malachi 3; 4). It is noteworthy that one of the reasons stated for providing these scriptures was that "it was wisdom in [God the Father] that they should be given unto *future generations*" (3 Nephi 26:2; emphasis added).

So stated, is it not imperative that due diligence be given to pondering Malachi's writings on such subjects as the restoration of the gospel and the covenant to pay tithes and offerings, as well as the importance of living righteously, of avoiding spiritual dis-content, of accepting the Atonement of the Son of Righteousness, of preparing for the Second Coming, and of knowing the significance of the mission of Elijah?

Malachi is the last prophet of the Old Testament. His writings are found not only in the Book of Mormon but are also quoted in other books of scripture (D&C 2; 110:14–16; 128:18; 133:64; Joseph Smith—History 1:36–39).

MANASSEH

This is the name of the eldest son of Joseph[1] (Genesis 41:50–51) and of the tribe of Israel named for him. Lehi[1] and his posterity were descendants from Joseph[1] through Manasseh (1 Nephi 5:14; Alma 10:3).

Manasseh is also mentioned in the writings of Isaiah[1] found in the Book of Mormon. The tribes of both Manasseh and his brother Ephraim are mentioned as being "against Judah" (2 Nephi 19:21). These two tribes of the northern kingdom of Israel are represented as having positioned themselves against the southern kingdom of Judah. This sibling infighting saddened and displeased the Lord, yet He was anxious to reach out and unite them once again: "For all this his anger is not turned away, but his hand is stretched out still" (2 Nephi 15:25).

See also Ephraim.

MANTI

One of four spies sent by Alma[2] to discover the plans and plots of the traitorous Amlicites who had risen up in rebellion against their fellow citizens, Manti joined with Zeram, Amnor, and Limher and "their men"

to gather this intelligence (Alma 2:21–22). They were "astonished and struck with much fear" when they discovered the rebel Amlicites had joined with the Lamanites in an attack on the Nephites (Alma 2:23–25). As a result of their report, Alma[2] was able to assemble his troops and defeat the invaders, saving many lives.

There is a subtle message that can be drawn from this experience. What if these men, who had been called as watchmen on the tower (see D&C 101:45), and sent out to discover the dangers facing the Nephites, had not followed through on their duty or reported back? Ponder how many lives were ultimately saved because a few faithful men fulfilled their callings or responsibilities! Is there not a modern-day application here for Latter-day Saints called as *watchmen on the tower,* such as home teachers, visiting teachers, and member missionaries?

MARY

The mortal mother of the Son of God is identified by *name* as well as by *calling* in the Book of Mormon. Six hundred years before the birth of the Divine Child, Nephi[1] was shown in vision "a virgin, and she was exceedingly fair and white." She was to become "the mother of the Son of God, after the manner of the flesh" (1 Nephi 11:13, 18). The Book of Mormon also provides second witness to Isaiah's prophecy that Christ would be born of "a virgin" (2 Nephi 17:14; Isaiah 7:14).

While skeptics and disbelievers cast doubt on the virgin birth, the fact remains that Christ was born of a mother who had not conceived Him through the seed of a mortal man. The Great God Elohim, Father of the spirits that inhabit the bodies of the human race, was also the Father of the *Only Begotten in the flesh,* even Jesus Christ. President Joseph F. Smith (1838–1918) testified: "God Almighty was the Father of His Son Jesus Christ. Mary, the virgin girl, who had never known mortal man, was his mother. God by her begot His son Jesus Christ" (Clark, *Messages of the First Presidency,* 4:329).

This virgin's name was to be *Mary.* Several hundred years after Nephi's writings, the prophet-king Benjamin identified her name: "His mother shall be called Mary" (Mosiah 3:8). Even later, the prophet Alma[2] gave second witness that this special woman, the mother of the Savior of the world, would be named "Mary . . . she being a virgin, a precious and chosen vessel" (Alma 7:10).

Following the conception of the Holy Child, Mary was married to Joseph the carpenter, who became a stepfather or earthly mentor to Jesus.

MATHONI

Mathoni is one of the twelve special disciples chosen by the resurrected Redeemer to lead His church in ancient America (3 Nephi 19:4). He is not mentioned by name again in the sacred record, but we can with assurance conclude that Mathoni participated in all of the acts performed by the Twelve as they labored in their ministry. Individuals do not need to be singled out by name in order to make a difference for good.

See also Disciples, Twelve.

MATHONIHAH

This brother of Mathoni was also selected as one of the twelve special disciples Christ designated to lead His church in ancient America (3 Nephi 19:4).

See also Disciples, Twelve.

MELCHIZEDEK

Although Melchizedek is one of the all-time great prophets, the world knows little about him. References to him in the King James Bible are very limited (Genesis 14:18–20; Hebrews 5:6; 7:1–3). However, latter-day revelation to the Prophet Joseph Smith has provided significant insights into the life of this forgotten man (JST Genesis 1:17–40; JST Hebrews 7:1–3; Alma 13:14–19; D&C 84:14; 107:1–4).

Melchizedek lived about 2000

B.C. and was called the "king of Salem" (Jerusalem). The King James Version of the Bible mentions that the patriarch Abraham paid tithes to Melchizedek (Genesis 14:18–20). The Joseph Smith Translation of that same chapter in Genesis adds significant information about Melchizedek, a sample of which follows:

"Now Melchizedek was a man of faith, who wrought righteousness; and when a child he feared God, and stopped the mouths of lions, and quenched the violence of fire.

"And thus, having been approved of God, he was ordained an high priest after the order of the covenant which God made with Enoch. . . . [And] he obtained peace in Salem, and was called the Prince of peace [a title foreshadowing Christ, who is the Prince of Peace].

"And his people wrought righteousness, and obtained heaven, and sought for the city of Enoch which God had before taken, separating it from the earth, having reserved it unto the latter days, or the end of the world" (JST Genesis 14:26–27, 33–34).

The Father and the Son thought so highly of Melchizedek that they placed his name on the high priesthood, which previously had been called "the Holy Priesthood, after the Order of the Son of God" (D&C 107:2–4).

The Book of Mormon teaches that all who receive this priesthood in mortality were foreordained to such an honor and responsibility in the premortal councils (Alma 13).

Alma[2] bore witness to the righteousness of Melchizedek in this succinct declaration: "There were many before him, and also there were many afterwards, but none were greater" (Alma 13:19).

MESSIAH

This title of Jesus Christ, which means "Anointed One," appears frequently in the Book of Mormon. About 600 B.C. Father Lehi[1] prophesied that the Messiah would come to redeem the world in six hundred years (1 Nephi 1:19; 10:4). Lehi[1] and others taught that many prophets before had testified of the coming of the Messiah (1 Nephi 10:5; Jacob 7:9–11; Mosiah 13:33). Christ Himself bore witness that the prophets had testified of His coming (3 Nephi 20:23–24).

Bearing witness of Jesus Christ as the promised Messiah (both for the First *and* Second Coming), is not limited to one who holds the *office* of prophet. The most humble member of Christ's Church who bears witness of Jesus as the Christ is declaring Him to be the Messiah. The Apostle John taught that "the testimony of Jesus [as the Christ] is the spirit of prophecy" (Revelation 19:10). And "no man can say that Jesus is the Lord, but by the Holy Ghost" (1 Corinthians 12:3).

The term *Messias* is the Greek equivalent of the Hebrew *Messiah*. When Jesus spoke to the woman at the well in Samaria, He declared, "I who speak unto thee am the Messias" (JST John 4:28).

See also Christ; Christ, Names of; Father, Jesus Christ As; God; Immanuel; Jehovah; Jesse, Stem of; Jesus; Lamb of God; Only Begotten of the Father; Prince of Peace; Redeemer; Savior.

MORIANTON[1]

Historically speaking, Morianton[1], a Jaredite king, is the first man to bear that name in the Book of Mormon (Ether 1:22–23). A brief account of his reign was found on the twenty-four gold plates that were translated by Moroni[2] into the book of Ether (Ether 10:9–13).

While little is written of this first Morianton, a significant statement is made which, in spite of the good things he did, implies much more might have been done if he had been worthy. Morianton[1] eased the burden under which the people had been living and became a popular ruler. However, *where he succeeded publicly he failed privately.* Moroni[2] tells us that Morianton[1] "did do justice unto the people, *but not unto himself* because of his many whoredoms; where-

fore he was cut off from the presence of the Lord" (Ether 10:11; emphasis added).

Morianton's life reminds us of the Savior's declaration, "For what shall it profit a man, if he shall gain the whole world, and lose his own soul?" (Mark 8:36).

MORIANTON[2]

Morianton[2] was an obviously powerful leader, but one who used his talents to lead people down the wrong path. When the Nephite system of being governed by judges had been in place about a quarter of a century, a border dispute broke out between the citizens of the lands of Lehi and Morianton. Rather than appeal to the reason or judgment of the law, the people in Morianton determined to solve the dispute with the sword, causing the people of Lehi to flee to the camp of Captain Moroni[1] for protection (Alma 50:25–27).

Upon hearing of the appeal to Moroni[1], the people of Morianton made plans to flee north, where they planned to set up their own community. They were led by a man named Morianton[2], who was an ill-tempered man given to angry outbursts. However, before their plan could be carried out, in what turned out to be a defining moment Morianton[2] beat one of his maidservants in a fit of anger. She fled to the camp of

Captain Moroni[1] and alerted him to the pending plans of Morianton[2] and his followers (Alma 50:28–31).

Moroni[1] feared that such plans, if successfully carried out, would ultimately place the freedom of the Nephites in jeopardy. He therefore sent an army to stop his opponents. The "stubborn" people of Morianton, led by the "flattering words" of the wicked Morianton[2], engaged in a battle with Moroni's army, but they were defeated and Morianton[2] was slain (Alma 50:33–35).

MORIANTON[2], PEOPLE OF

See Morianton[2].

MORMON[1]

The only mention of this man, who lived around A.D. 322, is as the father of the great prophet, military commander, and historian Mormon[2] (Mormon 1:5). The son gives no hint as to the kind of man his father was, but the fact that when Mormon[2] was "about ten years of age" Mormon[2] was selected to be the successor-recorder of the plates of Nephi must indicate that Mormon[2] did have the experience of being properly taught by someone (Mormon 1:1–3).

MORMON[2]

The name of Mormon[2] is synonymous with membership in The Church of Jesus Christ of Latter-day Saints. The Prophet Joseph Smith said the name means "more good" (*Teachings of the Prophet Joseph Smith,* 299–300).

Mormon[2] was named after his father and was the father of Moroni[2]. Mormon[2] stepped into the spiritual spotlight when but a boy. At the age of ten he was given charge of the sacred records from which the Book of Mormon would someday be translated (Mormon 1:2–4). In his sixteenth year he displayed such great capacity in both spiritual and temporal affairs that he saw the Savior (Mormon 1:15) and was chosen as the leader of the Nephite armies (Mormon 2:2).

In spite of living in one of the most degenerate of societies, Mormon[2] exercised his agency to follow God's ways. He remained unsullied from sin, a powerful example of righteous resistance to wrong. He proved that it is possible to live in the world and yet not be of the world (1 John 2:15). His commitment to the cause of righteousness was unsurpassed. Elder Sterling W. Sill (1903–1994) observed that "most of us have to be coaxed and begged and reminded to do our duty. Mormon had to be held back" (*The Upward Reach,* 249; Mormon 1:16–17).

"Under the direction of the Spirit of God, Mormon undertook the mammoth task of abridging all of the

Nephite records which had been handed down from 600 B.C. to his day, which was around A.D. 385. His abridgment consists of the books of Mosiah, Alma, Helaman, 3 Nephi, and 4 Nephi in the Book of Mormon. In addition to these writings, he wrote the Words of Mormon, the first seven chapters of Mormon, and contributed teachings or epistles found in chapters 7, 8, and 9 of his son Moroni's book.

"This great prophet-general was still leading the Nephite armies some fifty-eight years after he had first stood at their helm, and died with most of his people at the great battle of Cumorah (see Morm. 1–7; 8:3; Words of Mormon; Moro. 7–9)" (Brewster, *Doctrine & Covenants Encyclopedia*, 365).

MORON

This Jaredite king was the son of Ethem and the father of Coriantor (Ether 1:7–8). He followed the bad example of his father in doing "that which was wicked before the Lord" (Ether 11:14). For a time, because of a rebellion against him, he retained only half of his kingdom. He finally succeeded in reuniting the kingdom under his monarchy but was overthrown by a "mighty man" who placed Moron "in captivity all the remainder of his days" (Ether 11:15–18).

MORONI[1], CAPTAIN

Moroni[1] was only twenty-five years of age when he was appointed chief captain of the Nephite armies around 100 B.C. He is the hero known to millions of Latter-day Saints as "Captain Moroni," one of the most notable names in the Book of Mormon (Alma 43:16–17). He was not only a skilled military leader but was also a great patriot and a role model of righteousness.

His life and the impact for good he had in the society in which he lived could be summarized in the following statement:

"Yea, verily, verily I say unto you, if all men had been, and were, and ever would be, like unto Moroni, behold, the very powers of hell would have been shaken forever; yea, the devil would never have power over the hearts of the children of men" (Alma 48:17).

Oh, that our world today could be filled with men and women of the same caliber!

Captain Moroni's life was one filled with a succession of occasions in which his actions promoted peace and provided protection for a freedom-loving and righteous people. He prepared his armies with protective clothing and gear, in contrast to the invading armies, whose wicked leaders had not prepared them (Alma 53:19–20, 37–38). He sought divine direction from the "prophet" of his day, the leader of Christ's Church, the high priest Alma[2] (Alma 43:23).

In contrast to his treacherous adversary, Amalickiah, who obtained "power by fraud and deceit, Moroni . . . [prepared] the minds of [his] people to be faithful unto the Lord their God" (Alma 48:7).

He rallied the Nephite nation at a critical time, creating the "title of liberty," a national flag or standard, and he "prayed mightily" for divine assistance and intervention (Alma 46:11–13). He had the capacity to inspire his troops, driving fear from their hearts (Alma 43:14–50).

He was compassionate. When his armies had the upper hand, he ceased fighting and gave the enemy a chance to stop the bloodshed (Alma 43:54; 44:1, 6). He did not "delight in bloodshed" but rejoiced in "the liberty and the freedom of his country" (Alma 48:11). He was "firm in the faith of Christ" (Alma 48:13).

"In B.C. 56 the valiant Moroni, one of the greatest and most virtuous of God's sons, passed away from the state of mortality to the glories of eternity, at the early age of forty-three years. Some time before his death he had given the chief command of the armies of the Nephites to his son, *Moronihah,* who, from the history of later years, we judge to have been a worthy son of so illustrious a sire"

(Reynolds, *A Dictionary of the Book of Mormon,* 215).

MORONI[2]

Born and raised in a society that was steeped in the death throes of wickedness (Mormon 2:13–15), Moroni[2] proved that an individual can "Stand for Truth and Righteousness" (as the Young Women's motto of today states) regardless of the conditions of the world. Indeed, in a thankful father's tribute to his righteous son, Mormon[2] said, "My son, I recommend thee unto God" (Moroni 9:22).

Moroni[2] was the last of the Nephite record keepers, having received the plates from his father (Words of Mormon 1:1; Mormon 8:1). He translated and abridged the record of the Jaredites (Ether 1:1–2) and added his own writings (Mormon 8–9; Moroni 1–6, 10; Title Page) to complete the Book of Mormon. He hid the plates in the hill known as Cumorah. Centuries later, as a resurrected messenger sent from God, he delivered them into the hands of the Prophet Joseph Smith (Joseph Smith—History 1:27–60).

Moroni[2] served as a military leader under the direction of his father, striving to defend a people whose survival could not be assured because of their wickedness. He, like his father, also sought to bring the people to repentance in spite of their resistance. Indeed, Mormon² had emphasized the need to never give up on trying to change the hearts of their wayward neighbors:

"And now, my beloved son, notwithstanding their hardness, let us labor diligently; for if we should cease to labor, we should be brought under condemnation; for we have a labor to perform" (Moroni 9:6).

As one of the few surviving Nephites, Moroni² faced a number of pivotal points near the end of his life. The plight of his loneliness is expressed in his lament, "I am alone. My father hath been slain in battle, and all my kinsfolk, and I have not friends nor whither to go" (Mormon 8:5). His commitment to Christ was evidenced in the statement that the Lamanites "put to death every Nephite that will not deny the Christ. And I, Moroni, will not deny the Christ; wherefore, I wander whithersoever I can for the safety of mine own life" (Moroni 1:2–3).

Moroni² is a wonderful example of one who put his time to good use. Rather than spending his final days pining, dwelling on his unfavorable circumstances, he chose to add his contributions to the Book of Mormon. Without Moroni's diligence we would have suffered a tragic loss of valuable, inspiring scripture.

Some fourteen hundred years later, then as a resurrected being, he appeared to the teenager Joseph Smith and began the tutoring that led to the translation and publication of the book that has brought millions to Christ (Joseph Smith—History 1:27–54).

MORONIHAH¹

The son of Captain Moroni¹, Moronihah¹, like his father, was a righteous Nephite general (Alma 62:43). He served around 51 B.C. at a time when the secret combination of the Gadianton band raised its ugly head (Helaman 1). As a result of internal dissension among the Nephites, the Lamanites gained a military advantage over the Nephites, and Moronihah¹ had his armies in constant conflict with their enemies. His military victories seemed short-lived because of the contention and lack of spirituality among the people. He ultimately was able to regain only one-half of the territory lost to the invaders (Helaman 4:9–10).

Moronihah¹ left the military for a time to preach in an effort to get to the heart of the problems the Nephites were having. He joined forces with Nephi² and Lehi⁴ in preaching repentance and had sufficient success that he once again agreed to lead the military (Helaman 4:14–16). He is last mentioned as employing "all his armies in maintaining those parts which he had [re]taken" (Helaman 4:19).

MORONIHAH²

Moronihah² was among the Nephite military commanders who fell in the final battle with the Lamanites at Cumorah, each with their ten thousand troops (Mormon 6:14). One can only imagine the sorrow their leader Mormon² felt as he surveyed and reported on the terrible carnage of his people.

MOSES

Events in the life of this Old Testament prophet, as well as some of his declarations, are found sprinkled in the Book of Mormon (e.g., 1 Nephi 17:23–31, 42; Mosiah 13:5; 3 Nephi 20:23). One of the more significant references to Moses is the prophecy of Joseph¹, son of Jacob¹, who prophesied of the future missions of both Moses and Joseph Smith (2 Nephi 3).

Moses was born under a death threat. Rescued and raised by Pharaoh's daughter, he gave up his royal status to become an outcast, later returning to challenge the ruler of Egypt to free the enslaved Israelites. He was a prophet, miracle worker, author, lawgiver, and leader of wilderness wanderers. His was a multifaceted life, filled with demanding challenges which he successfully met.

Moses was born at the time Pharaoh's death decree for male Israelite babies was in effect. His life was saved through divine intervention when Pharaoh's daughter discovered the babe in a basket, hidden among the bulrushes of the river, and took him as her own child (Exodus 2:1–10). Raised in a royal household, he had the best educational opportunities; but he was also naturally gifted, for Luke tells us Moses "was mighty in words and in deeds" (Acts 7:22). A pivotal point for him came at age forty, when he went out to observe the Hebrew slaves and saw one being beaten by an Egyptian.

The text in the current book of Exodus implies that Moses stealthily slew the attacker, but the New Testament indicates that Moses was simply defending the one being attacked (cf. Exodus 2:11–12; Acts 7:24). As a result of the slaying, Moses had to flee Egypt. His propensity to defend the innocent was again displayed at a well in the land of Midian, when he came to the rescue of seven women being harassed by shepherds. This led to his marrying one of them (Exodus 2:15–21).

It was while serving his father-in-law Jethro (also known as Reuel, the priest of Midian) that Moses came into the presence of the Lord at the burning bush and received his calling to deliver the children of Israel from bondage (JST Exodus 3; 1 Nephi 17:24–26). This calling was a challenge for Moses. Whether out of modesty or because of real feelings of inadequacy, he replied, "Who am I, that I should go unto Pharaoh, and that I should bring forth the children of Israel out of Egypt?" (Exodus 3:11). In spite of his balking at the assignment, even when shown miracles by the Lord (Exodus 4), Moses grew from a reluctant messenger to a powerful prophet.

Truly he is an example of the oft-stated truism, "Whom the Lord calls, the Lord qualifies!"

The confrontation with Pharaoh begins in Exodus 5 and concludes in chapter 14, with Moses parting the waters of the Red Sea for the safety of the Israelites but then returning the waters for the destruction of Pharaoh's pursuing soldiers (1 Nephi 4:2; 17:26–27; Mosiah 7:19). God continued to perform miracles through Moses, but in a moment of prideful anger the prophet forgot who the Giver of the power was and took credit himself. The Lord chastised Moses and did not allow him to enter the Promised Land (Numbers 20:7–12).

Moses was later translated, not tasting of death, enabling him to continue in a postmortal ministry that included his appearance on the Mount of Transfiguration (Alma 45:19; Matthew 17). He was resurrected following the resurrection of Christ and restored the priesthood keys of the gathering of Israel to the Prophet Joseph Smith and Oliver Cowdery in the Kirtland Temple in 1836 (D&C 110:11).

MOSIAH[1]

We lack background information on this important person in the Book of Mormon because of the loss of the 116 pages of manuscript. King Mosiah[1] ruled in the land of Nephi sometime between 279 and 130 B.C. He was warned by the Lord to flee into the wilderness, taking with him those who were willing to "hearken unto the voice of the Lord" (Omni 1:12).

Certainly the obedience of Mosiah[1] and his people to respond to the Lord's warning was a critical point in their physical and spiritual survival. The righteousness of these people is evidenced by the fact that "they were led by many preachings and prophesyings" and the "power" of the Lord (Omni 1:13).

Eventually they arrived at a land known as Zarahemla, inhabited by "a people, who were called the people of Zarahemla" (popularly referred to as "Mulekites"). These people had fled Jerusalem in the Old World "at the time that Zedekiah, king of Judah, was carried away captive into

Babylon." They, like Lehi's party, had been brought across the ocean and led by the Lord to the New World (Omni 1:13–16).

The people of Zarahemla were a testimony of the significance of the Lord's command to Father Lehi[1] to have his sons obtain the plates of brass (1 Nephi 3:2–5). These people had no scriptural records with them, and as a result "they denied the being of their Creator" (Omni 1:17; see also Mosiah 1:3). Recall the Lord's pronouncement to Nephi[1], as he struggled with the command to slay Laban: "It is better that one man should perish than that *a nation should dwindle and perish in unbelief*" (1 Nephi 4:13; emphasis added). Had Nephi[1] not been successful in obtaining the scriptural record found on the plates of brass, the same fate of unbelief that came upon the people of Zarahemla might have befallen the Nephites.

The people of Zarahemla rejoiced "exceedingly" because King Mosiah[1] had the plates of brass with him (Omni 1:14). He taught this newfound people, and they joined with his people under Mosiah's leadership (Omni 1:18–19). Mosiah's ability as a seer was demonstrated when he was able to interpret a stone that had a partial account of the Jaredites, which had been in the possession of a man named Coriantumr[2], the last survivor

of that ancient civilization (Omni 1:20–22).

See also Mulek; People of Zarahemla.

MOSIAH[2]

While no mention is made of the mother of Mosiah[2] (consistent with their culture's approach to history and record keeping), we can be assured that he, like his ancestor Nephi[1], was "born of goodly parents" (1 Nephi 1:1). Both his father, King Benjamin, and his grandfather, King Mosiah[1], were holy men who diligently sought to lead their people in righteousness. We can assume with confidence that Mosiah's mother and grandmother were of the same celestial character as their husbands.

King Mosiah[2] was consecrated by his father in about 124 B.C. to rule over the people of Nephi. Like his father and grandfather before him, "King Mosiah did walk in the ways of the Lord, and did observe his judgments and his statutes, and did keep his commandments in all things whatsoever he commanded him" (Mosiah 6:6).

History has shown that when some individuals are elevated to positions of power and authority, they unrighteously set themselves above their subjects, imposing hardships upon them (see D&C 121:39). To be given a position of leadership is always a pivotal point in the newly called leader's life. He or she must choose whether to be a servant-leader or to act as a dictator or tyrant who selfishly seeks personal interests, imposing his or her will upon the subject-slaves.

Fortunately for his people, King Mosiah[2] chose to serve them. As a result, "they did wax strong in love towards Mosiah; yea, they did esteem him more than any other man; for they did not look upon him as a tyrant who was seeking for gain" (Mosiah 29:40).

Mosiah[2] sent an expedition led by Ammon[1] to the land of Lehi-Nephi in search of the colony of Zeniff. The searchers found the colony that at that time was ruled by King Limhi. However, the colony was in severe servitude to the Lamanites (Mosiah 7). With the assistance of Ammon[1], the people were able to escape and united under the leadership of King Mosiah[2] (Mosiah 22). It was during King Mosiah's reign that the colony of Alma[1] also escaped bondage from their persecutors and united with King Mosiah's people in the land of Zarahemla (Mosiah 24).

King Mosiah[2] granted Alma[1] permission to establish congregations of the church throughout the land (Mosiah 25:19). He also recognized Alma's stewardship and authority to judge ecclesiastical matters (Mosiah 26:1–12).

Mosiah[2] himself was a seer who "had a gift from God, whereby he could interpret" ancient records (Mosiah 21:28). Indeed, he translated ancient writings of the Jaredites by use of what obviously was a Urim and Thummim (Mosiah 28:11–19).

Mosiah[2] conferred these sacred implements upon Alma[2], as well as all the records that were in his possession, with a charge to "keep and preserve them, and also keep a record of the people" (Mosiah 28:20).

In a very significant move at the conclusion of his thirty-three-year reign before his death, Mosiah[2] proposed that the Nephite government by kings be done away with and that a new system of judges be instituted (Mosiah 29).

MOSIAH[2], SONS OF

The four sons of King Mosiah[2]—Ammon[2], Aaron[3], Omner, and Himni (Mosiah 27:34)—are grouped together for this entry because of their unique status of generally being referred to as a group (see Mosiah 27:8; 28:1; 29:3; Alma 17:1–2; 36:6). Separate entries for each are also included.

Although raised in the righteous home of King Mosiah[2], they chose the path of rebellion for a time. They "were numbered among the unbelievers" who were "seeking to destroy the church, and to lead astray the people of the Lord" (Mosiah 27:8–10).

Nevertheless, just like their fellow miscreant, Alma², the pivotal point that turned their lives to good was the appearance of an angel of the Lord calling them to repentance. While the written record focuses on Alma², the sons of Mosiah² were present and felt the same rebuke (Mosiah 27:11–20).

This incident is illustrative of a gospel truth taught by Elder Dallin H. Oaks of the Quorum of the Twelve Apostles (1932–): "The power of the Atonement and the principle of repentance show that we should never give up on loved ones who now seem to be making many wrong choices" (*Ensign*, November 2000, 34).

Following this miraculous occurrence, the sons of Mosiah² ("those who were with Alma at the time the angel appeared unto them") traveled about preaching the "good tidings of good," even though they now became the targets of persecution by the unbelievers (Mosiah 27:32–37).

We are reminded that those who find themselves in the right places, where they can partake of the fruit of the tree of life, will be subject to having the finger of scorn pointed at them by those who follow the ways of the world (1 Nephi 8:33).

So powerful was their change of heart that these once "very vilest of sinners" now "could not bear that any human soul should perish" (Mosiah 28:3–4).

The desire of the sons of Mosiah² to share the gospel with others was so strong that "they did plead with their father many days" for permission to leave home and go out among the Lamanites to preach the gospel (Mosiah 28:1–5). King Mosiah² made their request a matter of prayer and received the following answer:

"Let them go . . . for many shall believe on their words, and they shall have eternal life; and I will deliver thy sons out of the hands of the Lamanites" (Mosiah 28:7). Thus began a fourteen-year mission (Alma 17:4) filled with many trials and much suffering. Chapters 17 through 26 of Alma give an account of their missionary labors.

The Lord had forewarned them that their missions would not be easy: "Go forth among the Lamanites, thy brethren, and establish my word; *yet ye shall be patient in long-suffering and afflictions,* that ye may show forth good examples unto them in me, and I will make an instrument of thee in my hands unto the salvation of many souls" (Alma 17:11; emphasis added).

One example of the suffering endured by these persistent missionaries, who stood firm at pivotal points in their ministry, is found in the description of those who had been imprisoned: "They were naked, and their skins were worn exceedingly because of being bound with strong cords. And they also had suffered hunger, thirst, and all kinds of afflictions; nevertheless they were patient in all their sufferings" (Alma 20:29).

While the testimonies of the sons of Mosiah[2] may have been initiated by an angelic rebuke, those testimonies were retained and strengthened through their unwavering commitment to their mission, and because they "had searched the scriptures diligently," and "given themselves to much prayer, and fasting" (Alma 17:2–3).

See also Aaron[3]; Ammon[2]; Omner; Himni.

MULEK

This son of the Jewish King Zedekiah[1] escaped from Jerusalem at the time the Babylonian king slew Mulek's brothers, then put out the eyes of Mulek's father and carried him captive into Babylon (2 Kings 25:1–7). In some way not recorded in the biblical record, Mulek escaped the fate of his brothers and was brought by the hand of the Lord to ancient America. Father Lehi's group was led to the southern part of the promised land, and "the Lord did bring Mulek into the land north" (Helaman 6:10). Mulek's group came to be known as the people from the land of Zarahemla.

They were later discovered by the Nephites and united with them under the leadership of King Mosiah[1] (Omni 1:13–19). When they joined forces, the people of Zarahemla outnumbered the Nephites (Mosiah 25:2).

Regarding Mulek's age at the time of his escape, Elder George Reynolds (1842–1909) wrote: "Mulek . . . must have been very young, as his father was only 21 years old when he commenced to reign, and he reigned but eleven years in Jerusalem (II Chronicles 36:11; Jeremiah 25:1.) It is altogether probable that when Mulek attained a proper age he, on account of his lineage, was recognized as king or leader of the colony" (Reynolds, *Dictionary of the Book of Mormon*, 226).

See also Mulekites; People of Zarahemla; Zarahemla.

MULEKITES

"Mulekites" is a nonscriptural term—except as used in Book of Mormon chapter headings (Omni 1; Mosiah 25). The term refers to the descendants of the Jewish King Zedekiah's son Mulek, who was brought to ancient America about the same time as Father Lehi's group.

See also Mulek; People of Zarahemla; Zarahemla.

MULOKI

Muloki was one of three Nephite missionaries mentioned as being imprisoned by the Lamanites (Alma 20:2; see also 21:9–14). When Ammon[2] was successful in securing their release, "he was exceedingly sorrowful, for behold they were naked, and their skins were worn exceedingly because of being bound with strong cords. And they also had suffered hunger, thirst, and all kinds of afflictions; nevertheless they were patient in all their sufferings" (Alma 20:29).

Muloki's terrible experience in prison did not deter him from continuing his labors after being freed. He and his companions "went forth whithersoever they were led by the Spirit of the Lord, preaching the word of God in every synagogue of the Amalekites, or in every assembly of the Lamanites where they could be admitted" (Alma 21:16). What an example of faithfulness and a great model for present-day missionaries to consider whenever they are tempted to be discouraged because of rejection, persecution, unfavorable weather conditions, or any other reason!

N

NEHOR[1]

This man, a brother of Abraham (Abraham 2:2) is not mentioned in the Book of Mormon. However, his listing as Nehor[1] in the index of the Triple Combination necessitated listing the Book of Mormon Nehor with the superscript "[2]."

NEHOR[2]

This Nephite apostate is identified with the superscript "[2]" to distinguish him from the other Nehor listed in the index of the Triple Combination.

The number of recorded lines allotted to Nehor[2] in the Book of Mormon is minimal. However, his negative impact lived beyond his own miserable life and, therefore, affords a lesson to be learned.

Nehor[2] was brought before the chief judge Alma[2] about 92 B.C. to answer for his crimes. Nehor[2] is described as "a man who was large, and was noted for his much strength" (Alma 1:2). Like other false preachers, he evidently had sufficient speaking ability to gain a gathering of misguided followers. His success led to his being "lifted up in the pride of his heart, and to wear very costly apparel,

yea, and [he] even began to establish a church after the manner of his preaching" (Alma 1:6).

The nature of the apostate teachings of this "successful religious charlatan of the hour, to whom the unstable listened and the weak-minded flocked," are well described by Elder George Reynolds (1842–1909):

"Some of his theories were older than Idumea. They had been rejected in the counsels of heaven before Lucifer, the Son of the Morning, fell. He would save all men in their sins and with their sins; he abolished hell, established a paid order of priests, and taught doctrines so liberal that every man could be a member of his church and yet continue to gratify every vice his nature inclined to. For this liberality of doctrine, Nehor expected in return liberality of support for himself and assistants, in which anticipation he was not disappointed. Many adopted his heresies; his success fired his zeal, and developed his vanity. He was so used to the sycophancy of his converts that he was restive under contradiction, and when *Gideon,* the aged patriot and teacher in the true Church, one day met him in the streets of Zarahemla and upbraided him for his wicked course, neither respecting his great age nor his many virtues [at this pivotal point], Nehor drew his sword and smote him till he died" (*Dictionary of the Book of Mormon,* 229–30).

Although in gross error, Nehor² had the freedom to teach false doctrine, but he did not have the right to enforce it by the sword, which he tried when he took the life of the faithful Gideon (Alma 1:7–9). And so the life of Nehor² was required for this murder of an innocent man (Alma 1:10–15). Nehor's lasting negative impact was that the Order of Nehors, the preaching of priestcraft, persisted down through the centuries.

See also Nehors, Order of; Teachers, False.

NEHORS, ORDER OF

This was the cult that arose following the death of the apostate Nehor² and embraced his heresy. "Though Nehor's shameful life was . . . ended, unfortunately his doctrine did not die with him. It was too pleasant to those who desired to gain heaven by a life of sin. Consequently it spread widely through the teachings of his followers. In later years the traitorous Amlicites, the apostate Amalekites, the blood-thirsty Amulonites and Ammonihahites, were all believers in his soul-destroying doctrines. The bloodshed, the misery produced,

the treasure expended through the wickedness and folly of these base creatures, cannot be computed" (Reynolds, *Dictionary of the Book of Mormon,* 230).

See also Nehor².

NEPHI¹

The writings and personal history of Nephi¹, the son of Lehi¹ and Sariah, have provided inspiration to countless people since the first publication of the Book of Mormon in 1830. Perhaps one of the most quoted scriptures from this sacred book of scripture is Nephi's undeviating declaration of faith and commitment: "I, Nephi, said unto my father: I will go and do the things which the Lord hath commanded, for I know that the Lord giveth no commandments unto the children of men, save he shall prepare a way for them that they may accomplish the thing which he commandeth them" (1 Nephi 3:7).

Nephi¹ not only believed in the words of his prophet-father, Lehi¹, but he sought his own personal witness, "having great desires to know" for himself (1 Nephi 2:16; see also 1 Nephi 11:1–3). In contrast to his rebellious brothers, Laman¹ and Lemuel, Nephi¹ turned to the Lord and obediently followed divine direction, thus making correct choices at the many pivotal points he faced in his life.

Nephi[1] stood firm in the face of adversity, willing to try again when his first and even succeeding efforts failed to accomplish the task at hand. For example, when two successive efforts to obtain the brass plates failed and his discouraged brothers were ready to abandon the task, Nephi[1] refused to give up and ultimately succeeded (1 Nephi 3–4). An important aspect of his success was not only his persistence, but his willingness to be "led by the Spirit," as exemplified in his third attempt to obtain the plates of brass (1 Nephi 4:6).

Nephi's faith was certainly tried during times when his brothers physically assaulted him and even sought to take his life. Bound with cords, he was left "in the wilderness to be devoured by wild beasts." Yet Nephi[1] prayed with faith to be delivered and the cords were loosed, setting him free (1 Nephi 7:16–18).

A pivotal point in Nephi's faith— a true test of his willingness to endure severe hardship and yet remain steadfast—came during the voyage across the ocean. Rejecting their brother's pleas to turn their thoughts and actions to the Lord, Laman[1] and Lemuel tied Nephi[1] with cords and left him bound for four days. A "great and terrible tempest" raged during that time, and it wasn't until they feared being drowned that the rebellious brothers finally set Nephi[1] free.

Nephi's wrists and ankles were "swollen exceedingly . . . and great was the soreness thereof." It was at this point that Nephi[1] showed the depth of his spiritual strength, for in spite of his mistreatment and suffering he said, "I did look unto my God, and I did praise him all the day long; and I did not murmur against the Lord because of mine afflictions" (1 Nephi 18:9–16).

What a magnificent model to consider as one is faced with trials in his or her life. Suffering and mistreatment can lead a person to rely more fully upon God for strength and succor, thus increasing one's faith; or, for the faint of heart, such experiences could lead to a loss of faith and thus a loss of the blessings that might otherwise have been realized.

Another lesson to learn from Nephi[1] was his ability to forgive others in spite of their cruel treatment towards him (1 Nephi 7:21). He was an example of the principle the Savior would later teach on both the eastern and the western hemispheres: "Pray for them which despitefully use you, and persecute you" (Matthew 5:44; see also 3 Nephi 12:44).

As already mentioned, Nephi[1] had great faith in simply moving forward without doubt to accomplish whatever the Lord required of him. An additional example of this is when the Lord commanded him to build a ship, a task in which Nephi[1] had absolutely no experience. Yet his response was not to remind the Lord of his lack of experience or expertise. He simply asked for directions to find the necessary ore from which he could mold the tools needed in this major construction project (1 Nephi 17:7–9).

When ridiculed by his brothers, who said, "Our brother is a fool, for he thinketh that he can build a ship" (1 Nephi 17:17), Nephi's faith-filled reply was: "If God had commanded me to do *all* things I could do them" (1 Nephi 17:50; emphasis added).

Nephi[1] was not arrogant in his self-confidence, for he knew the Source from whence his skills, knowledge, and success came. He willingly admitted his own shortcomings. "I do not know the meaning of all things," he told an angel who was instructing him (1 Nephi 11:17). Furthermore, he acknowledged being "encompassed about, because of the temptations and the sins which do so easily beset me" (2 Nephi 4:18). Yet he knew to Whom he should turn for strength: "Why should I give way to temptations, that the evil one have place in my heart to destroy my peace and afflict my soul? . . . Rejoice, O my heart, and cry unto the Lord. . . . O Lord, wilt thou redeem my soul? Wilt thou deliver me out of the hands of mine enemies? Wilt thou make me

that I may shake at the appearance of sin. . . . O Lord, I have trusted in thee, and I will trust in thee forever" (2 Nephi 4:27–34).

Following the death of Father Lehi[1], the hostility of Nephi's brothers towards him continued. In fact, "their anger did increase . . . insomuch that they did seek to take away [his] life" (2 Nephi 5:1–2). Being warned of the Lord of his brother's hateful intent, Nephi[1] journeyed into the wilderness with "all those who would go with [him]." They settled in a land his followers called Nephi, and they petitioned him to be their king (2 Nephi 5:5–16). As they lived in righteousness, they prospered, for they "lived after the manner of happiness" (2 Nephi 5:27).

Nephi[1] maintained both the large and the small plates upon which he recorded the spiritual as well as historical matters and events pertaining to his people. He also copied many of the writings of Isaiah[1] from the plates of brass onto the records he was keeping. His sermons and writings provide much spiritual food upon which we may feast, and he consistently bears powerful witness of Jesus as the Christ, the Promised Messiah.

Before his death, Nephi[1] charged his brother Jacob[2] with the responsibility of maintaining the spiritual history of the Nephites on the small plates and "anointed a man to be a king and a ruler over his people, according to the reign of the kings" (Jacob 1:1–12).

Nephi's younger brother Jacob[2] gave a simple, yet fitting tribute to this great prophet of the ancient Nephite civilization; said he, Nephi[1] "labored in all his days for [his people's] welfare" (Jacob 1:10).

What more need be said?

See also Nephites.

NEPHI[2]

It is interesting that in almost 600 years of Nephite history, no other mention is made of another prophet or prominent man being named Nephi until Helaman gave his eldest son that name (Helaman 5:6). The life and ministry of this second Nephite prophet bearing that honored name certainly added luster to it. He was the son of Helaman[2] and brother of Lehi[4].

Nephi[2] served for a time as the chief judge among the Nephites, where he served with "justice and equity" (Helaman 3:37). Because of the spreading iniquity of the people, "he yielded up the judgment-seat, and took it upon him to preach the word of God all the remainder of his days" (Helaman 5:4). Nephi[2] turned away from the popular position of chief judge to devote full time to preaching the gospel and calling the people to repentance. In this sense, he followed the same path as Alma[2] the Younger, who in a previous time had taken a similar course of action (Alma 4:15–20).

Although Nephi[2] and his brother, Lehi[4], experienced great success in their missionary labors, they also suffered much rejection and persecution. At one point they were "cast into prison many days without food" and threatened with death (Helaman 5:22). A marvelous manifestation of God's power then took place and the two missionaries were surrounded by a protecting circle of what seemed like fire. A "voice of perfect mildness" (Helaman 5:30) spoke from the heavens, calling the persecutors to repentance, and a tremendous spiritual conversion followed (Helaman 5:23–51).

At a time when those of the wicked Gadianton conspiracy had control of the government, Nephi[2] was pouring his heart out from a tower at his house when a crowd of curious onlookers gathered to watch him. He courageously called them to repentance and prophesied their destruction unless they repented. As an indicator of their wickedness, he told them that their judge, whom he identified as a member of the infamous Gadianton band, had been murdered by his brother and was even then lying in his blood at the judgment seat. At first Nephi[2] was accused of being in conspiracy with whomever had slain the judge, but he was vindicated by the later confession of the murderer (Helaman 7–9).

Nephi² was burdened by the wickedness of the people he sought to save. Perhaps like his righteous namesake ancestor, his pillow was wet with his tears at night as he thought about his wayward people (2 Nephi 33:3). In any event, this loving yet forthright leader was "much cast down because of the wickedness of the people" (Helaman 10:3).

At this point, when Nephi's sorrow for their sins might have tempted him to turn away from his ministry, the Lord's voice spoke to him and commended him for his "unwearyingness" in the work. He was then given the promise that whatever he asked for would be granted, because he would "not ask that which is contrary to my will" (Helaman 10:3–5).

What confidence the Lord had in this faithful servant! And what a high degree of faith and righteousness Nephi² had that allowed the Lord to trust him completely!

Soon thereafter, seeing no other way to humble the people, Nephi² used this power that the Lord had conveyed to him and asked for the rains to cease and a famine to begin (Helaman 11:4). When the people began to perish because of want of food, their thoughts turned to God and to the warning words of Nephi². Thus they began to plead for deliverance. The Gadiantons were destroyed and the people repented, allowing Nephi² to once again intercede in their behalf (Helaman 11:5–17).

There is no mention that Nephi² himself was spared the consequences of the famine, and it is likely that he, too, suffered for want of food during the famine. Truly, he was a remarkable prophet who stood spiritually strong and steady under all conditions.

At the conclusion of his ministry, Nephi² simply "departed out of the land, and whither he went, no man knoweth" (3 Nephi 1:2–3; 2:9). Some believe that he, like Alma² the Younger, was "taken up by the Spirit, or buried by the hand of the Lord" (Alma 45:18–19).

NEPHI³

This eldest son of Nephi² and grandson of Helaman³ was one of the keepers of the sacred records that became the Book of Mormon (3 Nephi 1:2). He and all the true believers in the Messianic prophecies of Samuel² the Lamanite prophet were threatened with death by the unbelievers if the foretold signs of Christ's birth did not occur by a certain date (3 Nephi 1:9).

At this critical time, Nephi³ "cried mightily to his God in behalf of his people" and had a singular experience. He had the remarkable privilege of having "the voice of the Lord" come to him and announce His pending birth: "On this night shall the sign be given, and on the morrow come I into the world" (3 Nephi 1:11–14).

Many prophets and other righteous individuals foresaw or foretold the birth of the Son of God, but to our knowledge there was only one to whom the voice of the Lord spoke on the day before His divine birth. How exceptional this righteous follower of Christ must have been to receive such a singular manifestation!

Nephi's faith was so firm, and he testified with such power, that his words could not be disbelieved, even though many of the people failed to repent and turn from their wickedness (3 Nephi 7:17–18). Indeed, the power of Nephi's preaching was similar to the power of the disciple Stephen in the Holy Land, who, "full of faith and power, did great wonders and miracles among the people. . . . And they were not able to resist the wisdom and the spirit by which he spake" (Acts 6:8, 10).

Nephi[3] stood firm in the face of increasing wickedness, testifying "boldly" (3 Nephi 7:16). He performed many miracles, including raising his martyred brother from the dead. Angels visited him daily, and he heard the voice of the Lord (3 Nephi 7:15–20).

When the resurrected Christ visited the ancient inhabitants of the western hemisphere, He called Nephi[3] to be His chief disciple of the twelve He chose to lead His Church (3 Nephi 11:18–21; 19:4). It was Nephi's privilege to record the sermons and events of the Savior's ministry to this ancient civilization. Nephi[3] then had the glorious calling of being the prophet who led the people into the golden era of righteousness that followed the Savior's visit, a time when "there was no contention in the land, because of the love of God which did dwell in the hearts of the people. . . . [and] they were in one, the children of Christ, and heirs to the kingdom of God" (4 Nephi 1:15–17).

NEPHI[4]

This Nephite record keeper is identified in the heading to the book of 4 Nephi as "the son of Nephi—one of the disciples of Jesus Christ." The index to the Triple Combination states that Nephi[4] could "possibly [be the] same as Nephi[3], or his son."

He had the privilege of living in an era when "there could not be a happier people among all the people who had been created by the hand of God" (4 Nephi 1:16). When he died, his son Amos[1] took over the record-keeping responsibilities (4 Nephi 1:19).

NEPHI, UNNAMED KINGS

When Nephi[1], son of Lehi[1], neared the end of his life, "he anointed a man to be a king and a ruler over his people." Because of their great love for Nephi[1], the people named each successive ruler over them by the name of Nephi: "second Nephi, third Nephi, and so forth" (Jacob 1:9–11). This is the only mention of the first rulers who followed Nephi in our present edition of the Book of Mormon. The details of the lives of these succeeding kings were recorded in the Book of Lehi ("the other plates"), or what we know as the 116 pages of lost manuscript (1 Nephi 9:4).

NEPHIHAH

When Alma[2] decided to resign as the chief judge in the Nephite government, "he selected a wise man who was among the elders of the church, and gave him power according to the voice of the people, that he might have power to enact laws according to the laws which had been given, . . . and he was appointed chief judge" (Alma 4:16–17). This man's name was Nephihah.

It is of interest to note the process whereby Nephihah was selected as Alma's successor in the chief judge's seat. That process is strikingly similar to the revelatory process whereby ecclesiastical leaders in The Church of Jesus Christ of Latter-day Saints are selected today. The one with the proper priesthood keys prayerfully and by inspiration selects the person to fill a position. After receiving a sustaining witness by his associates in the presidency or the council over which he presides, he then presents the selected individual's name to a constituted body of believers to be sustained in the designated calling.

It is obvious that Nephihah's conduct and character qualified him for this position of trust. It is also clear that Nephihah met the challenge of integrity his position required, for at the end of his service it was said of him that he "filled the judgment-seat with *perfect* uprightness before God" (Alma 50:37; emphasis added).

Beyond the Savior, who was *absolutely* perfect in every way (Mosiah 15:5; D&C 20:22), there are few individuals in history who have had the appellation "perfect" ascribed to some aspect of their character or works. Nephihah is among those select few, which included Seth (D&C 107:43), Job (Job 1:1), and Captain Moroni[1] (Alma 48:11).

Very little is written about Nephihah, but his life is evidence that one's name does not have to *fill* the pages of history in order to make a difference for good in the world.

NEPHITE DISCIPLES

See Disciples, Twelve; Three Nephite Disciples.

NEPHITES

This group of people was one of two nations whose history comprises most of the Book of Mormon record. The other group was known as the Lamanites. Both of these nations originated with the Lehi[1] expedition that started in Jerusalem about 600 B.C. The original group, which consisted of the families of Lehi[1] and Ishmael[1], as well as a man named Zoram[1], were led by the Lord to a "land of promise" (1 Nephi 2:20) in ancient America.

The Nephites were originally those people who followed their prophet-leader Nephi[1] when he was warned by the Lord to separate himself and his followers from those who were plotting his death. Those who followed Nephi[1] included his brothers Sam, Jacob[2], and Joseph[2], his sisters, Zoram[1], "and all those who would go with [him]." They were "those who believed in the warnings and the revelations of God" as given through Nephi[1]. These believers took upon themselves the name "the people of Nephi" (2 Nephi 5:1–9).

The term *Nephite* may have been found upon the large plates of Nephi (the record kept by the kings). However, its first recorded use in our presently published Book of Mormon is in 2 Nephi 29:12. Later, Nephi's younger brother Jacob[2] used *Nephite* to designate "those who are friendly to Nephi." Those who sought "to destroy the people of Nephi" were called Lamanites (Jacob 1:14).

"Throughout the Book of Mormon the Nephites are those people from whom the record keepers are selected and from whom the prophets were generally called. During the golden era of peace following the visit of the resurrected Savior to the American continent, there were no categories of people and all were called the 'children of Christ' (4 Nephi 1:17).

"In A.D. 231, however, because of the previous revolt of some of the Church who took upon themselves the name of Lamanites, the 'true believers in Christ' were called Nephites, regardless of their original ancestry (4 Nephi 1:20–36). Their descendants were ultimately destroyed by the Lamanites. Mormon[2], one of the last surviving Nephites, 'hid up' many of the sacred records of their history about A.D. 385, and entrusted the records to his son Moroni[2] (Morm. 6). Moroni[2] finished the record and was among the last of his civilization to survive (Morm. 8:1–7). Nephite blood has been preserved through the lineage of the Lamanites and is sprinkled among them today" (Brewster, *Doctrine & Covenants Encyclopedia*, 381).

See also Jacobites; Josephites; Zoramites.

NEUM

Neum is among the Old Testament prophets ostensibly quoted from the plates of brass but whose names are presently missing in the biblical text as we now have it. Sometime before 600 B.C., Neum prophesied of the future crucifixion of the Son of God (1 Nephi 19:10), thus joining his voice with those of "all the holy prophets" in testifying of Christ's divine Sonship and forthcoming Atonement (Jacob 4:4).

NIMRAH

This Jaredite son of an extremely wicked father is mentioned but once in the history of that people. His father, King Akish, who had gained the monarchy upon the murder of his predecessor, became "jealous" of an unnamed son. Presumably, that son was more popular with the people. In any event, the son was put in prison and kept "upon little or no food until he had suffered death" (Ether 9:7).

It was at this point that "the brother of him that suffered death, (and his name was Nimrah) was angry with his father because of that which his father had done unto his brother" (Ether 9:8). Nimrah gathered "a small number of men" and fled his father's jurisdiction, finding refuge with the followers of a previously disposed king, Omer (Ether 9:9).

NIMROD[1]

This Old Testament man is mentioned in the Jaredite writings. The valley of Nimrod was named "after the mighty hunter" (Ether 2:1). Nimrod's prowess as a hunter is mentioned in JST Genesis 10:5, where he is described as "the mighty hunter in the land."

NIMROD[2]

Nimrod's father, Cohor, was killed in a Jaredite power struggle with a rival. Nimrod[2] then pledged his allegiance to the victor, Shule. Nimrod[2] gained favor with his new king, who bestowed "great favors upon him, and he did do in the kingdom of Shule according to his desires" (Ether 7:21–22). Inasmuch as Shule was one who protected the prophets and passed laws that brought the people to repentance, we can surmise that Nimrod[2] might also have been righteous (Ether 7:24–25).

NOAH[1]

This patriarch, who preserved the human race aboard the ark at the time of the great flood, is referred to several times in the Book of Mormon. The first occasion is in a sermon by the great missionary Amulek, who spoke of the destruction of the wicked by the flood "in the days of Noah" (Alma 10:22). The second occasion is when the resurrected Redeemer quoted from the writings of Isaiah[1]: "I have sworn that the waters of Noah should no more go over the earth" (3 Nephi 22:9; Isaiah 54:9). The third occasion is when the Jaredite barges were described as "tight like unto the ark of Noah" (Ether 6:7). Each of these references provides a *second witness* to the reality of the great flood that once encompassed the earth when the Lord destroyed the wicked (Genesis 6–8).

"Noah was born to save seed of everything, when the earth was washed of its wickedness by the flood" (*Teachings of the Prophet Joseph Smith*, 12).

Noah[1] was a grandson of Methuselah, from whom he received the priesthood at the age of ten (Genesis 5:25–29; D&C 107:52). As with many prophets, the wicked sought to slay Noah[1]. However, the Lord protected him. Noah[1] was described as "a just man, and perfect in his generation; and he walked with God, as did also his three sons, Shem, Ham, and Japheth" (Moses 8:18–27).

"The Prophet Joseph declared that Noah 'stands next in authority to Adam in the Priesthood' and is the angel Gabriel who was privileged to announce the forthcoming births and missions of John the Baptist and Jesus the Christ (*TPJS*, 157; Luke 1:5–38). . . .

"He is also known as Elias, in which capacity, according to Joseph Fielding Smith, he appeared in the Kirtland Temple on April 3, 1836, restoring the keys of the dispensation of Abraham to Joseph Smith and Oliver Cowdery (*AGQ* 3:138–41; D&C 110:12). He was among the 'congregation of the righteous' whom the Savior visited in the spirit world following his death on Calvary (D&C 138:38, 41)" (Brewster, *Doctrine & Covenants Encyclopedia*, 387).

NOAH[2]

This wicked Jaredite rebel was the son of Corihor[1]. He rebelled against King Shule and also his father, who then was a loyal subject of the king. Noah[2] was successful in obtaining a portion of Shule's kingdom and was crowned king "over that part of the land." In a subsequent battle with Shule, Noah[2] defeated him and carried him into captivity. Noah[2] was about to kill him when Shule's sons rescued their father and killed Noah[2] (Ether 7:14–18).

NOAH[3]

Noah[3] was the son of Zeniff, who was the first king of the group of Nephites that returned to the land of Lehi-Nephi from the land of Zarahemla around 200 B.C. (Mosiah

7:9). Noah³ succeeded his father as king over this colony of Nephites (Mosiah 11:1).

That righteous parents are not always successful in producing righteous children is illustrated in the life of King Noah³. After his father, Zeniff, conferred the kingdom upon him, Noah³ "did not walk in the ways of his father," nor did he "keep the commandments of God, but he did walk after the desires of his own heart. . . . And he did cause his people to commit sin, and do that which was abominable in the sight of the Lord" (Mosiah 11:1–2; see also 11:14).

King Noah's reign was one of debauchery. As a consequence, his wicked example was imitated by many of his followers. Certainly when wickedness encompasses the lives of the leaders selected to govern, the fallout on the people being governed is deadly and potentially disastrous. Noah's ascension to the throne was a fateful point for his subjects.

The Lord has declared: "When the wicked rule the people mourn. Wherefore, honest men and wise men should be sought for diligently, and good men and wise men ye should observe to uphold; otherwise whatsoever is less than these cometh of evil" (D&C 98:9–10).

The life of this carnal king provides several examples from which we can draw lessons for living. On the occasion when the prophet Abinadi stood before King Noah³ as his prisoner and boldly spoke against the king's wickedness, fear struck Noah's heart and he was about to set Abinadi free. However, he succumbed to flattery and pressure on the part of his wicked priests. Lifted up in pride, his darkened mind turned against Abinadi and he "delivered him up that he might be slain" (Mosiah 17:11–12).

The next example of a point in which Noah³ panicked was when he and his people were fleeing from the attacking Lamanites. Selfishly fearing for his own life, he commanded the men to leave their wives and children and save themselves. Fortunately, "there were many that would not leave them, but had rather stay and perish with them" (Mosiah 19:9–12).

Later regretting their cowardly decision, those who had deserted their families became "angry with the king, and caused that he should suffer, even unto death by fire" (Mosiah 19:20). Noah's manner of death fulfilled the prophecy of the martyred Abinadi, who foretold the king's death by fire (Mosiah 12:3; 13:10; 17:18).

NOAH³, PRIESTS OF

When Noah³ succeeded his father as king over the colony of Zeniff, "he put down all the priests that had been consecrated by his father, and consecrated new ones in their stead, such as were lifted up in the pride of their hearts" (Mosiah 11:5). These priests joined their leader in his "whoredoms and all manner of wickedness" (Mosiah 11:2).

They were "supported in their laziness, and in their idolatry, and in their whoredoms, by the taxes which king Noah[3] had put upon his people" (Mosiah 11:6). They joined the king in flattering the people to join them in iniquity (Mosiah 11:7).

Noah[3] fed the pride of his decadent priests by providing them ornamented seats of pure gold in his newly constructed "spacious palace" (Mosiah 11:9). The seats were constructed in such a way that they gave the priests a place where "they might rest their bodies and their arms . . . while they should speak lying and vain words to [the] people" (Mosiah 11:11–12).

At this time of terrible iniquity, the Lord sent the prophet Abinadi to call the people to repentance. Abinadi was eventually captured and imprisoned by the king and his priests. They held a council to consider what to do with him and determined to question him "that they might cross him" (Mosiah 12:1–19). Abinadi boldly withstood their efforts to ensnare him, and the king ordered his priests to kill him. However, for a time

Abinadi was protected by the power of God in order to finish his message (Mosiah 13).

We see in this event that in spite of the efforts of the wicked to prevent the work of the Lord from moving forward, "the works, and the designs, and the purposes of God cannot be frustrated, neither can they come to naught" (D&C 3:1). While the devil may seemingly have temporary victories, he knows "not the mind of God" (Moses 4:6) and will ultimately fail in his nefarious efforts to destroy God's work.

Abinadi's powerful sermon was to be delivered not only for the benefit— and condemnation—of Noah's wicked priests, but also for the blessing of "future generations" (Alma 37:14) who now read and ponder his words as recorded in the Book of Mormon.

Noah[3] was temporarily struck with fear after hearing the prophet's sermon and was about to release him, but the priests "stirred up" the king in anger, and he had Abinadi scourged and martyred by fire (Mosiah 17:11–20).

Abinadi's words did have an impact on one priest—Alma[1]. His heart had been touched by the prophet's words, and he even sought to intercede in his behalf, for which the king sought to slay him as well (Mosiah 17:1–4).

Following Abinadi's martyrdom, the cowardly king and his priests abandoned their families when an attacking Lamanite army came upon them. Noah³ was killed in an uprising by his followers, but the priests escaped by fleeing into the wilderness (Mosiah 19:23). They abducted twenty-four young daughters of the Lamanites, whom they took for wives (Mosiah 20:1–5). After a time, obviously when the hearts of the abducted women had been softened towards their captors, the priests joined forces with a Lamanite army. They discovered Alma¹ and his followers in a land called Helam and placed them in bondage, with the priests of King Noah³ as the taskmasters.

The leader of these wicked priests was a man named Amulon, who took particular devilish delight in persecuting his former associate Alma¹ (Mosiah 23:30–39; 24:8–9). Neither the devil nor his miscreant followers are pleased when former carnal colleagues repent and pursue the course of righteousness. Every effort is made to persecute and bring them down. Indeed, as Elder Neal A. Maxwell (1926–2004) once observed, "Babylon does not give exit permits gladly" (*Ensign,* November 1988, 33).

The Lord did intervene in behalf of Alma's people, and they were eventually able to escape. Some of the children of Amulon and his priests later repented and joined with the Nephites in worshipping the true and living God (Mosiah 25:12). However, the "iniquity of the fathers" (Exodus 20:5) continued with many of the descendants of Amulon, who became known as the Amulonites (Alma 21:3).

See also Amulon; Amulonites.

O

OMER

This righteous Jaredite king was the son of King Shule and the father of the treacherous Jared[2], who "rebelled against his father" (Ether 7:27; 8:1–2). King Omer was overthrown and placed in captivity by his rebellious son. Omer later had the kingdom restored to him through the intervention of his other sons, who made the fatal mistake of not executing their traitorous brother (Ether 8:4–6).

The king was once again betrayed by his son Jared[2], who, with Omer's unnamed granddaughter and a so-called friend of the king named Akish, entered into a conspiracy to kill his father (Ether 8:7–17). The Lord warned Omer, and he was able to escape the planned assassination (Ether 9:2–3).

It is evident that Omer was living a righteous life and therefore in tune with the Spirit at this critical time. It is significant that he did not delay responding to the spiritual warning that came to him but acted immediately to save his life. There is a lesson in this for all. When the Spirit warns of danger, it is time to take instant action.

Omer and loyal family members fled to another location, where they remained until the conclusion of a terrible war in which nearly all the people were destroyed. Omer was then restored to his position as king (Ether 9:12–13).

He later begat a son he named Emer, whom he anointed to be his successor. "And after that he had anointed Emer to be king he saw peace in the land for the space of two years, and he died, having seen exceedingly many days, which were full of sorrow" (Ether 9:14–15).

See also Akish; Jared[3]; Jared[3], Daughter of.

OMNER

Omner, together with his brothers Ammon[2], Aaron[3], and Himni, "were numbered among the unbelievers" around 100 B.C. (Mosiah 27:8). Omner was not a passive unbeliever, for he sought to "destroy the church" (Mosiah 27:10). While they were in the process of "rebelling against God," an angel appeared to them and their companion Alma[2] the Younger and called them to repentance (Mosiah 27:11–18).

The four had a complete change of heart and "traveled throughout all the land of Zarahemla . . . zealously striving to repair all the injuries which they had done to the church" (Mosiah 27:35). Omner was proffered the crown and a chance to be king, but he turned it down to join his brothers in a very challenging fourteen-year mission among the Lamanites (Mosiah 28:10; Alma 17:4). In spite of severe persecution, they were able to bring thousands to a true knowledge of Jesus Christ and His gospel.

Omner and his brothers were driven by a desire to change the hatred of the Lamanites towards the Nephites through the preaching of the gospel. "Now they were desirous that salvation should be declared to every creature, for they could not bear that any human soul should perish; yea, even the very thoughts that any soul should endure endless torment did cause them to quake and tremble.

"And thus did the Spirit of the Lord work upon them" (Mosiah 28:3–4).

Omner's testimony and the steadiness of his work as a missionary were not based alone on the miraculous experience he had of seeing an angel of God. He was one of "a sound understanding" because he "had searched the scriptures diligently [to]

know the word of God" (Alma 17:2). He rejoiced over the success of his missionary labors, for "the Lord had granted unto [Omner and his brothers] according to their prayers" (Alma 25:17).

The last mention of Omner is when he finally returned to the land of Zarahemla (Alma 35:14).

See also Aaron[3]; Ammon[2]; Himni; Mosiah[2], Sons of.

OMNI

This Nephite record keeper was the son of Jarom, who delivered the plates containing the history of Father Lehi's descendants to his son with the charge to keep them "according to the commandments of [his] fathers" (Jarom 1:15). The charge initially given by the original record keeper, Nephi[1], to the second record keeper, his brother Jacob[2], was to write *sacred* things upon the small plates and *historical* things upon the large plates (Jacob 1:1–4).

Why then did Omni write only three of the thirty verses in the little book that bears his name (Omni 1:1–3)? And why did he not record things of a sacred or spiritual nature?

Omni is quite frank in telling us: "I of myself am a wicked man, and I have not kept the statutes and the commandments of the Lord as I ought to have done" (Omni 1:2).

Omni's choice to live a life

offensive to the Spirit left the sacred record devoid of words of wisdom and inspiration that might otherwise have been ours to enjoy.

A personal decision to make wrongful choices does not remain *personal,* for its impact affects many others beyond the one making that choice. While serving as a member of the Quorum of the Twelve Apostles, Elder James E. Faust (1920–) observed: "Private choices are not private; they all have public consequences. . . . Our society is the sum total of what millions of individuals do in their private lives. That sum total of private behavior has worldwide public consequences of enormous magnitude. *There are no completely private choices*" (*Ensign,* May 1987, 80; emphasis added).

ONLY BEGOTTEN OF THE FATHER

This singular title, which only the Son of God may bear, can be found in all of the Standard Works (John 3:16; Jacob 4:11; D&C 49:5; Moses 1:6). While all mortals are begotten sons and daughters of our Father in Heaven in the spirit world (Hebrews 12:9), only Jesus Christ was also begotten of the Father in the flesh. In order for Christ to have control over life and death, and therefore choice between the two, it was necessary that He have mixed parentage. Elohim,

His Father, bequeathed to Him seeds of immortality and Mary, His mortal mother, gave Him the genetic disposition for death.

Elder James E. Talmage (1862–1933) wrote: "That Child . . . born of Mary was begotten of Elohim, the Eternal Father, not in violation of natural law but in accordance with a higher manifestation thereof; and, the offspring from that association of supreme sanctity, celestial Sireship, and pure though mortal maternity, was of right to be called the 'Son of the Highest'" (*Jesus the Christ,* 81).

See also Christ; Christ, Names of; Father, Jesus Christ As; God; Immanuel; Jehovah; Jesse, Stem of; Jesus; Lamb of God; Messiah; Prince of Peace; Redeemer; Savior.

ORIHAH

This first king of the Jaredite civilization was the son of Jared², who was the founder of the civilization that preceded the Nephite and Lamanite civilization in ancient America. Prior to his selection as king, Orihah's brothers and cousins had all declined the position (Ether 6:22–27). To his credit, and the blessing of his people, "Orihah did walk humbly before the Lord . . . and also taught his people how great things the Lord had done for their fathers" (Ether 6:30). His reign of righteousness lasted "all his days" (Ether

7:1). His son Kib succeeded him as king (Ether 7:3).

OTHER SHEEP

While visiting ancient America following His resurrection, the Savior told the inhabitants that they were the "other sheep" of whom He had testified to His disciples in the Holy Land during His mortal ministry (3 Nephi 15:13–24; John 10:16). He also told these ancient Nephites that He had still "other sheep, which are not of this land, neither of the land of Jerusalem," and that He had a charge from His Father to visit them "that they shall hear my voice, and shall be numbered among my sheep, that there may be one fold and one shepherd" (3 Nephi 16:1–3). The Savior identified these *other sheep* as "the lost tribes of Israel" (3 Nephi 17:4).

See also Israel, House of; Israel, Lost Tribes of; Lamanites; Nephites.

P

PAANCHI

About 52 B.C. the Nephite chief judge Pahoran[1] died, and a "serious contention" arose among three of his sons regarding who should succeed him in the judgment seat. The three—Pahoran[2], Paanchi, and Pacumeni—sought the position, creating "three divisions among the people." Pahoran[2] was victorious in the election, and his brother Pacumeni supported the will of the people (Helaman 1:1–6).

Paanchi and his supporters were angry with the outcome, and he "was about to flatter away those people to rise up in rebellion against their brethren." Before he was able to put his plan fully into effect, "he was taken, and was tried according to the voice of the people, and condemned unto death" for seeking to "destroy the liberty of the people" (Helaman 1:7–8).

Although Paanchi's rebellion was short-lived, the disastrous results of his treacherous scheming had long-term consequences. It was this plot against the duly elected Nephite government that led Paanchi's traitorous followers to send the infamous Kishkumen to kill the elected chief judge. From this small beginning came the abominable secret combination of the Gadiantons that ultimately proved to be the destruction of the Nephite nation (Helaman 1:9–12; 2:13; see also Ether 8:18–21).

PACHUS

About 62 B.C., at a very critical time in a long-running war to defend their lands against the invading Lamanites, the Nephites faced a serious rebellion against the government. Pachus, a man possessed of much flattery—that poisonous siren's song that seduces people to destruction—led a treacherous revolt that drove the chief judge from the seat of government and had himself crowned king (Alma 61:4; 62:6). He formed an alliance with the invading Lamanites and withheld supplies from his country's own defending forces (Alma 61:2–8).

In response to the exiled chief judge's plea for assistance, Captain Moroni[1] gathered an army of freedom-loving men and joined forces with the loyal followers of the chief judge. They were successful in defeating the followers of the traitor Pachus, who himself was killed in the battle for the return of freedom (Alma 62:3–8).

PACUMENI

One of three sons of the deceased chief judge Pahoran[1] who sought to succeed his father in the Nephite's judgment seat (Helaman 1:1–3). His brother Pahoran[2] was successful in the election, and Pacumeni gracefully and patriotically united "with the voice of the people" (Helaman 1:5–6). When his brother was later assassinated, "Pacumeni was appointed, according to the voice of the people, to be a chief judge and a governor over the people" (Helaman 1:13). It was but a short time later that a Lamanite attack on the Nephites occurred, and Pacumeni was killed by the leader of the invading army (Helaman 1:21).

PAGAG

Pagag was the firstborn son of the brother of Jared[2], whose father was the powerful spiritual leader of the Jaredite people. When the people asked that Pagag be anointed as their first king, he refused the offer. However, the people insisted that he be forced to serve. The wise father then counseled the people that no man should be constrained to be their king (Ether 6:22–25). This almost footnote in Book of Mormon history is a great example of the need to protect the righteous exercise of agency, that God-given gift over which a war in heaven was fought (Moses 4:3; Revelation 12:7–9).

PAGE, HIRAM

Hiram Page is not mentioned by name in the ancient text that comprised the Book of Mormon, but he was one of the "few" additional witnesses (Eight Witnesses) to the truthfulness of the Book of Mormon to whom Nephi[1] and undoubtedly Isaiah[1] referred (2 Nephi 27:12–13).

Hiram Page was the only one of the Eight Witnesses not to bear the family name of *Smith* or *Whitmer*. However, Hiram was a brother-in-law to the four Whitmer sons, having married their sister Catherine four years before he was privileged to become an eyewitness to the existence of the gold plates containing the record of the Book of Mormon.

There is an oft-quoted phrase used by real estate agents when asked what determines the value of a home: "location, location, location!"

Perhaps this same phrase might have application when considering how Hiram Page was selected to be one of the Eight Witnesses to the Book of Mormon. Hiram was living at his in-laws' home in Fayette at the time the Prophet Joseph and Oliver Cowdery arrived there in the spring of 1829 to pursue the work of translating and transcribing the Book of Mormon record.

It should be quickly added, however, that Hiram's presence at the Whitmer home was probably not coincidental. The Lord of the universe not only charts the course of planets and stars but is also intricately involved in plotting the paths of the people of this planet. It is, therefore, not beyond reason to believe that Hiram Page was chosen to be one of these select witnesses in premortal councils and that divine direction brought him into the presence of the Prophet Joseph Smith.

Just a few months after the Church was officially organized (restored), a critical point occurred in Hiram Page's life that could have led him quickly out of the Church. Contrary to divine order, which channels heavenly communications to the Church through the Prophet, Hiram claimed to be receiving revelation "concerning the upbuilding of Zion and the order of the Church" (D&C 28, heading).

Page possessed a "peep stone" through which the alleged revelations came. Unfortunately, he was successful for a time in duping Oliver Cowdery and other witnesses of the Book of Mormon into believing him.

In response, "the Prophet inquired earnestly of the Lord concerning the matter," and the revelation now found in section 28 of the Doctrine and Covenants was received. In it, the Lord instructed Oliver and the others that "no one shall be appointed to receive commandments and revelations in this church excepting my servant Joseph Smith, Jun." (D&C 28:2).

Oliver was charged to "take thy brother, Hiram Page, between him and thee alone, and tell him that those things which he hath written from that stone are not of me and that Satan deceiveth him" (D&C 28:11).

Fortunately, Hiram responded to the correction, and those who were deceived changed the course of their wayward thinking.

Learning from his corrective chastisement, Hiram Page remained true to the Prophet and the Church during the next few years. He followed the faithful to Ohio and then to Missouri, where he was once severely beaten and threatened with death because of his Church membership.

Perhaps the persecution became too much for him, for in 1838 he "severed his relations with the Church," and lived the remainder of his life away from the faith of which he had been such an important part (Roberts, *New Witnesses for God*, 2:324). For a time, he was nominally connected with apostate factions fostered by William E. McLellin and David Whitmer (*Ensign*, August 1979, 34).

How ironic that the Book of Mormon, the scriptural record of which he bore such strong witness, should include this warning:

"And now, my beloved brethren, after ye have gotten into this strait and narrow path, I would ask if all is done? Behold, I say unto you, Nay; for ye have not come thus far save it were by the word of Christ with unshaken faith in him, relying wholly upon the merits of him who is mighty to save.

"Wherefore, ye must press forward with a steadfastness in Christ, having a perfect brightness of hope, and a love of God and of all men. Wherefore, if ye shall press forward, feasting upon the word of Christ, and *endure to the end,* behold, thus saith the Father: Ye shall have eternal life" (2 Nephi 31:19–20; emphasis added).

Thus we see the importance of enduring!

To his credit, Hiram Page did remain true to his testimony regarding the Book of Mormon's divine origin. Many years after his death, his son Philander Page said the following of his father's continued adherence to that special witness:

"I knew my father to be true and faithful to his testimony of the divinity of the Book of Mormon until the very last. Whenever he had an opportunity to bear his testimony to this effect, he would always do so, and seemed to rejoice exceedingly in having been privileged to see the plates and thus become one of the Eight Witnesses" (Roberts, *New Witnesses for God,* 2:324).

See also Witnesses, Eight.

PAHORAN[1]

The third chief judge of the Nephites, Pahoran[1] was the son of the second chief judge, Nephihah (Alma 50:39–40). Unfortunately Pahoran[1] presided at a time when there was great conflict in the country because of civil rebellion as well as a war of aggression from the Lamanites.

Pahoran[1] was a righteous judge who refused to succumb to pressure by special interests ("those of high birth [who] sought to be kings") and to change the laws (Alma 51:8). His desire was to protect the people's rights and privileges. The matter was put to a vote, and those in favor of protecting liberty were victorious (Alma 51:2–8). A civil uprising (or, more accurately said, "rebellion") followed the election, and it took Captain Moroni[1] and the army to restore order (Alma 51:9–21).

Perhaps the most significant point in Pahoran's service was during the height of the war with the Lamanites. Because of continuing civil disobedience on the home front, the military was not getting the supplies and manpower they needed. It appeared to Captain Moroni[1] that Pahoran[1] was sitting comfortably safe at home without sending the necessary aid to those on the battlefront. As a result, Moroni[1] sent a scathing letter of rebuke to the chief judge in which he threatened to come to the Nephite capital and set matters straight, including removing the assumed neglectful chief judge from his office (Alma 60).

The magnanimity of Pahoran[1] is evidenced in his charitable reply. He explained to the military leader that dissenters had driven him from the judgment seat, which prevented him from sending the supplies and manpower needed by his country's defending forces.

His reply included this classic statement: "You have censured me, but it mattereth not; I am not angry, but do rejoice in the greatness of your heart" (Alma 61:9). What a superb example of pure Christian charity!

Captain Moroni[1] was able to join forces with Pahoran[1] and once again restore order to the government. After being placed back in the judgment seat, Pahoran[1] did not rest comfortably in ease, for he joined with Moroni[1] in leading the forces of freedom in further forays against the invaders (Alma 62:14). Following the conclusion of a successful military campaign against the invaders, Pahoran[1] returned to the judgment seat, where he later died (Alma 62:44; Helaman 1:2).

PAHORAN[2]

This son of Pahoran[1] had a brief reign as the chief judge of the Nephites. Following the death of his father, Pahoran[2] was elected to succeed his father in governing the Nephites (Helaman 1:2–5). Tragically, he was killed by an assassin sent by dissidents who sought to overthrow the government and "destroy the liberty of the people" (Helaman 1:7–9).

PASTORS OF MY PEOPLE

The title "pastors of my people" is found only once in all of current scripture. It is part of a restored introduction to Isaiah 49, which obviously was on the plates of brass from which Nephi[1] quoted (1 Nephi 21:1). These *wicked* pastors are described as being responsible for the waywardness of the children of Israel.

A pastor is *not* an ordained office in The Church of Jesus Christ of Latter-day Saints, but a *title* describing one's *function*. It is a title that refers to one who is a shepherd of a Church flock, who presides over a congregation or ecclesiastical unit of the Church. Thus, bishops, stake presidents, and mission presidents are pastors who are charged with the responsibility of shepherding the Lord's sheep.

Pastors who neglect or deliberately lead astray the flocks entrusted to their care are held accountable by the Lord. President John Taylor (1808–1887) declared: "If you do not magnify your callings, God will hold you responsible for those whom you might have saved had you done your duty" (in *Journal of Discourses*, 20:23).

PEKAH

Among the writings of Isaiah[1] recorded by Nephi[1] is the seventh chapter of Isaiah (2 Nephi 17). Mention is made of "Pekah the son of Remaliah, king of Israel" (v. 1). He is mentioned in conjunction with his joint invasion of Judah (the southern kingdom). This conniving king of Israel (the northern kingdom occasionally referred to as "Ephraim") came to power through assassinating his predecessor on the throne. He reigned for twenty years, doing "that which was evil in the sight of the Lord." His reign ended when he himself was assassinated in a conspiracy against him (2 Kings 15:25–32).

See also Ephraim; Ephraim, Head of; Remaliah.

PEOPLE OF AKISH

The murderous Jaredite King Akish came to the throne through the assassination of his father-in-law Jared[3]. His lust for power led him to even have his own son killed (Ether 9:5–7). His abominations had an influence on his subjects, for "the people of Akish were desirous for gain, even as Akish was desirous for power" (Ether 9:11). This led to many of them accepting bribe money to join with the sons of Akish in a revolt against their father. The result was a terrible war that led to "the destruction of nearly all the people of the kingdom, yea, even all, save it were thirty souls" (Ether 9:12).

PEOPLE OF AMMON[2]

See Anti-Nephi-Lehies.

PEOPLE OF AMMONIHAH

See Ammonihah, Citizens of.

PEOPLE OF AMULON

See Amulon.

PEOPLE OF ANTI-NEPHI-LEHI

See Anti-Nephi-Lehies.

PEOPLE OF ANTIPARAH

During the long wars recounted in the later chapters of the book of Alma, one of the Nephite cities that fell to the invading Lamanites was the city of Antiparah. The king of the Lamanites offered to free the city in exchange for the prisoners Helaman[2] had taken. Helaman[2] considered such an exchange a disadvantage to the Nephites and turned down the proposal, declaring he thought the strength of his army sufficient to take the city of Antiparah without such an exchange. The conquerors of Antiparah ("the people of Antiparah") were so fearful of the strength of Helaman's army that they deserted the city (Alma 57:1–4).

PEOPLE OF ANTIPUS

The people of Antipus were the soldiers who served under the leadership of the courageous Nephite military commander Antipus about 64 B.C. (Alma 56:53). They were part of a stratagem to lure the enemy into a trap. The plan put Antipus and his men at risk, and they "were about to fall into the hands of the Lamanites" when they were saved by the arrival of Helaman[2] and his stripling warriors (Alma 56).

See also Antipus.

PEOPLE OF CHRIST

The "people of Christ" is the title Moroni[2] used to describe members of Christ's Church, who had been received by baptism and the conferral of the gift of the Holy Ghost (Moroni 6:4, 7).

See also Chosen People; Covenant People of the Lord; People of God;

People of Jesus; Saints of the Church of the Lamb.

PEOPLE OF CORIANTUMR[2]

During the final days of the Jaredite civilization, the people divided into two camps of loyalty: the people of Coriantumr[2] and the people of Shiz (Ether 15:6). Shiz was the final opponent in the ongoing battles that consumed the reign of Coriantumr[2]. Both sides were filled with such rage towards the other that they were described as being "drunken with anger" (Ether 15:22). The end result was the total annihilation of the Jaredite people.

See also Coriantumr[2]; Shiz.

PEOPLE OF GIDEON

These were the people who lived in the land of Gideon, which was named after the righteous man who was slain by the anti-Christ Nehor (Alma 2:20; 6:7; 8:1). It was during a visit to the branch of the church in Gideon that Alma[2] delivered the powerful sermon in which he testified that Christ's Atonement was not just for sins and transgressions, but that He also took "upon him the pains and the sicknesses of his people" (Alma 7:11–13).

PEOPLE OF GOD

As Alma[1] baptized people, they became members of "the church of

God." They took upon them "the name of Christ, or of God" and "they were called the people of God. And the Lord did pour out his Spirit upon them, and they were blessed, and prospered in the land" (Mosiah 25:18–24). Through the covenants entered into in the waters of baptism, these converts became the "covenant people of the Lord" (1 Nephi 14:14; 15:14). They were committed to keeping the commandments of the Lord and, in fact, they had entered into sacred covenants to do so.

When an apostate group later broke away from the main body of the Nephites and took upon themselves the name of Amlicites, "the remainder were called Nephites, or the people of God" (Alma 2:11). They were led by the prophet Alma[2] and prevailed in their battle with the Amlicites, "being strengthened by the hand of the Lord, having prayed mightily to him" (Alma 2:28).

Later, the Anti-Nephi-Lehies were specifically referred to as the people of God. When they were ruthlessly attacked by an invading army, they refused to fight against the invaders because of a covenant they had made to never again take up arms. One thousand and five were murdered before the attackers ceased the slaughter. "And it came to pass that the people of God were joined that day by more than the number who had been slain" (Alma 24:16–29).

See also Chosen People; People of Christ; People of Jesus.

PEOPLE OF JARED[2]
See Jaredites.

PEOPLE OF JESUS
The faithful followers of Jesus Christ near the end of the golden era that followed His post-resurrection appearance in ancient America were called the people of Jesus (4 Nephi 1:34). This was a period when the people were once again divided into classes and built up churches that denied "the more parts of [Christ's] gospel" (4 Nephi 1:24–27). The false priests and teachers led the people into "all manner of iniquity. And they did smite upon the people of Jesus; but the people of Jesus did not smite again" (4 Nephi 1:34).

It was these people of Jesus who were the "true believers in Christ" (4 Nephi 4:36–37).

See also Chosen People; Covenant People of the Lord; People of Christ; People of God; Saints of the Church of the Lamb.

PEOPLE OF KING JACOB[4]
These were foolish followers of the apostate Nephite Jacob[4]. They formed a secret combination about 29–30 B.C. and chose Jacob[4] as their

king (3 Nephi 7:9–14). The Lord destroyed them at the time of the crucifixion.

"And behold, that great city Jacobugath, which was inhabited by the people of King Jacob, have I caused to be burned with fire because of their sins and their wickedness, which was above all the wickedness of the whole earth, because of their secret murders and combinations; for it was they that did destroy the peace of my people and the government of the land; therefore I did cause them to be burned, to destroy them from before my face, that the blood of the prophets and the saints should not come up unto me any more against them" (3 Nephi 9:9).

See also Jacob⁴.

PEOPLE OF KING LIMHI
See Limhi.

PEOPLE OF KING NOAH³

The people of King Noah³ were the citizens who lived under this monarch in the land of Nephi around 160 B.C. He lived in debauchery, and the people supported his abominations with their taxes. At one point while the prophet Abinadi was preaching to them, calling them to repentance, the Spirit of the Lord was so powerful upon Abinadi "that the people of King Noah durst not lay their hands on him" (Mosiah 13:5).

The more wicked followers of King Noah³ comprised the army that the king sent out to capture Alma¹ and the recent converts he had gleaned from among the people of King Noah³ (Mosiah 23:1–2; Alma 5:4).

See also Noah³.

PEOPLE OF LIBERTY
See Freemen.

PEOPLE OF LEHI

The title "people of Lehi" is used in two separate settings, identifying two different groups of people.

The *first* group identified as "the people of Lehi" were the inhabitants of the land of Lehi, which shared borders with the people of the land of Morianton. About 68 B.C., a "warm contention" arose when the people of Morianton claimed "a part of the land of Lehi." The contention escalated to the point where "the people of Morianton took up arms against their brethren, and they were determined by the sword to slay them" (Alma 50:25–26; see v. 28).

The people of Lehi sought refuge in the camp of Captain Moroni¹, where they "appealed unto him for assistance; for behold they were not in the wrong" (Alma 50:27). Moroni¹ was successful in defeating the uprising and restoring peace to both the people of Lehi and the people of Morianton (Alma 50:28–36).

As used in 3 Nephi 4:11, the *second* group referred to as "the people of Lehi" are the descendants of Father Lehi[1]. In a tragic description of the results of a fierce war between the Gadianton terrorists and the Nephites who were defending their families and country, the scribe recorded these words: "Great and terrible was the slaughter thereof, insomuch that there never was known so great a slaughter among all the *people of Lehi* since he left Jerusalem" (3 Nephi 4:10–11; emphasis added).

On the positive side of this terrible tragedy, the Nephites "were prepared to meet [the terrorists]; yea, in the strength of the Lord they did receive them. . . . [and] did beat them" (3 Nephi 4:10–13).

PEOPLE OF MORIANTON[2]

About 68 B.C., the Nephites who inhabited a land called Morianton were led by a man named Morianton[2]. A dispute arose concerning their shared border with the people of the land of Lehi. The people of Morianton claimed part of the land of Lehi and were prepared to slay their neighbors in order to obtain it (Alma 50:25–26).

Morianton[2], the leader of the people of Morianton, was "a man of much passion" (Alma 50:30). He led

his people astray with "his wickedness and his flattering words" (Alma 50:35). When Morianton[2] discovered that the people of Lehi had enlisted the help of Captain Moroni[1], he fled with his people to the land northward, which Moroni[1] perceived as a threat to the liberty of the Nephites. He therefore sent an army to head them off, and in the ensuing battle Morianton[2] was killed and his army defeated. "And upon their covenanting to keep the peace they were restored to the land of Morianton, and a union took place between them and the people of Lehi" (Alma 50:28–36).

See also Morianton[2]; People of Lehi.

PEOPLE OF MORONI[1]

Those Nephite patriots who followed the righteous leadership of Captain Moroni[1] in his battles with traitors, dissidents, and attacking armies (Alma 46:29) were sometimes called the people of Moroni[1].

PEOPLE OF MORONIHAH[1]

About 52 B.C., some Nephite dissenters stirred up the Lamanites "to war against the people of Moronihah[1], or against the army of Moronihah[1], in the which they were beaten and driven back again to their own lands, suffering great loss" (Alma 63:14–15).

It is a sad truth that dissidents are usually not content with rejecting people and principles to which they once gave allegiance, but they pursue a course of angry retribution in retaliation for alleged wrongs.

Bishop Glenn L. Pace (1940–) provided the following insight regarding this phenomenon: "It seems that history continues to teach us: You can leave the Church, but you can't leave it alone. The basic reason for this is simple. Once someone has received a witness of the Spirit and accepted it, he leaves neutral ground. One loses his testimony only by listening to the promptings of the evil one, and Satan's goal is not complete when a person leaves the Church, but when he comes out in open rebellion against it" (*Ensign*, May 1989, 26).

See also Moronihah.

PEOPLE OF MOSIAH¹
See Mosiah¹; Nephites.

PEOPLE OF MY SEED
See Nephites.

PEOPLE OF MY WRATH
In a revelation through the prophet Isaiah¹ (Isaiah 10:6), which was cited by Nephi¹ (2 Nephi 20:6), the Lord speaks of Israel as a "hypocritical nation" and "the people of my wrath." While professing to follow the God of Israel, the chosen people have fallen into the ways of the world—becoming like the heathen nations that surround them. Thus, rather than being the righteous exemplars they were intended to be, and partakers of the blessings intended for them, they have become a people who will suffer the righteous wrath of God.

PEOPLE OF NEPHI¹
See Nephites.

PEOPLE OF NEPHIHAH
At a time when the Nephite government was fighting to defend its people and lands from the war of aggression being waged by the Lamanites, the government also was weakened because of traitors among its citizens. In such a condition, the people of Nephihah (citizens and refugees who were then living in the city of Nephihah) were easy prey to the attacking armies, who killed them "with an exceedingly great slaughter" (Alma 59:5–7).

The loss of this great Nephite city caused Captain Moroni¹ to be "exceedingly sorrowful" and, not knowing of the contention caused by dissidents, he mistakenly thought the government had been indifferent to properly strengthening the city and assisting in the war effort (Alma 59:9–13). This event led to Moroni's stern letter of rebuke to the chief judge Pahoran[1] (Alma 60) and the magnanimous reply from the chief judge (Alma 61).

See also Pahoran[1]; Moroni[1].

PEOPLE OF SHIZ

See People of Coriantumr[2]; Shiz.

PEOPLE OF THE CHURCH

See People of God.

PEOPLE OF THE FIRST COVENANT

Near the end of his ministry, as he completed his recording of history and prophecies, Mormon[2] wrote to the Lamanites of the future:

"And ye will also know that ye are a remnant of the seed of Jacob; therefore *ye are numbered among the people of the first covenant;* and if it so be that ye believe in Christ, and are baptized, first with water, then with fire and with the Holy Ghost, following the example of our Savior, according to that which he hath commanded us, it shall be well with you in the day of judgment" (Mormon 7:10; emphasis added).

The "people of the first covenant" are all the descendants of the great patriarchs Abraham, Isaac, and Jacob[1] and are heirs, based upon their own obedience to the laws and ordinances of the gospel, to all of the promised blessings given anciently.

In an apostolic plea, Elder Bruce R. McConkie (1915–1985) uttered the following invitation: "Thus we say: Come, all ye house of Israel, all ye scattered sheep, all ye lost and fallen ones; come, ye of every tribe and family; believe the testimony of Joseph Smith and those upon whom his prophetic mantle has fallen. Come out of the world, out of the bondage of Egypt, and join The Church of Jesus Christ of Latter-day Saints, for this church administers the gospel, and the gospel is the plan of salvation. Come to the Lord's house and receive your blessings and inherit thereby the same blessings given to Abraham, Isaac, and Jacob and promised to all of their righteous children. All ye who 'are a remnant of the seed of Jacob,' know that 'ye are numbered among the people of the first covenant; and if it so be that ye believe in Christ, and are baptized, first with water, then with fire and with the Holy Ghost, following the example of our Savior, according to that which he hath commanded us, it shall be well with you in the day of judgment. Amen' (Morm. 7:1–10)" (*The Millennial Messiah*, 219).

PEOPLE OF THE HOUSE OF ISRAEL

See Israel, House of.

PEOPLE OF THE LAMANITES

See Lamanites.

PEOPLE OF THE LORD

See Chosen People; People of Christ; People of God; People of Jesus; Saints of the Church of the Lamb.

PEOPLE OF THE SEED OF MY BRETHREN

See Lamanites.

PEOPLE OF UNCLEAN LIPS

Quoting from an experience of the prophet Isaiah[1] found on the plates of brass, Nephi[1] cited the prophet's concern that he may have "unclean lips" and that he lives amidst "a people of unclean lips" (2 Nephi 16:5; Isaiah 6:5). Having had a vision where he saw the Lord, Isaiah[1] "was overwhelmed by his consciousness of the sins of himself and his people" (Isaiah 6:5, footnote 5*a*).

Latter-day Saints who seek the presence of the Lord in their lives through partaking of the sacrament—in which one promises to "always remember Him" (Moroni 4:3; 5:2)—and by being in temples, or houses of the Lord (D&C 97:15–17), must be very careful of their *everyday* thoughts, words, and conduct. One's lips should be clean not only in houses of worship and when on bended knees, but "at

all times and in *all* things, and in *all* places" (Mosiah 18:9; emphasis added).

PEOPLE OF THE ZORAMITES

See Zoramites[2].

PEOPLE OF ZARAHEMLA

This group of people was discovered during the reign of the Nephite King Mosiah[1] by the king and his followers. The people of Zarahemla were descendants of a group which had left Jerusalem at the time King Nebuchadnezzar conquered that city and surrounding land, taking the Jewish King Zedekiah[1] into captivity after killing his known sons and putting out the king's eyes. An otherwise unknown son of King Zedekiah[1] named Mulek and his group were led by the hand of the Lord to the northern part of the same promised land where Lehi[1] and his people were settled in the southern portion (Omni 1:12–16; Mosiah 25:2; Helaman 6:10; 2 Kings 25:1–7).

These people were discovered by King Mosiah[1] after he and his people, heeding a warning from the Lord, had fled the land of Nephi. "And at the time that Mosiah discovered them, they had become exceedingly numerous. Nevertheless, they had had many wars and serious contentions, and had fallen by the sword from time to time; and their language had become corrupted; and they had brought no records with them; and they denied the being of their Creator; and Mosiah, nor the people of Mosiah, could understand them" (Omni 1:17).

Their lack of belief in God, having "brought no records with them," is a strong testimony of the important role the plates of brass played among the Nephites. We are reminded of the Spirit's command to Nephi to slay the wicked Laban in order to obtain the plates: "It is better that one man should perish than that a nation should dwindle and *perish in unbelief*" (1 Nephi 4:13; emphasis added).

The people of Zarahemla united with the Nephites under Mosiah's leadership, and he taught them a common language (Omni 1:18). At the time the people of Zarahemla joined with the Nephites, the descendants of Mulek were the more numerous of the two groups (Mosiah 25:2).

The people of Zarahemla are commonly referred to as Mulekites (see chapter headings for Omni 1 and Mosiah 25).

See also Mulek; Mulekites; Zarahemla.

PEOPLE OF ZEMNARIHAH

The abominable Gadiantons, led by the robber Zemnarihah, found themselves at a distinct disadvantage during one of their attacks on the Nephites. Around A.D. 21, they had laid siege to the well-fortified and provisioned Nephites. The terrorists had no place of refuge and were vulnerable to forays by the Nephites that took a heavy toll on their attackers.

"And thus it became the desire of the people of Zemnarihah to withdraw from their design [siege], because of the great destruction which came upon them by night and by day" (3 Nephi 4:22).

Their retreat was cut off by the Nephites, who defeated the Gadiantons and hanged their leader.

See also Zemnarihah.

PEOPLE OF ZENIFF
See Zeniff.

PERDITION, SON OF

"Two persons, Cain and Satan, have received the awesome name-title *Perdition*. The name signifies that they have no hope whatever of any degree of salvation, that they have wholly given themselves up to iniquity, and that any feeling of righteousness whatever has been destroyed in their breasts. Both had great administrative ability and persuasive power in pre-existence, but both were rebellious and iniquitous from eternity. (D. & C. 76:25–27; 2 Ne. 2:17–18.) Both came out in open rebellion against God having a perfect knowledge that their course was contrary to all righteousness" (McConkie, *Mormon Doctrine,* 566; see also Moses 5:24).

The singular title "*son* of perdition" was used by the Savior during His post-resurrection visit to ancient America. He sorrowfully spoke of a future generation that would be "led away captive by [the devil] even as was the son of perdition; for they will sell me for silver and for gold, and for that which moth doth corrupt and which thieves can break through and steal. And in that day will I visit them, even in turning their works upon their own heads" (3 Nephi 27:32).

The footnote to "son of perdition" in this verse refers to Christ's great intercessory prayer, in which He spoke of His select disciples as having been "kept, and none of them is lost, but the son of perdition" (John 17:12). This seems to be an obvious reference of Christ's betrayal at the hands of the Apostle Judas Iscariot, who sold his soul for thirty pieces of silver (Matthew 26:14–16).

Elder Bruce R. McConkie (1915–1985) provided the following commentary on the relationship between choosing coins over Christ: "When men set their hearts upon the wealth of the world and the good things of the earth in preference to the things of the Spirit, they thereby sell Christ for silver and gold and lose their own souls" (*The Mortal Messiah,* 4:386).

Regarding the question as to whether or not Judas is a son of perdition, one commentary provides the following insights: "According to Matthew, the distraught Judas sought to undo his crime by returning the thirty pieces of silver. He then committed suicide by hanging. (Matt. 27:3-5.) Luke, probably reflecting John's less charitable view of Judas, describes his death as resulting from an accidental fall on property he had purchased with the bribery money. (Acts 1:16-20.) JST Matt. 27:6 combines the two accounts. Satan is called perdition. (D&C 76:26.) Therefore, *all who yield to his enticings and die in their sins are sons (or daughters) of perdition and will have to suffer in hell for a given length of time.* (Moses 7:37–39.) The risen Christ compared Nephite apostates to Judas: 'For they are led away captive by him [Satan] even as was the son of perdition; for they will sell me for silver.' (3 Ne. 27:32.) Those Gentiles who deny Christ 'shall become like unto the son of perdition, for whom there was no mercy.' (3 Ne. 29:7.) 'No mercy' means they must bear the full weight of divine justice (the wrath of God or hell) before being saved. *They are temporary sons or daughters of perdition as opposed to those who, failing to ever repent, are termed the 'filthy still'* (D&C 88:35, 102) and are consigned to the fullness of the second death (D&C 29:27-30, 41). Likening Nephite and Gentile sinners to Judas suggests that there is hope for him as well. Consequently, whether or not Judas committed the unpardonable sin and is, in fact, a son of perdition in the direst sense of the term is debatable. Although an apostle, he had received neither the baptism nor the gift of the Holy Ghost. Like Peter, he was not yet converted. (Luke 22:32.) Then too, if, as Matthew suggests, he attempted to repent—something a totally lost son of perdition would not do (D&C 29:44)—he may yet obtain some measure of salvation. This issue has had proponents among Church leaders on both sides of the question" (Rodney Turner in Jackson and Millet, *Studies in Scripture, Vol. 5: The Gospels,* 426–27; emphasis added).

See also Angels of the Devil; Demons; Satan.

PHARAOH

In a second witness to the biblical account of the armies of Pharaoh being drowned in the midst of the Red Sea, Nephi[1] refers to this event as an example of the Lord's willingness to help His children accomplish His purposes (1 Nephi 4:2; 17:27).

There are nine or ten different Pharaohs or Egyptian kings mentioned in the Old Testament. However, the Pharaoh who sought to destroy Moses and the children of Israel in their exodus from Egyptian bondage is generally thought to be Menephthah II, the pharaoh who succeeded Ramses II (LDS Bible Dictionary, 661, 750).

The current text in the King James Version of the Bible mistakenly places the hardness of Pharaoh's heart upon the Lord, but the Prophet Joseph Smith corrected the mistranslated passages to indicate that the Lord simply *foretold* that Pharaoh by his own choice would harden his own heart (e.g., JST Exodus 4:21; 7:3).

The conflict between Pharaoh and the Lord's servants—Moses and Aaron—is found in Exodus 5–10, when the defeated ruler finally allowed Israel to leave. Nevertheless, Pharaoh's pride fueled his anger, and he pursued the departing people, leading to the death of the Egyptian army in the Red Sea (Exodus 14).

PRINCE OF PEACE

The title "prince of peace" is found two times in the Book of Mormon. One citation refers directly to Jesus Christ (2 Nephi 19:6) and the other to the great high priest Melchizedek (Alma 13:18).

Melchizedek was a prototype of the Son of God, He who was to come to earth "after the similitude of Melchisedec" (Hebrews 7:15). Thus Melchizedek was honored to be called both the "Prince of Peace" and "King of Peace" in the similitude of Christ (Alma 13:18; JST Genesis 14:33, 36).

In recorded scripture, the prophet Isaiah[1] is the first who pronounced Christ to be the "Prince of Peace" (Isaiah 9:6). This was later recited by Nephi[1] (2 Nephi 19:6).

Jesus Christ will ultimately reign as the Prince of Peace during the Millennium, when warfare and conflict will be nonexistent because of the peace that will prevail in the hearts of the people.

"The gospel is the only answer to the problems of the world. . . . We may cry peace. We may hold peace conferences. And I have nothing but commendation for those who work for peace. But it is my conviction that peace must come from within. It cannot be imposed by state mandate. It can come only by following the teachings and the example of the Prince of Peace" (Ezra Taft Benson, *Improvement Era*, June 1961, 432–33).

After quoting John 14:27 (see also John 16:33), wherein the Savior said: "Peace I leave with you, my peace I give unto you: not as the world giveth, give I [peace] unto you," President Harold B. Lee explained: "The Savior was not speaking of the kind of peace which is won with armies or navies or force; nor was He speaking of the kind of peace which can be negotiated in the halls of congresses. He was speaking of the kind of peace we each can have in our hearts only when we live His commandments to such a degree that we know He is pleased with us" (quoted in *Ensign*, November 1982, 70).

See also Christ; Christ, Names of; Father, Jesus Christ As; Immanuel; Jehovah; Jesse, Stem of; Jesus; Lamb of God; Melchizedek; Messiah; Only Begotten of the Father; Redeemer; Savior.

PROPHET

In a very general sense, a prophet is one "who has the testimony of Jesus" (*Teachings of the Prophet Joseph Smith*, 119, 269; see also Revelation 19:10). "In this respect, anyone is a prophet who has had the witness of the Spirit that Jesus is the Christ (1 Cor. 12:3). Thus, if those who profess to be the Saints of God are worthy of such a witness, there should be one prophet for every member of record in The Church of Jesus Christ of Latter-day Saints. What a strength there would be if the prayer of Moses were granted: 'Would God that all the

Lord's people were prophets, and that the Lord would put his spirit upon them!' (Numbers 11:29)" (Brewster, *Doctrine & Covenants Encyclopedia,* 445).

In a more specific sense, a prophet is an ecclesiastical priesthood leader, endowed with authority from God to preside over His Church, to teach the true nature of Deity, to explain and expound upon His principles and commandments, to counsel the people, and to administer the saving and exalting ordinances of the gospel of Jesus Christ. As the LDS Bible Dictionary notes, "As a rule a prophet [is] a *forthteller* rather than a *foreteller*" (page 754). In other words, a prophet spends more time being forthright— preaching repentance and teaching divine principles—than he does predicting the future.

In our day, the men called of God to serve in the First Presidency and the Quorum of the Twelve Apostles of The Church of Jesus Christ of Latter-day Saints are the Lord's recognized prophets on the earth. One of them, the senior Apostle, is sustained as the President of the Church. He is [the] "prophet, seer, and revelator" who holds and is authorized to exercise all restored priesthood keys.

In ancient days, as directed by the Lord, prophets of God often appear to have functioned independent of priesthood councils. For example, consider virtually every spokesman whom the Lord called to minister to the people of ancient America. Examples include the following: Lehi[1], Nephi[1], Jacob[2], Enos[2], Mosiah[1], King Benjamin, Abinadi, Alma[1], Alma[2], Helaman[2], Nephi[2], Samuel[2], Nephi[3], Mormon[2], Moroni[2], and the brother of Jared[2]. There were also a number of *unnamed prophets* who served among the people of ancient America (Enos 1:22; Jarom 1:10–11; Words of Mormon 1:16–18; Alma 37:30; Helaman 13:24; 3 Nephi 6:25; 7:14; Ether 7:23; 9:28; 11:1, 12, 20. However, whether named or unnamed, true prophets of the Lord *always* come to their callings according to divine directions: "We believe that a man must be called of God, by prophecy, and by the laying on of hands by those who are in authority, to preach the Gospel and administer in the ordinances thereof" (Articles of Faith 1:5).

See also Holy Men; Prophets, False.

PROPHETESS

The term *prophetess* is found once in the Book of Mormon, in the writings of Isaiah[1] as recorded by Nephi[1]: "And I went unto the prophetess; and she conceived and bare a son" (2 Nephi 18:3).

The "prophetess" in this verse is

Isaiah's wife. "It is reasonable to assume that Isaiah's wife had heard him speak often of the coming of the Messiah and that she too had a testimony of Christ. In this respect, it is of interest to note the words of President Wilford Woodruff: 'Anybody is a prophet who has a testimony of Jesus Christ, for that is the spirit of prophecy.' . . . The term 'prophetess' is also used to identify other faithful women of the Bible such as Miriam (Exodus 15:20), Deborah (Judges 4:4–5), and Anna (Luke 2:36–38)" (Brewster, *Isaiah Plain & Simple,* 76).

PROPHETS, FALSE

In Jesus' renowned Sermon on the Mount, much of which He repeated to the ancient inhabitants of America (the Book of Mormon gives us the inspired translation), He warned of "false prophets, who come to you in sheep's clothing, but inwardly they are ravening wolves" (3 Nephi 14:15; Matthew 7:15). In another sermon near the end of His mortal ministry, Christ once more spoke of false prophets who would arise and "deceive many" prior to His Second Coming (Matthew 24:11, 24).

"False prophets always arise to oppose the true prophets and they will prophesy so very near the truth that they will deceive almost the very

chosen ones" (*Teachings of the Prophet Joseph Smith,* 365).

"Today we warn you that there are false prophets and false teachers arising," said Elder M. Russell Ballard (1928–) of the Quorum of the Twelve Apostles, "and if we are not careful, even those who are among the faithful members of The Church of Jesus Christ of Latter-day Saints will fall victim to their deception" (*Ensign,* November 1999, 62).

President Joseph F. Smith (1838–1918) counseled: "We can accept nothing as authoritative but that which comes directly through the appointed channel, the constituted organizations of the priesthood, which is the channel that God has appointed through which to make known his mind and will to the world. . . .

"And the moment that individuals look to any other source, that moment they throw themselves open to the seductive influences of Satan, and render themselves liable to become servants of the devil; they lose sight of the true order through which the blessings of the Priesthood are to be enjoyed; they step outside of the pale of the kingdom of God, and are on dangerous ground. Whenever you see a man rise up claiming to have received direct revelation from the Lord to the Church, independent of the order and channel of the priesthood, you may set him down as an imposter" (*Gospel Doctrine*, 42).

The arising of "many priests and false prophets" around A.D. 200 was one of the stumbling blocks that led to the ultimate downfall and annihilation of the Nephite civilization (4 Nephi 1:34).

See also Prophet.

R

RAHAB

The name *Rahab* appears in a citation from Isaiah's writings (2 Nephi 8:9; Isaiah 51:9). The verse occurs in the context of a plea from Israel for the God of Israel to come to the defense of the people as He did anciently in having "cut Rahab, and wounded the dragon."

"The psalmist also mentioned the utter defeat of Rahab. (Psalm 89:10.) The 'dragon' is easily identified as Satan. (Revelation 12:7–9; 20:2.) The identity of 'Rahab' is a little more difficult. Some scholars suggest Rahab represents Egypt while others say it is a sea monster representing Satan. Footnote reference 'c' in the Book of Mormon text cites Isaiah 27:1 as a cross-reference, which speaks of 'leviathan that crooked serpent.' The footnote identifies 'leviathan' as 'a legendary sea-monster representing the *forces of chaos that opposed the Creator.*' (LDSKJ, Isaiah 27:1, footnote *c*)" (Brewster, *Isaiah Plain & Simple,* 221; emphasis added).

REDEEMER

Another of the sacred and descriptive titles by which Jesus Christ is known is that of Redeemer. Anciently, Job was the first prophet known to have used this title when he declared, "I know that my redeemer liveth, and that he shall stand at the latter day upon the earth" (Job 19:25). Later, speaking through the prophet Isaiah[1], the Great Jehovah Himself declared His role as the Redeemer (Isaiah 41:14; 43:14; 44:6).

Father Lehi[1] bore witness that a great number of prophets had "testified . . . concerning this Messiah . . . or this Redeemer of the world" (1 Nephi 10:5). The Book of Mormon declares that the day will come, in the Lord's "own due time," that the house of Israel shall "know their Redeemer, who is Jesus Christ, the Son of God; and then shall they be gathered in from the four quarters of the earth" (3 Nephi 5:25–26).

Literally one-half of the total scriptural uses of this sacred title are found in the Book of Mormon. Curiously, it does not appear in either the New Testament or the Pearl of Great Price.

"Christ is the Redeemer because he redeems mankind from the effects of death and personal transgression (D&C 29:40–46; 93:38; 2 Nephi 2:26–27). All will be redeemed from death (1 Cor. 15:22), but only those whose garments are 'purified' and 'cleansed from all stain' (Alma 5:21) will be redeemed from the effects of personal transgression, for they cannot be redeemed 'in their sins' (Hel. 5:10–11; D&C 19:15–20)" (Brewster, *Doctrine & Covenants Encyclopedia,* 456).

The appellations "Redeemer" and "Savior" are essentially the same. However, the title "Redeemer" has the significance of *ransom* attached to its meaning. Christ's Atonement was a *ransom* price He paid to purchase us out of the bondage of sin and the chains of death. His blood, which oozed from "every pore" of His holy body (Mosiah 3:7; D&C 19:18; JST Luke 22:44) was the *precious ransom* He paid to redeem us.

See also Christ; Christ, Names of; Father, Jesus Christ As; Father of Heaven and Earth; God; Immanuel; Jehovah; Jesse, Stem of; Jesus; Lamb of God; Messiah; Only Begotten of the Father; Prince of Peace; Savior; Spirit of the Lord.

REMALIAH

This character of the Old Testament is mentioned in both the Book of Mormon and the Bible only in conjunction with his son Pekah, who is referred to as "the son of Remaliah" (2 Nephi 17:1, 4, 5, 9;

18:6; 2 Kings 15:25; 16:1; Isaiah 7:1).

REMALIAH, SON OF

The son of Remaliah is mentioned in the writings of Isaiah copied from the plates of brass (2 Nephi 17:5, 9). "Ephraim was the lead tribe of the northern kingdom and Pekah was the king. Isaiah appears to show his disdain for King Pekah by not mentioning his name, referring to him as 'the son of Remaliah.' That Pekah deserved this scorn is evident by this description of him: 'And he did that which was evil in the sight of the Lord: he departed not from the sins of Jeroboam . . . , who made Israel to sin.' (2 Kings 15:28)" (Brewster, *Isaiah Plain & Simple,* 66).

See Pekah; Remaliah.

REZIN

Rezin, a king of ancient Syria, is mentioned in the writings of Isaiah[1] copied from the plates of brass onto the Nephite record (2 Nephi 17:1, 4, 8; 18:6; 19:11). He joined in an alliance with Pekah, king of the northern kingdom of Israel (referred to as Ephraim), in an attack on the southern kingdom of Judah. Rezin is referred to as the "head of [the city of] Damascus" (2 Nephi 17:8).

The southern kingdom, in turn, entered into an alliance with Assyria, offering its king the "treasures of the king's house" as a present. The Assyrian king, Tiglath-pileser, responded by attacking Damascus and killing Rezin (2 Kings 15:7–9).

RIPLAKISH

The unrighteous use of agency is demonstrated in the brief account of Riplakish, a Jaredite king who was the son of Shez[1] (Ether 1:24). Just as his father's life illustrated that one raised in wickedness need not follow that same wayward path, so did Riplakish show that righteous homes do not always guarantee that all children raised in such homes will follow the proper path.

While serving as a member of the Quorum of the Twelve Apostles, President Gordon B. Hinckley (1910–) said: "I recognize that there are parents who, notwithstanding an outpouring of love and a diligent and faithful effort to teach them, see their children grow in a contrary manner and weep while their wayward sons and daughters willfully pursue courses of tragic consequence. For such I have great sympathy, and to them I am wont to quote the words of Ezekiel: 'The son shall not bear the iniquity of the father, neither shall the father bear the iniquity of the son' (Ezek. 18:20)" (*Ensign,* November 1978, 19.)

Riplakish succeeded his righteous father, Shez[1], as king of the Jaredite people. Tragically, he "did not do that which was right in the sight of the Lord," pursuing a carnal course of corruption and sinfulness (Ether 10:4–5). In his lust for power and prominence, he levied a heavy tax on his people and threw into prison those who could not pay the tax. His wicked forty-two-year reign is summarized in this statement: *"He did afflict the people with his whoredoms and abominations"* (Ether 10:7; emphasis added). He was killed when the people finally rose up in rebellion against him (Ether 10:8).

ROCK, THE
See Abraham.

ROD OUT OF THE STEM OF JESSE

In one of Isaiah's Messianic prophecies recorded in the Book of Mormon, he speaks of the coming forth of "a rod out of the stem of Jesse" (2 Nephi 21:1; Isaiah 11:1).

The Lord revealed to the Prophet Joseph Smith the *general* identity of this "rod": "Behold, thus saith the Lord: It is a servant in the hands of Christ, who is partly a descendant of Jesse as well as of Ephraim, or of the house of Joseph, on whom there is laid much power" (D&C 113:3–4).

One esteemed gospel scholar suggested the *specific* identity of this individual: "Joseph Smith must be the person referred to. . . . He is . . . the 'rod,' the servant in the hands of Christ. . . . We can therefore, understand why Moroni would have occasion to quote all of Isaiah 11 to the young Prophet Joseph Smith" (Sperry, *Doctrine and Covenants Compendium,* 617).

See also Stem of Jesse.

S

SAINTS OF THE CHURCH OF THE LAMB

In one of the great visions of the prophet Nephi[1], he saw the "power of the Lamb of God" descending "upon the saints of the church of the Lamb, and upon the covenant people of the Lord, who were scattered upon all the face of the earth; and they were armed with righteousness and with the power of God in great glory" (1 Nephi 14:14).

Nephi[1] foresaw the faithful Latter-day Saints, those whose testimony of the restored Church of Jesus Christ would lead them to the waters of baptism, where they would receive this saving ordinance by the authority of the priesthood of God. These are they who, through their righteousness, will have a powerful impact for good in the far-flung communities in which they live.

Elder Neal A. Maxwell (1926–2004) suggested ways in which the Saints of the Lamb can make a difference for good in a world that is floundering in wickedness and despair:

"It takes faith to withstand the secular society. We who seek to serve in this day and time are, for instance, asked to be more loving at a time when the love of many waxes cold. We are asked to be more merciful, even as the Saints are persecuted. We are asked to be more holy as the world ripens in iniquity. We are asked to be more filled with hope in a world marked by growing despair because of growing iniquity. When, as in the world, there is more impatience, we are asked to be patient and full of faith even as other men's hearts fail them. We are asked to be peacemakers even as peace has been taken from the earth. We are asked to have enough faith to have fidelity in our marriage and chastity in dating even as the world celebrates sex almost as a secular religion" (*Men and Women of Christ*, 106).

Speaking of Nephi's prophecy, President Ezra Taft Benson (1899–1994) said: "The Book of Mormon prophet Nephi foresaw the day when the Saints would be scattered in stakes all over the world. He saw the time when the Lord would extend His protection to them when menaced by storms of destruction that threatened their existence" (*Come unto Christ*, 104).

See also Chosen People; Covenant

People of the Lord; People of Christ; People of God; People of Jesus; People of the First Covenant; Zoramites[2].

SAM

Dramatic productions such as movies and plays generally have a few well-defined main characters, who are always on center stage occupying the audience's attention. However, there is usually a supporting cast of virtually unknowns who also appear in the scene or on stage. Those in supporting roles have fewer lines to speak and often seem to just blend in with the scenery. Yet they are important to the drama's final outcome.

Sam, the third-born son of Lehi[1] and Sariah (1 Nephi 2:5), served in a supporting role in the real-life drama that took place in the beginning pages of the Book of Mormon. Unlike his two oldest brothers, Laman[1] and Lemuel, Sam was never rebellious or critical of his younger brother Nephi[1]. In fact, on one occasion when Nephi[1] was being flogged by Laman[1] and Lemuel with a rod, Sam sided with Nephi[1] and was also beaten (1 Nephi 3:28).

Later, after the family of Ishmael[1] had joined Father Lehi's family in the wilderness, Sam is specifically identified as siding with Nephi[1] in a disagreement with the rebellious members of the group (1 Nephi 7:6). At every critical point, Sam is identified as supporting his younger brother Nephi[1].

Nephi[1] taught Sam that which the Lord had manifested to him, and his older brother believed Nephi's testimony (1 Nephi 2:17).

Father Lehi[1] commended his son Sam for his faithfulness. In his final blessing to his children prior to his death, this patriarch of the family promised Sam that he would "be blessed in all [his] days" (2 Nephi 4:11). Sam is later included with his three younger brothers in being described as "just and holy men" (Alma 3:6).

SAMUEL[1]

The Old Testament prophet Samuel[1] is mentioned once in the Book of Mormon. He has the significant honor of being mentioned by name when the resurrected Savior speaks of the prophets who have testified of Him (3 Nephi 20:24).

Samuel[1] had the distinction of having been promised as a lifelong, consecrated servant of the Lord before he was born. His faithful mother, Hannah, vowed that if the Lord would take away her barrenness and give her a son, she in turn would give the child to the Lord for as long as he lived (1 Samuel 1). True to her vow, she presented her young son to the priest Eli as soon as he had been weaned (probably at the age of three).

One night, probably in the early morning hours, the child heard a voice calling him. Assuming it was Eli, he ran to the priest's room and said, "Here am I." The older man denied calling the boy and sent him back to bed. Again the voice called, with the same results. However, the third time the voice called, Eli discerned that it was the Lord calling the child. If the voice called again, Eli instructed Samuel[1] to reply, "Speak, Lord; for thy servant heareth." The child obeyed, and thus began a new phase of Samuel's life (1 Samuel 3:2–10).

From that point on, "Samuel grew, and the Lord was with him, and did let none of his words fall to the ground [he was absolutely obedient]. And all Israel from Dan even to Beersheba knew that Samuel was established to be a prophet of the Lord. And the Lord . . . revealed himself to Samuel" (1 Samuel 3:19–21).

SAMUEL[2]

This powerful preacher of Messianic prophecies first arrived in the Nephite land of Zarahemla around 6 B.C. At this time the Nephites were steeped in wickedness and the Lamanites were more righteous. While he is commonly referred to as "Samuel *the* Lamanite," the scriptural text calls him "Samuel, *a* Lamanite" (Helaman 13:2, 5; 14:1;

16:1). His ministry and prophecies are found in Helaman chapters 13 through 15.

Samuel's initial attempt to call the people to repentance was rejected, and he was cast out (Helaman 13:1–2). He was "about to return to his own land," undoubtedly discouraged, when he had an experience analogous to that which Alma[2] had after being rejected by the people of Ammonihah (Alma 8:10–18). Samuel[2] was told by the Lord to return to Zarahemla. He obeyed but found his way barred (Helaman 13:2–4).

A less committed disciple might have said, "Well, I tried," and given up. Samuel[2], however, was serving with *all* his "heart, might, mind and strength" (D&C 4:2; emphasis added), and could not be deterred from fulfilling his mission. He climbed on top of the city wall, where he began to preach a sermon of repentance, prophesying of the people's impending destruction (Helaman 13:4–39). He asked the wicked inhabitants, "How long will ye choose darkness rather than light?" (Helaman 13:29).

His most powerful prophecies were Messianic, foretelling signs of the birth of the Son of God and of His later death, as well as testifying that salvation can come only through Christ (Helaman 14). A portion of his prophecy was not recorded at that time, and the resurrected Savior later ensured that it was added to the record (Helaman 14:25; 3 Nephi 23:9–13; see also Matthew 27:52–53).

Samuel's second effort, returning to preach to the people who had already rejected him, bore fruit. The hearts of some of the people were touched, and they repented and sought baptism. Others, however, were angry and sought to kill Samuel[2] by slinging stones and shooting arrows at him; "but the Spirit of the Lord was with him, insomuch that they could not hit him with their stones neither with their arrows" (Helaman 16:1–2). Samuel[2] escaped their efforts to capture him, and he returned to "preach and to prophesy among his own people" (Helaman 16:7).

SARAH (SARAI)

Sarah, the wife of Abraham, is mentioned in the writings of Isaiah[1] found in the Book of Mormon (2 Nephi 8:2; Isaiah 51:2). Through Isaiah, the Lord made an appeal for the posterity of Abraham and Sarah to follow their ancestors' righteous examples. In the verse preceding the one in which this ancient couple are mentioned by name, the Lord declared: "Look unto the rock from whence ye are hewn, and to the hole of the pit from whence ye are digged" (2 Nephi 8:1).

Abraham is likened to "the rock" and Sarah to "the hole of the pit" or rock quarry. It is of interest to note that "the God of Abraham, Isaac, and Jacob is the very One who was born in the lineage of Abraham and Sarah and who Himself is the Stone of Israel. (Genesis 49:24; Psalm 118:22; Matthew 21:42; D&C 50:44)" (Brewster, *Isaiah Plain & Simple,* 216).

First known as *Sarai,* the Lord changed the name of the wife of Abraham to *Sarah* just prior to the conception of her first child.

Perhaps the most prominent pivotal point in Sarah's life came when she overheard the good news that at the advanced age of ninety she was to be blessed with a child. While the King James Version of the Bible identifies Sarah's response as laughing (Genesis 18:12), it must be understood that the word could mean "rejoicing" (see JST Genesis 17:23). Furthermore, could it be that after seventy years of being barren she may have "believed not for joy" (see Luke 24:41)? As promised, she and her husband have become the honored ancestors of a numerous posterity. There is much yet to be revealed about this faithful woman, who died at age 127.

SARIAH

One of the relatively unsung heroines of the Book of Mormon, Sariah was the wife of Father Lehi[1] and the mother of the sons who became the forefathers of two nations of people—the Nephites and Lamanites. Sariah left the comforts of her home in Jerusalem, as well as the majority of her possessions, to follow her prophet-husband into the wilderness, where she faced harsh conditions and endured much suffering.

She is first mentioned as her son Nephi[1] lists the members of his father's family who initially accompanied him into the wilderness (1 Nephi 2:5). A critical point for her came when her husband sent her sons back to Jerusalem to obtain the plates of brass. She complained against her husband, fearing her sons had perished. However, she was comforted by the counsel of her husband and "was exceedingly glad" when her sons returned successfully from their mission. This experience gave her the assurance that her husband was acting by divine direction, and she testified of that truth (1 Nephi 5:1–8).

She was later seen in vision by her husband as one who willingly responded to the invitation to come and partake of the fruit of the tree of life (1 Nephi 8:14–16).

While little is written of her in our present edition of the Book of Mormon, she was one who behind the scenes supported her husband in his divinely appointed calling. And, in spite of the rebellion of Laman[1] and Lemuel, it is evident from the lives of Sam, Nephi[1], Jacob[2], and Joseph[3] that Sariah taught her children proper principles. The lack of references to Sariah could be considered in light of two facts.

First, the culture of the times did not give as much "press coverage" to the women as it did the men. And second, the book of Lehi, which was contained in the 116 pages of lost manuscript, focused more on the *history* of Lehi[1] and Sariah's family and day-to-day experiences than does the present record found in the forepart of the Book of Mormon.

A fitting tribute was paid to Sariah by President Gordon B. Hinckley (1910–), who named her as one of "the greatest characters of scripture" (*Ensign,* November 2004, 83).

SATAN

This is one of the names by which the devil is known and appears throughout the Book of Mormon as well as in the other Standard Works of the Church. It is a formal Hebrew title for the devil and means the slanderer, or he who is the adversary or the opponent of the Lord.

We look forward to that future

day when "Satan shall have power over the hearts of the children of men no more" (2 Nephi 30:18).

See also Devil; Dragon; Evil One; Lucifer; Perdition, Son of; Son of the Morning.

SAVIOR

One of the sacred, descriptive titles of Jesus Christ is that of Savior. Near the beginning of his ministry as one of the Lord's prophets, Father Lehi[1] taught that "a prophet would the Lord God raise up among the Jews—even a Messiah, or, in other words, a Savior of the world" (1 Nephi 10:4). Some six hundred years later, "an angel of the Lord" would announce to the humble shepherds in the fields near Bethlehem the "good tidings of great joy, which shall be to all people" that a Holy Child was "born this day in the city of David, a Savior who is Christ the Lord" (JST Luke 2:8–11).

Almost two millennia later, then as a resurrected, glorified Being, this former Babe of Bethlehem would declare to the Prophet Joseph Smith, "Behold, I am Jesus Christ, the Savior of the world" (D&C 43:34).

"He is the Savior in two senses: first, he saves all mankind from the grip of the grave, for all will be resurrected (2 Ne. 9:6–11; 1 Cor. 15:20–22); second, the Savior saves us from the stain of sin *if* we will repent.

"'He shall not save his people in their sins,' said Amulek. 'Therefore the wicked remain as though there had been no redemption made, except it be the loosing of the bands of death.' (Alma 11:36, 41.)" (Brewster, *Doctrine & Covenants Encyclopedia*, 492).

See also Christ; Christ, Names of; Father, Jesus Christ As; Father of Heaven and Earth; God; Immanuel; Jehovah; Jesse, Stem of; Jesus; Lamb of God; Messiah; Only Begotten of the Father; Prince of Peace; Redeemer; Spirit of the Lord.

SEANTUM

This Nephite member of the abominable band of Gadianton robbers murdered his own brother Seezoram, who was the chief judge (Helaman 9:6). This occurred at a time when many people were gathered to listen to and to contend with Nephi[2], who was praying and calling the wicked to repentance (Helaman 7–8). During the course of his preaching, Nephi[2] announced the murder of their chief judge and even identified the killer as the judge's brother, although the citizens initially did not seem to grasp that piece of information (Helaman 8:27–28). When the judge was found dead, Nephi[2] was then accused of conspiring with another to kill him. Once more he identified the real killer as Seantum and even revealed that they would find blood on the skirts of his cloak. Thus, the murderer was apprehended, although nothing is recorded as to his punishment or fate (Helaman 9:19–38).

SECRET COMBINATIONS
See Gadianton.

SEER, CHOICE
See Choice Seer; Smith, Joseph, Jr.

SEEZORUM
Seezorum was elected chief judge at a time "Gadianton robbers [were] filling the judgment-seats" (Helaman 7:4). Both he and his brother Seantum belonged to that terrorist band of murderers and robbers, which probably led to Seezorum's murder at the hands of his brother (Helaman 8:27–28). This was truly a dark time for the Nephites as they rejected the words of their prophet Nephi[2]. Darkness and wickedness will always flourish when people reject the message and the messengers God has sent to them.

SERAPHIM
Nephi[1] recorded the words of Isaiah[1] where he spoke of seeing seraphim in the presence of the Lord (2 Nephi 16:2, 6–7; Isaiah 6:2, 6–7). "The Book of Mormon provides the correct rendering, 'seraphim.' Seraph is singular and seraphs or seraphim plural. Perhaps these unusual six-winged creatures seen by Isaiah have some association with the strange beasts John the Revelator saw near the throne of God. (Revelation 4:2–10; 5:11–14.) Joseph Smith explained that wings of the latter beasts 'are a representation of power, to move, to act, etc.' (D&C 77:2–4.) The Prophet further stated: 'John heard the words of the beasts giving glory to God, and understood them. God who made the beasts could understand every language spoken by them.' (*TPJS*, 291–92).

"In his dedicatory prayer of the Kirtland Temple, the Prophet pleaded that the Saints might have power to 'mingle our voices with those bright, shining seraphs around thy throne, with acclamations of praise, singing Hosanna to God and the Lamb!' (D&C 109:79.) His description of 'shining seraphs' is consistent with the Hebrew root of *seraph*, which is 'burning.' Thus, seraphs are burning (shining) or fiery beings" (Brewster, *Isaiah Plain & Simple*, 56.)

SETH[1]
This son of Adam and Eve is not mentioned in the Book of Mormon and is only cited here because of his

inclusion in the Triple Combination index as Seth[1], which necessitated identifying the Jaredite man named Seth with the superscript "[2]."

SETH[2]

This Jaredite was the son of Shiblom[1] (also identified as Shiblon) and the father of Ahah (Ether 1:10–11; 11:9–10). The brief reference to him in the translated record does not identify him as a Jaredite king, although both his father and his son were monarchs. The record states that Seth[2] "was brought into captivity, and did dwell in captivity all his days."

Since Seth[2] appears to have been captured at the time of Shiblom's death, and since Seth[2] remained in captivity until Ahah took the throne, and since Ahah was succeeded by Ethem and then Moron, it doesn't appear that Seth[2] was ever monarch himself.

SHARED

Shared was among those who rebelled against the Jaredite King Coriantumr[2]. While the record does not identify him as one of the robbers and murderers belonging to the secret combinations, it is likely that he was associated with that infamous group of terrorists. That band was "fighting against Coriantumr that they might obtain the kingdom" (Ether 13:15, 18).

We do not know what led Shared to a life of violence and wickedness, but we do know he lusted for power. We also know that he was a man possessed of "great anger" (Ether 13:23, 27). These characteristics were certainly key factors in the ensuing "war upon all the face of the land, every man with his band fighting for that which he desired" (Ether 13:25). While Shared was successful in overthrowing Coriantumr[2] once, he was finally defeated and killed (Ether 13:23–30).

SHEARJASHUB

This son of Isaiah[1] is mentioned in the writings Nephi[1] copied from the plates of brass (2 Nephi 17:3; Isaiah 7:3). On the occasion when Isaiah[1] was told by the Lord to meet the king of Judah by Jerusalem's water supply, Isaiah[1] was also instructed to bring Shearjashub with him. His name means "the remnant shall return," and his presence on this occasion may have been a symbolic reminder to the king that the kingdom of Judah, though destined to be destroyed and scattered, would ultimately be restored.

SHEM[1]

This son of Noah[1] is not mentioned in the Book of Mormon and is cited here only because of his inclusion in the Triple Combination index as Shem[1], which necessitated identifying the Nephite military commander Shem with the superscript "[2]."

SHEM[2]

The only mention of Shem[2] is as one of the Nephite military commanders who was killed with his ten thousand during the last great battle that destroyed that civilization around 385 A.D. (Mormon 6:14).

SHEMNON

The single mention of this righteous man is as one of the special twelve disciples whom the resurrected Savior called to preside over His Church in ancient America (3 Nephi 19:4). While the record does speak of the ministry of these special witnesses as a group, it is silent in identifying the individual actions of all but Nephi[3], who was their leader. One does not need specific recognition in order to accomplish good in the world.

See also Disciples, Twelve.

SHEREM

Although many of the numerous dissidents and apostates identified throughout the Book of Mormon were anti-Christs, meaning that they came out in opposition to Christ, His gospel, and His servants, Sherem is one of the more visible of these enemies of God. He openly proclaimed "that there should be no Christ . . . ; and this he did that he might overthrow the doctrine of Christ" (Jacob 7:2). Of significance is that "he was learned [and] . . . could use much flattery, and much power of speech, according to the power of the devil" (Jacob 7:4).

The prophet Nephi[1] had earlier warned of the danger that lies in placing one's trust in the learning of the world while rejecting the wisdom of God:

"O that cunning plan of the evil one! O the vainness, and the frailties, and the foolishness of men! When they are learned they think they are wise, and *they hearken not unto the counsel of God, for they set it aside, supposing they know of themselves,* wherefore, their wisdom is foolishness and it profiteth them not. And they shall perish.

"But to be learned is good *if* they hearken unto the counsels of God" (2 Nephi 9:28–29; emphasis added).

The Lord has counseled us to "seek learning, even by study *and also by faith*" (D&C 88:118; emphasis added).

Learning is not the problem. Forgetting faith is!

Sherem challenged Jacob[2] to a debate, hoping "to shake [him] from the faith," but Jacob[2] declared "I could not be shaken" (Jacob 7:5). Jacob[2] simply confounded his adversary as "the Lord God poured in his Spirit into [Jacob's] soul" (Jacob 7:8). Note that Jacob² did not debate the anti-Christ on the common but fallible grounds of the learning of the world, but fought him armed with the "sword of the Spirit, which is the word of God" (Ephesians 6:17).

In the futility of his position, Sherem finally asked for a "sign," a physical show of God's power. Jacob's response was that he would not succumb to a carnival-like sideshow to satisfy the whims of a wicked man. However, Jacob² indicated that if it was God's will, Sherem would be smitten. The evil man immediately "fell to the earth," where "he was nourished for the space of many days" (Jacob 7:13–15).

When he had regained a little strength, Sherem publicly confessed his falsehoods. He admitted "he had been deceived by the power of the devil" and "lied unto God," whereupon he then "gave up the ghost" (Jacob 7:16–20).

See also Anti-Christ; Teachers, False.

SHEZ¹

Shez¹ was a Jaredite king who was the son of Heth and the father of Riplakish (Ether 1:24–25). He came to power following a period of terrible famine that had been brought upon

by the wickedness of the people (Ether 9:28–35).

Unlike his predecessor, who embraced the secret combinations of wickedness the devil had established anciently (Ether 9:26), Shez¹ was a righteous leader who "began to build up again a broken people" and establish "a righteous kingdom" (Ether 10:1–2). He walked "in the ways of the Lord" and lived "to an exceedingly old age" before dying (Ether 10:3–4).

SHEZ²

The brief mention of this man in the Jaredite history is not a happy one. Although raised in a righteous home, Shez² rebelled against his father. He was ultimately killed by a robber "because of his exceeding riches" (Ether 10:3).

We are reminded of the Lord's counsel to "lay not up for yourselves treasures upon earth, where moth and rust doth corrupt, and thieves break through and steal; but lay up for yourselves treasures in heaven, where neither moth nor rust doth corrupt, and where thieves do not break through nor steal" (3 Nephi 13:19–20).

SHIBLOM¹

This Jaredite king was the son of Com (Ether 11:3–4). Because of what appears to be a typographical mistake in the original manuscript, Shiblom[1] is identified as "Shiblon" in the listing of Jaredite kings (Ether 1:12). For our purposes we shall consider "Shiblom" to be the correct spelling.

Shiblom[1] succeeded his father as king but was troubled in his reign by the rebellion of his unnamed brother, whose wickedness included killing the prophets (Ether 11:4–5). This was a period of "great calamity" and "great destruction" for the Jaredites (Ether 11:6). "And they hearkened not unto the voice of the Lord, because of their wicked combinations" (Ether 11:7). Towards the end of his reign, "the people began to repent," but Shiblom[1] was killed and his son Seth[2] placed in captivity (Ether 11:8–9).

SHIBLOM[2]

Shiblom[2] was one of the many Nephite military commanders who with their ten thousand troops were killed at the final battle of the Nephite civilization in 385 A.D. (Mormon 6:14).

SHIBLON

The name Shiblon appears under three headings in the Book of Mormon. It is used once to identify a Jaredite king (Ether 1:11–12), who thereafter is identified as Shiblom[1] (Ether 11:3–9). The name is also used as a Nephite coin (Alma 11:15, 19). However, its main use is as the name

of one of Alma[2] the Younger's sons (Alma 31:7).

Shiblon accompanied his father on a mission around 74 B.C. Little is known of his mission experience other than that he patiently bore "bonds" and was even "stoned for the word's sake" (Alma 38:4).

Shiblon was later cited as a good example of steadiness, faithfulness, and diligence in keeping the commandments of God (Alma 39:1). The grateful father Alma[2] commended his son, saying, "I trust that I shall have great joy in you, because of your steadiness and your faithfulness unto God; for as you have commenced in your youth to look to the Lord your God, even so I hope that you will continue in keeping his commandments; for blessed is he that endureth to the end" (Alma 38:2).

Shiblon's example is a reminder to youth that the time to set one's feet on the path of righteousness— spiritual safety—is in one's youth.

This faithful son did not get the news coverage that his older brother, Helaman[2], did, but he was a steady, consistent contributor to the cause of Christ. One does not need center stage nor to be prominently mentioned in bold headlines to make a difference for good in the world. Shiblon's life of steady service points out that not all role models and true heroes receive deserved and acclaimed recognition!

Shiblon's continued righteousness was evident when he was later entrusted with the sacred records. "And he was a just man, and he did walk uprightly before God; and he did observe to do good continually, to keep the commandments of the Lord his God" (Alma 63:1–2). Before he died around 53 B.C., Shiblon conferred the sacred records on his nephew Helaman[3] (Alma 63:11–12).

SHIZ

If one were to make a record of examples of unrelenting wickedness and cruelty in the Book of Mormon, certainly the name of the Jaredite Shiz would have to be listed. He was the brother of Lib, a murderer and member of a secret combination who had been killed in battle with the monarch Coriantumr[2] (Ether 14:10, 16–17). Just as Gilead followed his brother Shared in wickedness, so, too, did Shiz follow his brother Lib.

The wickedness of Shiz knew no bounds, as he slew "both women and children, and he did burn the cities" (Ether 14:17). His terrorist tactics created great fear among the people as he carried out what today might be called a "scorched earth" approach to warfare (Ether 14:18). The war he commenced was so devastating that "the whole face of the land was covered with the bodies of the dead," the stench of which troubled the survivors "day and night" (Ether 14:21–23).

There were numerous points at which Shiz made horribly wrong choices, but two seem to stand out in testimony of his evil nature. Shiz received a conciliatory letter from Coriantumr[2], in which the king offered to give up the throne if Shiz would cease the slaughter of the people. However, Shiz said the only way he would spare the lives of the people would be if Coriantumr[2] would give himself up to be personally slain by Shiz's sword. Coriantumr[2] refused and the war continued (Ether 15:4–6).

After much continued bloodshed, Coriantumr[2] wrote a second letter to Shiz. But "the Spirit of the Lord had ceased striving with them, and Satan had full power over the hearts of the people; for they were given up unto the hardness of their hearts, and the blindness of their minds that they might be destroyed; wherefore they went again to battle" (Ether 15:18–19).

One of the driving forces of the continued war was the *anger* which Shiz, Coriantumr[2], and all the people allowed to consume them, for "they were *drunken with anger,* even as a man who is drunken with wine" (Ether 15:22; emphasis added). This "drunkenness," and their over-all wickedness, led to the total destruction of the nation, with Shiz being slain by Coriantumr[2] (Ether 15:29–31).

SHULE

This Jaredite king was the son of Kib and the father of Omer (Ether 1:30–31). Shule was born during the captivity of his father. He "became mighty as to the strength of a man; and he was also mighty in judgment" (Ether 7:8).

Shule raised an army that successfully defeated King Corihor[1], an older brother of Shule who had imprisoned their father (Ether 7:8–9). The grateful father "bestowed upon [Shule] the kingdom; therefore he began to reign in the stead of his father" (Ether 7:10).

Shule was a righteous leader and very forgiving; he even gave his repentant brother Corihor[1] "power in his kingdom" (Ether 7:11–13). One of Corihor's sons, Noah[2], later rebelled against both his father and King Shule and obtained a portion of the kingdom. The rebel eventually succeeded in placing Shule in captivity and was about to kill him when Shule's sons slew Noah[2] and restored their father to the "throne in his own kingdom" (Ether 7:14–18). The son of Noah[2] retained control in his part of the kingdom, and thus "the

country was divided; and there were two kingdoms" (Ether 7:20). Shule later defeated this upstart son and the kingdom was reunited.

To his credit, Shule protected the prophets against those who sought to mock and revile them, which helped to bring the people to repentance (Ether 7:23–26). "And there were no more wars in the days of Shule; and he remembered the great things that the Lord had done for his fathers in bringing them across the great deep into the promised land; wherefore he did execute judgment in righteousness all his days" (Ether 7:27).

Shule was succeeded as king by his righteous son Omer (Ether 8:1).

SMITH, HYRUM

Hyrum Smith is not mentioned by name in the ancient text which comprised the Book of Mormon, but he was one of the "few" additional witnesses (Eight Witnesses) to the truthfulness of the Book of Mormon to whom Nephi[1] and undoubtedly Isaiah[1] referred (2 Nephi 27:12–13).

Hyrum Smith not only saw the plates, but he was one of the trusted guardians of the manuscript as it was being printed in Palmyra.

He would later declare, "I thank God that *I felt a determination to die, rather than deny the things which my eyes had seen, which my hands had handled, and which I had borne testimony to*" (*History of the Church,* 4:46; emphasis added).

In the Publisher's Preface to a biography on Hyrum Smith, I wrote the following: "In the annals of history there may be no individual who exceeds Hyrum Smith in absolute integrity of heart and in loyalty to God and His chosen servants. Hyrum was and is an unsung hero who sought neither position nor recognition. He was content to serve in the shadow of and in a supportive role to his younger brother [Joseph Smith, Jr.].

"In a world where men and women jealously compete for position and place, Hyrum Smith was a breath of fresh air. He did not suffer from the elder brother syndrome of spitefulness and jealousy so classically evident in the sons of Jacob, who sold their younger brother Joseph into slavery, or in the elder brothers of Nephi, who so often complained about their young brother's perceived favored status" (Corbett, *Hyrum Smith—Patriarch,* iii-iv).

Just as Joseph Smith Sr. and Lucy Mack Smith had been carefully preselected or foreordained to be the parents of the Prophet Joseph Smith, it is my strongly held conviction that Joseph's older brother Hyrum was similarly foreordained to serve by the Prophet's side.

The Lord needed one who would stand steady in the face of opposing hurricane forces of mobocracy, persecution, and other forms of constant adversity. However, Hyrum was not only to stand in a supportive role but he would also jointly hold the keys of priesthood authority (of course, as *second* elder) with his prophet-brother (see D&C 124:91–95; Brewster, *Prophets, Priesthood Keys, and Succession,* 45–47).

Of the eleven men (the Three and Eight Witnesses) specially selected to provide their living testimonies of the Book of Mormon to the world, Hyrum was the only one to seal his testimony with his blood. He and his prophet-brother Joseph were martyred by a mob in Carthage, Illinois, on June 27, 1844.

It is of interest to note that one of the last things Hyrum did prior to leaving for Carthage and his pending martyrdom was to read from the Book of Mormon. He quoted Ether 12:36–38.

"Hyrum Smith was forty-four years old in February, 1844, and Joseph Smith was thirty-eight in December, 1843; and henceforward their names will be classed among the martyrs of religion; and the reader in every nation will be reminded that the Book of Mormon, and [the] Doctrine and Covenants of the church, cost the best blood of the nineteenth century to bring them forth for the salvation of a ruined world" (D&C 135:6).

"The testators are now dead, and their testament is in force," wrote future President of the Church John Taylor (D&C 135:5).

"The sealing of the testimony through the shedding of blood would not have been complete in the death of the Prophet Joseph Smith alone," said President Joseph Fielding Smith (1876–1972); "it required the death of Hyrum Smith who jointly held the keys of this dispensation. It was needful that these martyrs seal their testimony with their blood, that they 'might be honored and the wicked might be condemned' [D&C 136:39]" (*Doctrines of Salvation,* 1:219).

See also Witnesses, Eight.

SMITH, JOSEPH, JR.

Joseph Smith Jr. was the prophet chosen before the world was to bring forth the Book of Mormon: Another Testament of Jesus Christ. He stood among the "noble and great ones" in premortal councils (Abraham 3:22). His foreordination as a prophet, including his name—Joseph—was foretold by the ancient patriarch and prophet Joseph[1], who was sold by his brothers into Egyptian slavery (2 Nephi 3:6–15; JST Genesis 50:26–33).

Other ancient prophets also foretold of Joseph Smith's future mission. Isaiah[1], for example, foresaw the historical event when a "learned" man, Professor Charles Anthon, would reject the writings of the Book of Mormon because it had been revealed by an angel of God to an "unlearned" man, even the Prophet Joseph Smith (Isaiah 29:11–12; 2 Nephi 27:9–10, 15–22; Joseph Smith—History 1:63–65).

Moroni[2], the last keeper of the sacred Nephite records, wrote to the Prophet Joseph Smith. He commanded him not to touch that portion of the plates which was sealed. Moroni[2] also informed the future translator that he would be supported by the testimony of the Three Witnesses who would be shown the plates (Ether 5).

Jesus Christ Himself made veiled reference to the future mission of the Prophet Joseph Smith, including his martyrdom, during His post-resurrection ministry to the ancient inhabitants of the Americas (3 Nephi 21:9–11; see also footnotes 10 and 11).

Centuries after the prophet Moroni[2] hid the plates containing the Book of Mormon record, he returned as a resurrected angel or messenger of God, appeared to the teenage Joseph Smith, and began the tutoring process that would eventually lead to the translation and publication of this second witness of Jesus Christ (Joseph Smith—History 1:29–54).

The translation process was not without challenges, including the tragic loss of the first 116 pages of translated manuscript known as the Book of Lehi (see D&C 3; 10). Joseph had to be constantly on guard against adversarial attempts to get the plates from him and to destroy the sacred work. Upon the completion of the translation, the plates were returned to the care of the angel Moroni[2].

The Prophet not only translated the ancient Nephite record, but also ancient papyri that contained writings of the patriarch Abraham. Furthermore, as directed by the Lord, Joseph Smith undertook a project of translating or correcting numerous passages in the Bible. This publication, previously known as the Inspired Version of the Bible, is now called the Joseph Smith Translation of the Bible. It has brought a restoration of truths that clarify and enhance the power of this book of scripture revered by the Christian world. The Prophet also received many revelations that are recorded in the Doctrine and Covenants and the Pearl of Great Price. Elder Stephen L Richards (1879–1959) commented on the extent of the Prophet's contributions to scriptural canon by saying, "He produced more scripture, that is, the

revealed word of God, than any other man of whom we have record. Indeed, his total scriptural productions would almost equal those of all others put together" (*Handbook of the Restoration,* 49).

The priesthood of God, which is the authority to act in His name and to administer the saving and exalting ordinances of the gospel, including the keys, was restored to the Prophet Joseph Smith (D&C 13; 27:12; 110:11–16; Joseph Smith—History 1:68–73). The Lord commissioned him to organize "the only true and living church upon the face of the whole earth" (D&C 1:30; 20:1), even The Church of Jesus Christ of Latter-day Saints (D&C 115:4).

Speaking of Joseph's foreordained calling to be the Prophet of the Restoration and the careful tutoring the Lord ensured the Prophet would have, President Brigham Young (1801–1877) declared: "It was decreed in the counsels of eternity, long before the foundations of the earth were laid, that he [Joseph Smith] should be the man, in the last dispensation of this world, to bring forth the word of God to the people, and receive the fulness of the keys and power of the Priesthood of the Son of God. The Lord had his eye upon him, and upon his father, and upon his father's father, and upon their progenitors clear back to Abraham, and from

Abraham to the flood, from the flood to Enoch, and from Enoch to Adam. He has watched that family and that blood as it has circulated from its fountain to the birth of that man. He was foreordained in eternity to preside over this last dispensation" (in *Journal of Discourses*, 7:289–90).

Canonized scripture declares that "Joseph Smith, the Prophet and Seer of the Lord, has done more, save Jesus only, for the salvation of men in this world, than any other man that ever lived in it" (D&C 135:3).

While he, along with his brother Hyrum, died martyrs' deaths, the work he was commissioned to do was complete. It continues to roll forward under the leadership of successor prophets of God, who likewise were foreordained to their sacred callings.

The devil persists in his fruitless efforts to destroy the work of the Prophet Joseph Smith, particularly through futile attempts to defame and discredit both the man and the work he brought about. In this respect, we ponder and take peaceful comfort in the observation of a latter-day Apostle of the Lord Jesus Christ:

"Those who revile Joseph Smith will not change Joseph's status with the Lord (see 2 Nephi 3:8)—merely their own!" (Neal A. Maxwell, *Ensign*, November 1983, 56).

See also Choice Seer.

SMITH, JOSEPH, SR.

Centuries before the birth of Joseph Smith (Sr.) on July 12, 1771, the name that Asael and Mary Duty Smith would give to their newborn son had already been predetermined or foreordained. An ancient seer who bore the name of *Joseph* had prophesied that this child would have his same name and would one day become the father of a son whom he would also name *Joseph* (2 Nephi 3:6, 15).

When God has a great work to perform, He not only is very careful about the individual whom He calls to bring the work about, but He is also very selective in placing His chosen servant among those whom He implicitly trusts. Thus, just as our Heavenly Father carefully selected the carpenter named *Joseph* to be the earthly caregiver of His Divine and Only Begotten Son, Jesus Christ, so, in a similar fashion, God chose Joseph Smith Sr. to be the trusted father of the boy who would be raised up to translate the ancient record that would be "Another Testament of Jesus Christ."

Joseph Smith Sr. was the first one to whom the young Prophet Joseph related the story of the Angel Moroni's visits on the night of September 21, 1823, and a subsequent visit the next morning.

Here, indeed, was a defining

moment. A father of less faith and spiritual stature might have dismissed his son's story as a dream or the effect of a fanciful imagination. However, this foreordained and faithful father responded to his son's testimony by declaring, "My son, these things are of God; take heed that you proceed in all holiness to do His will" (Cannon, *Life of Joseph Smith*, 38).

Thus, Joseph Smith Sr. became literally the second earthly witness to know of the existence of the records that would one day be translated into the Book of Mormon.

A few years later, Joseph Smith Sr. would be chosen to be an *official* witness of the Book of Mormon. He was selected as one of the Eight Witnesses who saw the plates from which the book was translated, but he did not see the angel Moroni[2], which privilege was reserved for the Three Witnesses. A day or two after the Three Witnesses had been shown the gold plates by the angel, Father Smith (as Joseph Smith Sr. was affectionately called by the members of the Church) and seven other selected men were invited by the Prophet Joseph to view the plates. No longer did these men simply *believe* in their existence from a spiritual perspective. Faith was supported by physical evidence and absolute temporal knowledge.

I hasten to add that while this eyewitness account may be considered by a skeptical, scientific-evidence seeking world to be more plausible than "believing without seeing," the experience did not take priority over the depth of the witness Joseph Smith Sr. had already received through the Spirit. As inspired seers have long taught, "Believing is seeing!"

The strength of Father Smith's testimony was powerfully illustrated on one occasion. A man came to the home of Joseph Smith Sr. claiming to have a note from Father Smith's creditors and demanding immediate payment of $14. The Smiths were told that if full payment was not made immediately, Father Smith would go to debtor's prison. Joseph Sr. offered the man $6, all the money he then possessed, and promised to pay the rest as soon as he was able. His wife, Lucy, even offered to give the man her gold jewelry in payment, but the offers were refused.

The evil motives of the creditor then became apparent, as he offered an infamous compromise. "Renounce your testimony of the Book of Mormon and burn all copies of that book in your possession, and I will forgive your full debt. But if not," warned the wicked man, "I shall have the constable who accompanied me here put you in jail."

The faithful father of the Prophet refused the abominable offer, and as a result he spent the next month in jail. Lucy was left to fend for herself and her family during this time, which included an instance of a mob invading their home (Dewey, *Joseph Smith: A Biography*, 81).

The continued faithfulness of Joseph Smith Sr. throughout his life is attested to by a divine declaration of the Lord following the death of this great and good man on September 14, 1840 at the age of sixty-nine: "Joseph Smith, Sen., . . . sitteth with Abraham at his right hand, and blessed and holy is he, for he is mine" (D&C 124:19).

See also Witnesses, Eight.

SMITH, SAMUEL H.

Samuel Smith is not mentioned by name in the ancient text that comprised the Book of Mormon, but he was one of the "few" additional witnesses (Eight Witnesses) to the truthfulness of the Book of Mormon to whom Nephi[1] and undoubtedly Isaiah[1] referred (2 Nephi 27:12–13).

Samuel Harrison Smith, born on March 13, 1808, was the fourth son of Joseph Sr. and Lucy Mack Smith. While visiting the Prophet in Pennsylvania, in May 1829, Samuel was informed "that the Lord was about to commence his latter-day work."

Not being immediately persuaded, Samuel was at a pivotal point that would determine the course for the remainder of his mortal life, and for that matter eternity, would take. On the very day the Aaronic Priesthood was restored to his prophet-brother, Samuel retired to a private place in the woods near the Susquehanna River to pray and "obtain from the Lord wisdom to enable him to judge for himself; the result was that he obtained revelation for himself sufficient to convince him of the truth of the testimony of his brother Joseph" (Smith, *History of Joseph Smith by His Mother*, 337).

As Joseph Smith and Oliver Cowdery were returning from the banks of the Susquehanna River, where the Aaronic Priesthood had just been restored and where each had been baptized by that authority, "they overheard Samuel engaged in secret prayer. Joseph said that he considered that a sufficient testimony of his being a fit subject for baptism; and as they had now received authority to baptize, they spoke to Samuel upon the subject, and he went straightway to the water with them, and was baptized by Oliver Cowdery, he being the third person baptized in the last dispensation" (*History of Joseph Smith by His Mother*, 337).

Just as Samuel was completely immersed in water for the remission of sins, he completely immersed himself in the work of the Restoration. In addition to being selected as one of the Eight Witnesses to the Book of Mormon, he was one of the six original members when The Church of Jesus Christ of Latter-day Saints was organized on April 6, 1830.

Perhaps most notable in his participation in the work of the Restoration is his often referenced title as "the first missionary" of the Church. It was Samuel Smith who shortly after the publication of the Book of Mormon set out on a missionary journey to share the book with potential converts.

There is a lesson of hope to be learned from Samuel's first missionary journey. Samuel did not baptize anyone during that journey, but he did place two copies of the Book of Mormon that had far-reaching effects. The books were given to Phineas Young (a brother to Brigham Young) and to John P. Greene (whose wife Rhoda was a sister to Brigham Young). These two books were eventually "the means of converting a whole neighborhood, including Brigham Young and his family and Heber C. Kimball and his family" (*Ensign,* September 2002, 16).

Many a modern-day missionary has returned from his labors seemingly without measurable results. Yet the seeds planted by a faithful missionary may simply have delayed germination that later will sprout and blossom into full fruit.

It should be comforting to every missionary, and to every person who has faithfully fulfilled a calling in the Lord's kingdom, to reflect upon the words of the Lord to Samuel Smith regarding his missionary labors, where the Lord referred to him as "my servant Samuel H. Smith, with whom I am well pleased" (D&C 61:35).

Little known to most people is the fact that Samuel Smith can also be classified with the martyrs who have given their lives for the cause of Christ. "Along with other members of the family, the Prophet's younger brother, Samuel H. Smith, suffered greatly for his testimony of the Savior and the divine work of his prophet-brother. 'On the day a malicious mob murdered his brothers, Joseph and Hyrum, Samuel was relentlessly pursued by a contingent of that mob. Because of the severe fatigue brought on by that chase, a fever was contracted which, according to John Taylor, "laid the foundation for his death, which took place on the 30th of July [1844]."' . . . Thus, although not felled by bullet or blade, Samuel might also be considered a martyr to the cause of Christ" (Brewster, *Martyrs of the Kingdom,* 83).

See also Witnesses, Eight.

SOLDIER WHO STOOD BY

An unnamed, anonymous Nephite soldier stepped forward at a critical point in the life of Captain Moroni[1] and prevented his potential death. This hero is simply described as "one of Moroni's soldiers," or "the soldier who stood by" (Alma 44:12–13).

At this moment when Captain Moroni's life was in danger this alert and prepared, unnamed soldier stepped forward. He saved his leader from the treachery of the Lamanite military leader Zerahemnah, who had previously surrendered his sword, and then suddenly picked it up and sought to slay Moroni[1]. "The soldier who stood by" disarmed the attacker, and in the process scalped him. Furthermore, "the soldier who stood by" took the severed scalp and, placing it on the point of his sword, held it high in the air, proclaiming: "Even as this scalp has fallen to the earth, which is the scalp of your chief, so shall ye fall to the earth except ye will deliver up your weapons of war and depart with a covenant of peace" (Alma 44:14).

His actions not only saved his righteous leader, but also caused that "there were many" who immediately responded to his challenge and threw down their weapons, agreeing to covenant not to attack the Nephites in the future (Alma 44:15).

Speaking of this unnamed hero in another publication, I wrote: "In a critical and defining moment that meant so much to the cause of freedom, an unnamed soldier displayed his preparation for such a moment. Because he *stood by, ready* to respond, his alertness saved the life of his leader and, perhaps, his people as well" (Brewster, *Defining Moments,* 22; emphasis in original).

See also Zerahemnah.

SOLOMON

This Old Testament figure, king of Israel, is mentioned several times in the Book of Mormon. Nephi[1] built a "temple after the manner of the temple of Solomon save it were not built of so many precious things; for they were not to be found upon the land" (2 Nephi 5:16; cf. 1 Kings 5–8). The opulence of Solomon's temple and kingdom is referred to in the resurrected Lord's sermon to the Nephites (3 Nephi 13:28–29).

Solomon's sin of whoredoms is cited by Jacob[2] when he called the Nephites to repentance for pursuing the same carnal course (Jacob 1:15; 2:23–24). It should be remembered that the transgression of Solomon and David was not in having multiple wives, for the Lord had given them permission to practice polygamy. The sin came in their taking "those things which they received not of [the Lord]" (D&C 132:38). "For if I will, saith the Lord of Hosts, raise up seed unto me, I will command my people; otherwise they shall hearken unto these things" (Jacob 2:30).

Solomon was the son of King David and of Bathsheba, whom David had taken to wife following his murder of her righteous husband, Uriah (2 Samuel 11). Solomon was the second child, and first legitimate child, born to his parents, and "the Lord loved him" (2 Samuel 12:24).

In response to Solomon's personal plea to the Lord to give him "an understanding heart to judge [and] discern" (1 Kings 3:9), "God gave Solomon wisdom and understanding exceeding much" (1 Kings 4:29). The classic example of his wisdom was when he judged rightly between two women, both of whom were claiming to be the mother of an infant (1 Kings 3:16–28).

Sadly, Solomon let sin overpower wisdom and he lost a crown more precious than his earthly one (1 Kings 11). He forgot his spiritual roots and the Source of his wisdom and lost his crown in the "royal courts on high." ("O My Father," *Hymns*, 292.)

SON OF PERDITION
See Perdition, Son of.

SON OF THE MORNING
The title "son of the morning" is used once in the Book of Mormon in connection with Lucifer (2 Nephi 24:12). It is a direct quotation from Isaiah (4:12) and is symbolically comparing the fallen king of Babylon to Lucifer and his ill-fated attempt "to usurp the position and power of God for his own evil ends, for which he and his followers were cast out" (Brewster, *Isaiah Plain & Simple*, 139–40).

The Doctrine and Covenants refers to Lucifer as "a" son of the morning (76:26–27). President George Q. Cannon (1827–1901) observed: "Some have called him 'the' son of the morning, but here it is 'a' son of the morning—one among many, doubtless. This angel was a mighty personage. . . . The [scripture] shows that he occupied a very high position, that he was thought a great deal of and that he was mighty in his sphere. . . . His plan . . . was so plausible and so attractive that out of the whole hosts of heaven one-third accepted his plan and were willing to cast their lot with him" (*Gospel Truth*, 1:4–5).

SONS OF HELAMAN[2]
See Helaman[2], Sons of.

SONS OF MOSIAH[2]
See Mosiah[2], Sons of.

SPIRIT OF THE LORD
The "spirit of the Lord" could refer to the premortal spirit body of

Jesus Christ, in which form He appeared to prophets prior to His mortal birth (Moses 1:1–2). It could also refer to the Light of Christ, which is not a personage (Alma 28:14; Moroni 7:18; D&C 88:7), and to the Holy Ghost, who is a personage of spirit (D&C 130:22).

Nephi[1] was "caught away *in* the Spirit [power, influence] of the Lord" (1 Nephi 11:1; emphasis added) to a mountain top where he was instructed by *the* Spirit of the Lord who "was in the form of a man" (1 Nephi 11:11). There have been differing opinions as to the identity of this "Spirit of the Lord." Some have suggested it was the premortal Jesus Christ, while others have suggested it was the Holy Ghost. In either event, it was a marvelous spiritual experience that provided Nephi with an unparalleled vision not found anywhere else.

The premortal Christ did visit the brother of Jared[2], and the veil was pierced so that he saw the finger of the Lord. The surprised prophet declared, "I knew not that the Lord had flesh and blood," to which the Lord replied, "Because of thy faith thou hast seen that *I shall take upon me flesh and blood*" (Ether 3:6–9; emphasis added). He further stated, "Never have I showed myself unto man whom I have created, for never has man believed in me as thou hast" (Ether 3:15).

Among the many possible meanings behind the Lord's declaration of never having showed Himself to man, Elder Jeffrey R. Holland (1940–) has suggested the following possibilities:

"[One] interpretation of this passage is that the faith of the brother of Jared was so great he saw not only the *spirit* finger and body of the premortal Jesus (which presumably many other prophets had also seen) but also some distinctly more revealing aspect of Christ's body of flesh, blood, and bone. Exactly what insight into the temporal nature of Christ's future body the brother of Jared could have had is not clear, but Jehovah did say to him, 'Because of thy faith thou hast seen that I shall take upon me flesh and blood,' and Moroni said that Christ revealed himself in this instance 'in the likeness of the same body even as he showed himself unto the Nephites.' Some have taken that to mean literally 'the same body' the Nephites would see—a body of flesh and bone. A stronger position would suggest it was only the spiritual likeness of that future body. In emphasizing that this was a spiritual body being revealed and not some special precursor simulating flesh and bone, Jehovah said, 'This body, which ye now behold, is the body of my spirit . . . and even as I appear unto thee to be in the spirit will I appear unto my people in the flesh.' Moroni also affirmed this, saying, 'Jesus showed himself unto this man in the spirit.'

"A final explanation—and in terms of the brother of Jared's faith the most persuasive one—is that Christ was saying to the brother of Jared, 'Never have I showed myself unto man in this manner, without my volition, driven solely by the faith of the beholder.' As a rule, prophets are invited into the presence of the Lord, are bidden to enter his presence by him and only with his sanction. The brother of Jared, on the other hand, seems to have thrust himself through the veil, not as an unwelcome guest but perhaps technically as an uninvited one" (*Christ and the New Covenant*, 22–23).

See also Holy Ghost; Holy Spirit.

SPOKESMAN

Joseph[1], the seer who was sold into slavery by his brothers, prophesied of the future mission of Moses to deliver the children of Israel out of bondage (2 Nephi 3:9–10). He prophesied, however, that Moses would not be "mighty in speaking" and therefore the Lord would "make a spokesman for him" (2 Nephi 3:17).

Aaron[1], the brother of Moses, was appointed by the Lord to be that spokesman (Exodus 4:10–16).

Joseph[1] of old also prophesied that the Lord would raise up one of his descendants to be a spokesman for the writings of another of his descendants (2 Nephi 3:18). Elder Bruce R. McConkie (1915–1985) provided the following insightful explanation as to the identity of both the writer and the spokesman that would come from "the fruit of [Joseph's] loins":

"The missions and labors and names of Moses, Aaron, and Joseph Smith were all revealed to our ancient father Joseph. Moses was named as the one who would deliver Israel from Egyptian bondage and unto whom the Lord would give his law. However, his tongue would not be loosed so as to make him mighty in speaking. Joseph Smith is described as the seer who would be like unto Joseph of old and who would bring salvation unto the Lord's people. . . . Aaron is identified as the spokesman for Moses in that he would proclaim the law, given to his younger brother, Moses, by revelation.

"That, in this setting of one person writing the Lord's law and another proclaiming it, the Lord said to Joseph of old: 'I will raise up unto the fruit of thy loins; and I will make for him a spokesman.' As Moses wrote and Aaron proclaimed the law given in the Old World, so someone in the New World, someone of the seed of Joseph, would write the Lord's law, and yet another, a spokesman, would declare it. In this case the writer and the spokesman are not identified by name; rather, we are left, based on our knowledge of what has transpired in this and previous dispensations, to identify those whose missions were of such import as to have them revealed thousands of years before the events transpired. Mormon wrote the Book of Mormon, quoting, condensing, and summarizing from many ancient records as the Spirit directed. And Joseph Smith translated the ancient word by the gift and power of God and proclaimed it to all men, and to the seed of Joseph in particular, as the mind and will and voice of Him by whom salvation comes.

"With this in mind, note these words of the Lord: 'And I, behold, I will give unto him [Mormon] that he shall write the writing of the fruit of thy loins [the Nephites], unto the fruit of thy loins [the Lamanites]; and the spokesman of thy loins [Joseph Smith] shall declare it.' That is, Mormon wrote the Book of Mormon, but what he wrote was taken from the writings of the Nephite prophets; and these writings, compiled into one book, were translated by Joseph Smith and sent forth by him unto the Lamanites unto whom, as the title page of the Book of Mormon attests, they were originally written. And further, they are sent forth to all the seed of Joseph, whether in the Lamanite branch of Israel or not.

"'And the words which he [Mormon] shall write shall be the words which are expedient in my wisdom should go forth unto the fruit of thy loins.' They were selected by inspiration, and they contain that portion of the word that is designed to bring fallen Israel again into the true sheepfold, where they will be taught the deeper doctrines, including the mysteries of the kingdom. 'And it shall be as if the fruit of thy loins [the Nephites] had cried unto them [their Lamanite brethren, in particular] from the dust; for I know their faith.' Many were the ancient Book of Mormon prophets who pled with the Lord that the gospel might go in due course and in his providences to the remnant of Lehi's seed.

"'And they [the Nephites] shall cry from the dust [for as a nation they have been destroyed and have no living voice with which to speak]; yea, even repentance unto their brethren even after many generations have gone by them. And it shall come to pass that their cry [in the Book of Mormon] shall go, even according to the simpleness of their words. Because of their faith their words [in the Book of Mormon] shall proceed forth out of my mouth'—the Book of Mormon is the word of the Lord; it is as though the words fell from his own lips—'unto their brethren [the Lamanites] who are the fruit of thy [Joseph's] loins; and the weakness of their words will I make strong in their faith, unto the remembering of my covenant which I made unto thy fathers.' (2 Nephi 3:4–21.) With Joseph's fathers—Abraham, Isaac, and Jacob—the Lord covenanted that in them and in their seed all generations shall be blessed. These blessings are now available to the seed of Joseph because of the coming forth of the Book of Mormon and the restoration of the gospel" (McConkie, *A New Witness for the Articles of Faith,* 425–26).

Ultimately, it is the power of the Holy Ghost that gives spiritual substance to whatever is spoken, "for when a man speaketh by the power of the Holy Ghost the power of the Holy Ghost carrieth it unto the hearts of the children of men" (2 Nephi 33:1).

The humblest servant of the Lord (leader, teacher, missionary, Church member) can speak and bear testimony with "*power* and authority" (Mosiah 13:6; emphasis added). And when one speaks and another hears by the "*power* of the Holy Ghost" (1 Nephi 10:17; emphasis added),

"the truth is woven into the very fibre and sinews of the body [of the listener] so that it cannot be forgotten" (Smith, *Doctrines of Salvation,* 1:48).

See also Aaron[1]; Witnesses, Many.

STEM OF JESSE

The writings of Isaiah[1] as recorded in the Book of Mormon foretell that a rod "shall come forth . . . out of the *stem* of Jesse, and a *branch* shall grow out of his roots" (2 Nephi 21:1; Isaiah 11:1; emphasis added). Christ is the One spoken of in this verse as the *Stem* (D&C 113:1–2); and He is also the *Branch,* the Messianic King David, who was prophesied to come forth in the last days (see Jeremiah 23:5). Christ is a descendant of Jesse, who was the father of King David (Ruth 4:17; Matthew 1:5–6). The "rod," identified elsewhere in this commentary, is the Prophet Joseph Smith.

See also Rod Out of the Stem of Jesse.

STRIPLING WARRIORS

See Helaman[2], Sons of.

T

TABEAL

The single mention of Tabeal is in the writings of Isaiah[1] found in the Book of Mormon (2 Nephi 17:6; Isaiah 7:6). Rezin, king of Syria, and Pekah, king of the northern kingdom of Israel, conspired to attack the southern kingdom of Judah, where they intended to install a puppet king, "the son of Tabeal," on the conquered throne. It is of interest to note the lack of respect the intended conquerors had for this puppet king, for they did not even refer to him by name but only as "the *son* of Tabeal."

TABEAL, SON OF

See Tabeal.

TEACHERS, FALSE

While the specific title "false teachers" appears only twice in holy writ (2 Nephi 28:12; 2 Peter 2:1), the appellation applies to all who teach falsehoods and seek to lead the children of our Father in Heaven astray. Before they repented, Alma[2] and the sons of Mosiah[2] were false teachers who sought deliberately to "lead astray the people of the Lord" (Mosiah 27:10). Obviously the anti-Christs Sherem (Jacob 7) and Korihor (Alma 30) were classic examples of false teachers.

The Apostle Paul warned of a time of apostasy when people "will not endure sound doctrine; but after their own lusts shall they heap to themselves teachers, having itching ears; and they shall turn away their ears from the truth, and shall be turned unto fables" (2 Timothy 4:3–4). He warned, "from such turn away" (2 Timothy 3:5).

"'Having itching ears' describes the false teachers in this English translation, but in Greek the participle can only modify 'they.' That is, Christian believers (the topic of Timothy's instructions) will have fickle ears for new teachers that please them. The result is simply corruption of the Christian gospel. . . . Every false doctrine is brought by a false teacher" (Richard Lloyd Anderson, *Ensign*, August 1976, 52).

Latter-day Saints have been frequently counseled to follow the living prophet and those whom he has authorized to serve and teach in the kingdom of God on earth. Under the direction of the First Presidency and the Twelve Apostles, stake and mission presidents are called and set apart with proper priesthood authority to administer their areas of stewardship. They in turn call and give presiding priesthood authority to bishops, branch presidents, and other priesthood leaders to administer in their stewardships. These priesthood leaders then by inspiration call, set apart, and oversee the work of priesthood and auxiliary leaders and teachers, who each function within their stewardships. The kingdom of God is one of order, for "God is not the author of confusion" (1 Corinthians 14:33).

The basic principles governing teaching in the Church can be found in the following scriptures:

"I say unto you, that it shall not be given to any one to go forth to preach my gospel, or to build up my church, except he be ordained by some one who has authority, and it is known to the church that he has authority and has been regularly ordained by the heads of the church" (D&C 42:11).

"And this is the ensample unto them, that they shall speak as they are moved upon by the Holy Ghost" (D&C 68:3).

"And the Spirit shall be given unto you by the prayer of faith; and if ye receive not the Spirit ye shall not teach" (D&C 42:14).

Spiritual and doctrinal safety for members of The Church of Jesus Christ of Latter-day Saints lies in following the counsel of the Apostle Paul: "But continue thou in the things which thou hast learned and hast been assured of, *knowing of whom thou hast learned them*" (2 Timothy 3:14; emphasis added.)

See also Prophets, False.

TEANCUM

This great patriot and Nephite military commander was feared by his enemies and loved by his troops. He served during the war years that were initially precipitated by the rebellion of the traitor Morianton[2] and his fellow dissidents. In the ensuing battle, Teancum slew the wicked Morianton (Alma 50:35).

A new group of dissidents soon raised its ugly head, this time led by the rebel Amalickiah, who joined forces with the Lamanites in attacking his countrymen. Teancum defeated the invaders in a battle and then sneaked into the enemy camp, where he killed their evil leader without being detected (Alma 51:29–36). There followed a few victories for the Nephite armies, but the overall war continued for several more years (Alma 52).

When Captain Moroni[1] returned to the capital city to assist the chief judge in putting down yet another rebellion, he left the trusted Teancum and Lehi[3] in charge of the ongoing battles with the Lamanites (Alma 61:15).

Still later, Teancum became "exceedingly angry" with the apostate leader of the Lamanite armies and "in his anger" sneaked into their camp in an effort to kill him. However, while he was successful in slaying the wicked leader, he was caught before he could escape and was killed (Alma 62:35–36).

While Teancum was "a man who had fought valiantly for his country, yea, a true friend to liberty" (Alma 62:37), perhaps his anger clouded his judgment of the potential risk of his foray into the enemy camp, which led to his death. There is surely a lesson to be learned from this experience. When anger overtakes one, regardless of the circumstances, rash actions can lead to terrible consequences.

"He that is slow to anger is better than the mighty; and he that ruleth his spirit than he that taketh a city" (Proverbs 16:32).

TEN LOST TRIBES

See Israel, Lost Tribes of.

TEOMNER

This Nephite military leader first appears on the scene about 63 B.C., serving under the direction of Helaman² (Alma 58:16). He and his troops were part of a successful plan to lure a Lamanite army out of their strongholds and secure them (Alma 58:16–23). This event is the only mention of him in the current record.

THREE NEPHITE DISCIPLES

One of the most intriguing stories of the Book of Mormon is the account of the three Nephite disciples who sought to have their lives extended so they could continue in their special ministry. When the resurrected Lord visited ancient America, He chose Nephi³ and eleven others to be His special witnesses and priesthood leaders among those people (3 Nephi 11:18–22; 12:1–2; 18:36–37). They were specifically charged to "testify that ye have seen me, and that ye know that I am" (3 Nephi 12:2). In other words, they were to be "special witnesses" of the *living* Christ.

Following His brief ministry among these ancient people, the Savior invited the twelve to express their desires to Him before He returned to be with His Father. Nine of the twelve asked that when they had "lived unto the age of man," concluding their earthly ministry, they could "speedily come unto [Him] in [His] kingdom."

Christ granted their desire, saying this would occur when they reached the age of "seventy and two years" (3 Nephi 28:1–3).

The remaining three "sorrowed

in their hearts, for they durst not speak unto him the thing which they desired" (3 Nephi 28:5). However, nothing can be withheld from the Son of God, and He knew their unspoken desire was the same as that which His Apostle John had desired of Him—to remain in mortality and continue in the special ministry. He granted their deep desire and promised that they would "never taste of death" but would "be changed in the twinkling of an eye from mortality to immortality" at the time of His Second Coming (3 Nephi 28:7–8). Subsequently, these three were given special powers that placed them in a paradisiacal state where they were not subject to death, sickness, pain, or sorrow "save it be for the sins of the world" (3 Nephi 28:4–9, 36–40).

In later years, when disbelievers sought to imprison, bury, burn, or otherwise kill them, these three disciples escaped without harm (3 Nephi 28:19–22). When the state of wickedness among the people reached such terrible depths, the Lord did not allow them to continue serving openly among the people. Both Mormon[2] and Moroni[2] had the privilege of seeing and being ministered to by these three special disciples hundreds of years after the three were transfigured (3 Nephi 28:26; Mormon 8:10–11).

The prophet-historian Mormon[2] was about to record the names of the three, "but the Lord forbade" (3 Nephi 28:25). However, he did provide the following prophecy regarding the three Nephite disciples:

"And behold they will be among the Gentiles, and the Gentiles shall know them not.

"They will also be among the Jews, and the Jews shall know them not.

"And it shall come to pass, when the Lord seeth fit in his wisdom that they shall minister unto all the scattered tribes of Israel, and unto all nations, kindreds, tongues and people, and shall bring out of them unto Jesus many souls, that their desire may be fulfilled, and also because of the convincing power of God which is in them.

"And they are as the angels of God, and if they shall pray unto the Father in the name of Jesus they can show themselves unto whatsoever man it seemeth them good.

"Therefore, great and marvelous works shall be wrought by them, before the great and coming day when all people must surely stand before the judgment-seat of Christ;

"Yea even among the Gentiles shall there be a great and marvelous work wrought by them, before that judgment day" (3 Nephi 28:27–32).

Through the years many anecdotal stories (which may more accurately be characterized as "urban legends") have circulated regarding the disciples commonly called "the Three Nephites." While according to Mormon's prophecy there obviously have been true appearances of these special three disciples, there have also been unsubstantiated, sensational, and false claims of such appearances. In this respect, it is well to keep in mind a general principle pertaining to true revelation. It is given for the specific blessing of an individual or people and should be spoken of with great care, even divine permission.

Perhaps the words of a newly called Apostle provide the guidelines for one who might have been privileged—for God's purposes—to be visited by not only the three Nephite disciples but any heavenly messenger. Said Elder Boyd K. Packer (1924–) regarding his call to the Quorum of the Twelve:

"Occasionally during the past year I have been asked a question. Usually it comes as a curious, almost an idle, question about the qualifications to stand as a witness for Christ. The question they ask is, 'Have you seen Him?'

"That is a question that I have never asked of another. I have not asked that question of my brethren in the Quorum, thinking that it would be so sacred and so personal that one would have to have some special in-

spiration, indeed, some authorization, even to ask it.

"There are some things just too sacred to discuss. We know that as it relates to the temples. In our temples, sacred ordinances are performed; sacred experiences are enjoyed. And yet we do not, because of the nature of them, discuss them outside those sacred walls.

"It is not that they are secret, but they are sacred; not to be discussed, but to be harbored and to be protected and regarded with the deepest of reverence" (*Ensign,* June 1971, 87).

TIMOTHY

Timothy was called as one of the twelve special disciples whom the resurrected Christ called to lead His Church in ancient America. Timothy was the brother of Christ's chief disciple, Nephi[3], and had experienced the miracle of having been raised from the dead through the priesthood power of his righteous brother (3 Nephi 19:4). Timothy had been stoned to death by the wicked in the tumultuous period that preceded Christ's visit to ancient America (3 Nephi 7:19).

For His divine purposes, the Lord allows some to be raised from the dead or from beds of affliction while others are allowed to die or suffer.

Timothy was raised from the dead to continue a yet to be completed mission, while Abinadi and Joseph Smith, for example, were allowed to be slain when their divinely designated missions were complete. Again, for the Lord's divine purposes, one such as Elder Neal A. Maxwell (1926–2004) received a brief extension of his life or what he called "a delay en route" when he was suffering from the death grips of cancer (*Ensign*, November 1997, 22).

In the Lord's eternal perspective, and *always* doing that which is best for the individual, He responds to prayerful and priesthood petitions offered in behalf of His children. "And if they die they shall die unto me," He declared, "and if they live they shall live unto me" (D&C 42:44).

See also Disciples, Twelve.

TUBALOTH

The single mention of this Lamanite king who lived around 51 B.C. was when he appointed the apostate Coriantumr³ to be the leader of his invading army in the land of the Nephites (Helaman 1:16–17). Tubaloth was the son of the Nephite apostate Ammoron, who was the brother of the treacherous Amalickiah, who had brought so much suffering and death among the people (Alma 52:3).

"And thus we see," to borrow a frequent Book of Mormon phrase, how the sins of the fathers continue to be perpetuated by their posterity!

TWELVE APOSTLES

See Apostles, Twelve.

TWELVE DISCIPLES

See Disciples, Twelve.

— U —

URIAH THE PRIEST

This man is mentioned in the writings of Isaiah[1] copied from the plates of brass onto the Nephite record (2 Nephi 18:1–2; Isaiah 8:1). Uriah the priest was one of two men the prophet Isaiah[1] chose to witness the prophecy found in the inscription of his son's name on a tablet. (The son's name was Maher-shalal-hash-baz, which means "Destruction is imminent.") The priest's name is spelled with a "j" (Urijah) in earlier writings in the Old Testament (2 Kings 16:10–16). He worked as a priest in the temple at Jerusalem.

See also Maher-shalal-hash-baz.

W

WHITMER, CHRISTIAN

While the Three Witnesses to the Book of Mormon have received much notoriety, less visible, but certainly key in the Lord's law of witnesses (D&C 6:28), were the Eight Witnesses. Christian Whitmer, the oldest of the five Whitmer sons (born January 18, 1798), was one of these witnesses. The Eight Witnesses did not see the Angel Moroni² or hear the voice of the Lord, as did the Three Witnesses, but they did see and handle the gold plates from which the Book of Mormon was translated.

Although Christian Whitmer is the first name listed among the Eight Witnesses to the Book of Mormon, he is probably the least known among this select group of men. He was baptized shortly after the Church was organized in 1830 and followed the Latter-day Saints in their moves to Ohio and Missouri, courageously suffering persecution from marauding mobs.

He served as a member of the first high council organized in Missouri. However, his service and his life were both cut short when he died on November 27, 1835, from a painful growth on his leg.

The life and works of Christian Whitmer occupy very little space in the history books, but his faithfulness to the end is noteworthy and a monument to his character. When thinking of this man, it is well to ponder the words of Elder Neal A. Maxwell (1926–2004): "Greatness is not measured by coverage in column inches, either in newspapers or in the scriptures" (*Ensign*, May 1978, 10).

See also Witnesses, Eight.

WHITMER, DAVID

Centuries before David Whitmer (1805–1888) was born, prophets foretold of the special calling that would go to "three witnesses" who would testify of the truthfulness of the record that was to become known as the Book of Mormon (2 Nephi 27:12; Ether 5:3–4). David was to be one of those special witnesses. He would join his friend and future brother-in-law, Oliver Cowdery, along with a well-to-do farmer named Martin Harris in etching their names indelibly in the annals of history as the Three Witnesses.

The paths of David Whitmer and

Oliver Cowdery crossed through a divine chain of events that was far from coincidental. Just as the Lord placed Amulek in the path of Alma² the Younger (Alma 8:14–22) for His divine purposes, so a seemingly chance meeting between two strangers on the streets of Palmyra one day led to a fast friendship between David and Oliver.

The result of that bond was that at a critical time in Joseph Smith's efforts to find a haven where he could safely work on the translation of the Book of Mormon, such a place was found on a farm in Fayette, New York, at the home of Peter Whitmer Sr.

Harassment had become so disruptive in Harmony, Pennsylvania, that the Prophet was in desperate need of a new location where he and his scribe, Oliver Cowdery, could work without interruption. Oliver wrote to his newfound friend, David Whitmer, and asked if it would be possible for the Whitmers to not only share their home for such a purpose, but to come to Harmony and provide the transportation for the move.

David's father, Peter Whitmer Sr., felt impressed to grant the request, but he reminded his son that certain farmwork had to be accomplished before he could make the trip from Fayette to Harmony.

The very next day, when David went to plow the fields, he discovered

five to seven acres had already been mysteriously and miraculously taken care of during the night. Returning to the fields the following day to apply fertilizer, David discovered this task had already been completed. His sister, Catherine Page, told him that on the previous day she had watched "three strangers . . . with great skill and speed" spread the fertilizer. With the work completed, David's father said, "There must be an overruling hand in this, and I think you [had] better go down to Pennsylvania" (interview of Joseph F. Smith and Orson Pratt with David Whitmer, as reported in the *Millennial Star* [December 9, 1878] 40:772).

The miracle of the plowed and fertilized fields was soon followed by what David Whitmer would surely consider further faith-promoting miracles.

At the conclusion of his three-day trip from Fayette to Harmony, David was surprised to find the Prophet Joseph and Oliver Cowdery walking out to meet him, as if they had anticipated his arrival at that very moment. David later bore testimony of the spiritual significance of that experience. Said he, "Oliver told me that Joseph had informed him when I started from home, where I had stopped the first night, how I read the sign at the tavern, where I stopped the second night, etc., and that I would be there that day before dinner" (*Millennial Star* 40:772).

An additional miraculous manifestation took place during the return trip from Harmony to Fayette. During the journey, they met "a very pleasant, nice-looking old man" who greeted them in a friendly manner. He declined their invitation to ride with them saying, "No, I am going to Cumorah" (*Millennial Star* 40:772). This was the first time David had ever heard the name *Cumorah*. He asked the Prophet Joseph for an explanation of the encounter and was told the stranger David had just met was Moroni[2]. The Prophet further explained that Moroni[2] was carrying the Book of Mormon plates, which Joseph had given him for temporary safe keeping.

The Prophet Joseph soon received a revelation promising David the privilege of being one of the Three Witnesses to the Book of Mormon (D&C 17).

David's testimony, together with the other witnesses to the Book of Mormon, has been published in tens of millions of copies of that sacred record, which since 1830 have "flooded the earth."

Although David Whitmer would later lose his allegiance to the Church in which he was one of the charter members, he had moments of courage in which he bore strong witness to the truthfulness of the Book of Mormon in the face of danger and death.

During the dark days of the marauding mobs in Missouri, David was among other Church leaders who were taken prisoner and told they would never see their families again. The men were taken to the public square in Independence at bayonet point, where they were stripped and covered with tar and feathers.

"The commanding officer then called twelve of his men, and ordering them to cock their guns and present them at the prisoners' breasts, and to be ready to fire when he gave the word,—he addressed the prisoners, threatening them with instant death, unless they denied the book of Mormon and confessed it to be a fraud; at the same time adding, that if they did so, they might enjoy the privileges of citizens. David Whitmer, hereupon, lifted up his hands and bore witness that the Book of Mormon was the Word of God. The mob then let them go" (quoted in *Ensign,* February 1989, 38).

Of this momentous experience, David would later recount: "The testimony I gave to that mob made them fear and tremble, and I escaped from them" (Journal History, 23 August 1883; quoted in *Ensign,* August 1979, 38).

Despite his initial faithfulness, perhaps the persecution suffered in the trying days of Missouri became too much for David Whitmer. What did cause this once stellar pillar in the Church to slide from divine favor to his excommunication from the Church on April 13, 1838?

A review of history indicates David Whitmer fell prey to pride, which Elder Boyd K. Packer (1924–) has identified as "the most deadly spiritual virus" (*Ensign*, May 1989, 59). David's involvement in leadership had been very prominent in the early years of the Church. He was called to preside over the Saints in Missouri while the Prophet Joseph was still in Kirtland. For a brief period of time, July through December 1834, the Prophet Joseph had even designated David Whitmer as his successor in the event something should happen to him (Brewster, *Doctrine & Covenants Encyclopedia*, 631). Unfortunately, David saw himself on a par with Joseph Smith and refused to accept the Prophet's counsel, or that of other designated priesthood leaders.

His rebellion led to his excommunication. He unsuccessfully sought to gain followers in his efforts to foster a new church, and he never returned to "the only true and living church" (D&C 1:30).

To his credit, and in spite of his disaffection from Joseph Smith and his successors in the leadership of The Church of Jesus Christ of Latter-day Saints, David did remain firm in his witness of the divine origin and truthfulness of the Book of Mormon. Throughout the remainder of his life he willingly and frequently gave interviews in which he reaffirmed his witness of the gold plates shown to him by the Angel Moroni[2].

On one occasion, he wrote a letter to his local newspaper, the *Richmond Conservator*, to clarify a false rumor then circulating. Said he: "I wish now, standing as it were, in the very sunset of life, and in the fear of God, once for all to make this public statement:

"That I have never at any time denied that testimony or any part thereof, which has so long since been published with that Book, as one of the three witnesses. Those who know me best, well know that I have always adhered to that testimony. And that no man may be misled or doubt my present views in regard to the same, I do again affirm the truth of all my statements, as then made and published.

"'He that hath an ear to hear, let him hear'; it was no delusion! What is written is written, and he that readeth let him understand" (quoted in *Ensign*, February 1989, 41–42).

See also Witnesses, Three.

WHITMER, JACOB

Centuries before his birth on January 27, 1800, a special event in the life of Jacob Whitmer was fore-seen by an ancient Nephite prophet. Having prophesied of the raising up of "three witnesses" to the Book of Mormon, the prophet also said "none other . . . shall view it, save it be *a few* according to the will of God, to bear testimony of his word" (2 Nephi 27:12–13; emphasis added). Jacob Whitmer was one of those "few" (eight) men whom the Lord raised up to bear testimony of the existence of the gold plates from which the Book of Mormon was translated.

Jacob Whitmer was baptized less than one week after the Church was organized on April 6, 1830. He, like his brothers, followed the main body of the Church from New York to Ohio and from there to Missouri. He served on the high council in Missouri and as a member of the building committee appointed to consider a temple in Far West, Missouri.

Unfortunately, the excommuni-cation of several of his brothers be-came a pivotal point for Jacob. He be-came disaffected from the society of the Saints and drifted into inactivity. Nevertheless, as with all of the wit-nesses to the Book of Mormon, he never denied his special experience. Speaking of his father's witness, Jacob's son later said, "My father, Jacob Whitmer, was always faithful and true to his testimony to the Book

of Mormon, and confirmed it on his death bed" (Anderson, *Investigating the Book of Mormon Witnesses,* 129).

While it is good that Jacob re-mained "faithful and true to his testi-mony to the Book of Mormon," it is sad that he did not remain equally true to his testimony of the prophet-ic calling of Joseph Smith and of the truthfulness of the Church Joseph was commissioned by the Lord to establish.

See also Witnesses, Eight.

WHITMER, JOHN

"Next to his brother David, John [Whitmer] was the most prominent and able man among the Whitmers, and rendered efficient service to the Church in various ways, as long as he remained faithful," wrote Church his-torian Andrew Jenson (1850–1941) (Brewster, *Doctrine & Covenants Ency-clopedia,* 632). Born on August 27, 1802, John Whitmer was three years older than the Prophet Joseph Smith. He was one of those who served briefly as a scribe to the Prophet in the translation of the Book of Mormon, and he was later called as the first official Church historian.

John was one of the earliest to embrace the message of the restora-tion of the gospel and was baptized shortly after priesthood authority was restored to Joseph Smith and Oliver Cowdery by the resurrected John the

Baptist. His early faithfulness earned him a place among the select group of eight men who were shown and handled the gold plates from which the Book of Mormon was translated.

The testimony of these men has been translated into scores of languages as the Book of Mormon has been published among the nations of the earth. "We give our names unto the world," they declared, "to witness unto the world that which we have seen. And we lie not, God bearing witness of it" ("The Testimony of Eight Witnesses").

John Whitmer started off in "the fast lane" of Church service and faithfulness. He held responsible positions of Church leadership in Ohio and Missouri and seemed to always be in the forefront of faithful activity.

The depth of his conviction of the truthfulness of the gospel was demonstrated during a critical moment of mob persecution in Missouri. "He and five others offered themselves to be whipped or killed if the mobs would leave the rest of the Saints alone" (Garr, *Encyclopedia of Latter-day Saint History,* 1336).

Unlike the Apostle Paul, who both "fought a good fight" and "finished [his] course," (2 Timothy 4:7), John Whitmer faded and failed to endure. On March 10, 1838, he was excommunicated from the Church he had once so faithfully served.

What could lead one from unfaltering faith to the point where he failed to finish?

Although the official verdict of the high council that excommunicated him was that he was guilty of conduct unbecoming a Christian, it appears that *greed and pride* became stumbling blocks to his once-solid faith. The lure of personal gain tempted him to take personal title to Church property at Far West, Missouri (*Encyclopedia of Latter-day Saint History,* 1336; *Ensign,* February 1989, 41).

Failing to acknowledge his transgression, John slid further into sin. Following his spiritual severance from the Church, he refused to return the Church records and documents in his possession.

See also Witnesses, Eight.

WHITMER, PETER, JR.

Born September 27, 1809, Peter Whitmer Jr. was the youngest of the Whitmer sons. He was one of the first to be baptized for remission of sins following the restoration of the priesthood, and he provided the Prophet Joseph with some assistance in his work of translating the Book of Mormon. Most notably, he was one of the Eight Witnesses to the Book of Mormon.

Peter was a faithful follower of the Prophet Joseph Smith. Unlike some others who had been specially chosen to serve as witnesses, including family members, Peter did not waver in his steadfast adherence to the Prophet and the restored Church. There were undoubtedly times when his faith was put to the test, but he remained true to his testimony.

To some degree, Peter may be considered a martyr to the cause of the Restoration. Suffering from exposure brought on by the mob persecutions in Missouri, Peter died of consumption just days before he was to have turned twenty-six, on September 22, 1836.

Writing of the faithfulness of both Christian and Peter Whitmer Jr., their brother-in-law Oliver Cowdery wrote: "By many in this church, our brothers were personally known: they were the first to embrace the new covenant, on hearing it, and during a constant scene of persecution and perplexity, to their last moments, maintained its truth—they were both included in the list of the eight witnesses in the Book of Mormon, and though they have departed, it is with great satisfaction that we reflect, that they proclaimed to their last moments, the certainty of their former testimony. . . . May all who read remember the fact, that the Lord has given men a witness of himself in the last days, and that they, have faithfully declared it till called away"

(*Latter-day Saints' Messenger and Advocate* 3 [December 1836]: 426). *See also* Witnesses, Eight.

WITNESSES, A FEW
See Witnesses, Eight.

WITNESSES, EIGHT

In quoting from the inspired writings of the prophet Isaiah[1] (chapter 29), as originally recorded on the plates of brass, Nephi[1] wrote of "three witnesses" who would see the record from which the Book of Mormon was to be translated. He then testified, "There is none other which shall view it, save it be *a few* according to the will of God, to bear testimony of his word" (2 Nephi 27:12–13; emphasis added).

These "few" would obviously include the eight witnesses who, with the Lord's sanction, were privileged to be able to see the plates from which the Book of Mormon was translated. In contrast to the Three Witnesses, who were shown the plates by an angel of God, the Eight Witnesses would be shown the plates by the Prophet Joseph Smith ("The Testimony of Eight Witnesses").

These eight men were Christian Whitmer; Jacob Whitmer; Peter Whitmer, Jun.; John Whitmer; Hiram Page; Joseph Smith, Sen.; Hyrum Smith; and Samuel H. Smith. Three of these witnesses failed in their faithfulness to the Church, but none ever denied the sure witness he had received in personally viewing the plates from which the Book of Mormon was translated.

It is interesting to note the use of the word "few" as it relates to the great flood and Noah's family. The Apostle Peter recorded that "few, that is, *eight* souls were saved by water" (1 Peter 3:20; emphasis added; see also D&C 138:9).

See also Page, Hiram; Smith, Hyrum; Smith, Joseph, Sr.; Smith, Samuel H.; Whitmer, Christian; Whitmer, Jacob; Whitmer, John; Whitmer, Peter, Jr.

WITNESSES, MANY

In the context of writing of future witnesses of the Book of Mormon, and quoting from a more complete record of Isaiah 29 than currently exists in the Bible, Nephi[1] wrote of "three witnesses" and "a few" who would be privileged to view the sacred plates from which the book was translated (2 Nephi 27:12–13). He then declared, "Wherefore, the Lord God will proceed to bring forth the words of the book; and in the mouth of as *many witnesses* as seemeth him good will he establish his word; and wo be unto him that rejecteth the word of God" (2 Nephi 27:14; emphasis added).

Does not every individual who reads, prays, and ponders the words of the Book of Mormon, and then receives the promised testimony of its truthfulness (Moroni 10:3–5), become one of the "many witnesses" to whom Nephi[1] referred?

Indeed, each one so converted then has an obligation to share that witness with others, "to flood the earth" with the testimony of the Book of Mormon's truthfulness.

President Ezra Taft Benson (1899–1994) declared, "Now, my good Saints, we have a great work to perform in a very short time. We must *flood the earth with the Book of Mormon*—and get out from under God's condemnation for having treated it lightly. (See D&C 84:54–58.)" (*Ensign,* November 1988, 5; emphasis added).

This prophet of the Lord uttered the following blessing upon Latter-day Saints: "I bless you with increased desire to flood the earth with the Book of Mormon, to gather out from the world the elect of God who are yearning for the truth but know not where to find it" (*Ensign,* May 1987, 85).

President Benson further stated: "May I commend you faithful Saints who are striving to flood the earth and your lives with the Book of Mormon. Not only must we move forward in a monumental manner more copies of the Book of Mormon, but we must move boldly forward into our own lives and throughout the earth more of its marvelous messages" (*Ensign,* May 1989, 4).

"Few men on earth," said Elder Bruce R. McConkie (1915–1985), "either in or out of the Church, have caught the vision of what the Book of Mormon is all about. Few are they among men who know the part it has played and will yet play in preparing the way for the coming of Him of whom it is a new witness. . . . The Book of Mormon shall so affect men that the whole earth and all its peoples will have been influenced and governed by it. . . . There is no greater issue ever to confront mankind in modern times than this: Is the Book of Mormon the mind and will and voice of God to all men?" (*Millennial Messiah,* 159, 170, 179).

See also Spokesman.

WITNESSES, THREE

In addition to raising up the promised seer—Joseph Smith Jr.—who would translate the Book of Mormon record, three special witnesses were also foreordained to add their testimonies to the truthfulness of his second witness of Jesus Christ. Nephi[1] quoted an inspired rendition of Isaiah 29. It included reference to "three witnesses" who "by the power of God" would see the book, or the plates from which it would be translated, "and they shall testify to the truth of the book and the things therein" (2 Nephi 27:12).

Hundreds of years later, Moroni[2], the last scribe of the sacred record, wrote some instructions to the future translator and told the Prophet Joseph Smith that he would be able to allow three to view the plates, which would enable them to "know of a surety that these things are true" (Ether 5:2–3).

Some sixteen hundred years later, the Lord revealed to the Prophet Joseph that "in addition to your testimony," the world would be blessed by "the testimony of three of my servants, whom I shall call and ordain, unto whom I will show these things, and they shall go forth with my words that are given through you" (D&C 5:11). And so it was that at the designated time, three witnesses— Oliver Cowdery, David Whitmer, and Martin Harris—were shown the plates containing the Book of Mormon record. They also saw "an angel of God" (Moroni[2]), heard the voice of God declaring the truthfulness of the record, and viewed "the breastplate, the sword of Laban, the Urim and Thummim, . . . and the miraculous directors [Liahona]" ("The Testimony of Three Witnesses"; D&C 17:1).

While all three would later fall away from the Church which the Prophet Joseph Smith organized as directed by the Lord, none of them ever denied the immutable witness they had received. Two of the three, Oliver Cowdery and Martin Harris, later repented and rejoined the faith from which they had strayed.

See also Cowdery, Oliver; Harris, Martin; Whitmer, David.

Z

ZARAHEMLA

While the kingdom of Judah was ruled by King Zedekiah[1], the Babylonian King Nebuchadnezzar attacked and destroyed Jerusalem. Most of the sons of King Zedekiah[1] were murdered as their helpless father watched, and then his eyes were put out (2 Kings 25:1–7). But one son, Mulek (who was probably an infant), was either unknown or undiscovered. Mulek was rescued by an unknown individual or group who were then led by the Lord to ancient America (Helaman 6:10).

They established a colony that came to be known as the people of Zarahemla. At the time of their discovery by the people of the Nephite King Mosiah[1], they were led by a man named *Zarahemla* who was a descendant of Mulek (Mosiah 25:2). The two groups united under Mosiah's leadership. Zarahemla and his people rejoiced to learn that Mosiah[1] had the plates of brass, which contained a record of the history of the Jews up to the time of King Zedekiah[1]. Zarahemla was able to give Mosiah[1] "a genealogy of his fathers, according to his memory" (Omni 1:13–19).

See also Mulek; People of Zarahemla.

ZARAHEMLA, PEOPLE OF

See Mulek; Mulekites; People of Zarahemla.

ZECHARIAH, THE SON OF JEBERCHIAH

This Zechariah is one of two witnesses Isaiah[1] called upon to attest to the veracity of his son's name as recorded on a tablet (2 Nephi 18:1–2; Isaiah 8:1–2).

"Little is known of Zechariah, other than that he was the son of Jeberechiah and was considered to be a *faithful witness*. He may have been the same Zechariah who was King Ahaz's father-in-law and the grandfather of King Hezekiah. The fact that Isaiah would have two witnesses, as required by law (Deut. 17:6; 19:15), to the inscription of his son's name on a tablet indicates that he wanted the public to know that the Lord had indeed fulfilled the sign given in 7:14–16. The two witnesses could later testify that Isaiah himself had inscribed the tablet and could confirm the date of inscription" (Parry, Parry, and Peterson, *Understanding Isaiah*, 82).

ZEDEKIAH[1]

Zedekiah[1] was the reigning and last king in the southern kingdom of Judah. His name was given to him by his conquerors, who placed him as a vassal or puppet king on the throne. Earlier he was known as Mattaniah (2 Kings 24:17). Conquerors often changed the names of those they installed as their puppet rulers as a reminder to them that they were beholden to the ones who had placed them in positions of authority.

Zedekiah[1] reigned during the time of the prophets Jeremiah[1] and Lehi[1]. Jeremiah[1] was the more visible prophet during the reign of King Zedekiah[1]. At several critical points, the weak-willed king succumbed to the will of the "princes," who imprisoned the prophet Jeremiah[1] for his unpopular prophecies. However, Zedekiah[1] showed some mercy towards the prophet. On several occasions he changed Jeremiah's imprisonment to more favorable circumstances, even saving the prophet's life (Jeremiah 37:15–21; 38:4–16).

Eventually the ultimate turning point for Zedekiah[1] was when he disregarded the prophet Jeremiah's plea: "Obey, I beseech thee, the voice of the Lord, which I speak unto thee" (Jeremiah 38:20). Fearing disfavor with his friends if he followed the prophet's counsel, Zedekiah[1] rejected "the voice of the Lord" and paid the price for disobedience. The kingdom of Judah was destroyed, his sons were murdered, and his eyes were put out (Jeremiah 52:1–11).

The following is a summary of why Zedekiah[1] fell and stands as a warning to all who reject "the voice of the Lord" as it is uttered through the mouth of a prophet of God: "And he did that which was evil in the sight of the Lord his God, and humbled not himself before Jeremiah the prophet speaking from the mouth of the Lord" (2 Chronicles 36:12).

While Lehi[1] is not mentioned by name in the writings of the Old Testament, his history, including a unique connection with Zedekiah[1], is recorded in the Book of Mormon. About 600 B.C., Lehi[1] prophesied of the impending destruction of Jerusalem, which led to attempts on his life (1 Nephi 1:4, 19–20). Lehi[1] and his family fled Jerusalem before it was destroyed and Zedekiah's sons were slain. Unknown to the Babylonian king, one son, a boy named Mulek, escaped the death decree. He and his protectors were led by the Lord to ancient America, where they ultimately joined with the descendants of Lehi[1] (Helaman 6:10; 8:21; Mosiah 25:1–3).

ZEDEKIAH[2]

Zedekiah[2] was one of the twelve special witnesses called to be the resurrected Savior's governing council of His church in ancient America (3 Nephi 19:4). Zedekiah[2] and the other eleven were given specific priesthood authority by the Savior (3 Nephi 11:19–22; 12:1–2; 18:36–37).

See also Disciples, Twelve.

ZEEZROM

The servants of God are always confronted by the uninformed, the misinformed, and the willfully wicked who seek to destroy them and their message. Such was the case with Alma[2] and Amulek's labors among the people of Ammonihah, who sent their "wise lawyers" (Alma 10:24) to contend with the Lord's missionaries. "Foremost to accuse Alma[2] and Amulek" was a skilled lawyer named Zeezrom (Alma 10:31).

He "was expert in the devices of the devil," seeking to trick and even bribe Alma[2] and Amulek into saying something contradictory to their testimonies (Alma 11:21). However, his cunning and expertise were no match for these two men who were guided by the Spirit. In fact, Amulek boldly rejected Zeezrom, calling him a "child of hell" (Alma 11:23).

The power of the rebuking testimony of Amulek was such that Zeezrom "began to tremble under a consciousness of his guilt" (Alma 12:1). This was a critical point for this crafty lawyer. The Spirit had broken through his hard shell of wickedness and warned him of the destructive course he was following. However, history is filled with stories of individuals who have experienced such moments of truth but have failed to respond in a positive way. To Zeezrom's credit, following the confirming testimony of Alma, "he was convinced more and more of the power of God," and he "began to inquire of them diligently, that he might know more concerning the kingdom of God" (Alma 12:7–8).

Take note of the process that changed Zeezrom's heart. His conscience was pricked, he perceived the rightful priesthood power of these two missionaries, and he began to "diligently" (Alma 12:8) seek to know more. The fact that his change of heart was sincere is evidenced in his effort to defend these two from the charges and insults of his former colleagues, as well as in his willingness to be reviled and cast out for his newfound faith (Alma 14:6–7).

He was later healed of a "burning fever," which had been caused by "the great tribulations of his mind on account of his wickedness," was baptized, and joined Alma[2] and Amulek in their missionary labors (Alma 15:1–12). Once again we see the power of repentance and the need to never give up on anyone. A modern-day Apostle underscored this when he pleaded, "Never give up on a loved one, never!" (Richard G. Scott, *Ensign,* May 1988, 61).

ZEMNARIHAH

About eighteen years after they saw the sign of the Savior's birth in ancient America, the Nephites became embroiled in conflict with the infamous Gadianton robbers. Because of the careful preparations for defense made by the wise and righteous leader of the Nephites, Lachoneus, the Gadiantons found themselves at a significant disadvantage (3 Nephi 3–4). The robber leader Giddianhi was killed, and he was succeeded by Zemnarihah, who laid siege to the people of Nephi (3 Nephi 4:16–17).

His siege was ill conceived, for it left the robbers open to nighttime forays against them by the Nephites. Weakened by their loss of men and want of food, their leader Zemnarihah ordered a retreat. However, their weakness was quickly assessed by the righteous Nephite prophet-commander Gidgiddoni, who surrounded the remaining robbers and defeated them. Zemnarihah was taken and hanged upon a tree, which was felled once he was dead (3 Nephi 4:17–28).

The felling of the tree with the dead body on it was consistent with traditions from Mosaic law:

"And if a man have committed a sin worthy of death, and he be put to death, and thou hang him on a tree:

"His body shall not remain all night upon the tree, but thou shalt in any wise bury him that day; (for he that is hanged is accursed of God;) that thy land be not defiled, which the Lord thy God giveth thee for an inheritance" (Deuteronomy 21:22–23).

The accompanying footnote to the above scripture (in the LDS edition of the Bible) states, "According to Rabbinical commentaries, to leave a body hanging was a degradation of the human body and therefore an affront to God, in whose image man's body was made."

ZENEPHI

This wicked Nephite military commander confiscated provisions that were intended for the relief of widows and their children during the final war of the Nephites and Lamanites (Moroni 9:16). Some may think his actions were justified, as he was looking after his troops, but the Lord and His prophets seem to have always placed a priority on the needs of women and children (see Exodus 22:22–23; James 1:27).

Zenephi seems to have forgotten the counsel recorded in earlier Nephite records by one righteous leader: "Now there was a great number of women, more than there was of

men; therefore king Limhi commanded that every man should impart to
the support of the widows and their
children, that they might not perish
with hunger; and this they did because of the greatness of their number
that had been slain" (Mosiah 21:17).

ZENIFF

The closing comments on the
small plates of Nephi mention "a certain number" who left the land of
Zarahemla to return to the land of
Nephi. They were led by a "stiffnecked man" whose bloodthirsty and
contentious disposition caused a
battle in which all but fifty of what
must have been a rather large group
were killed. Zeniff was a leader of the
opposition that prevailed in the conflict. The survivors returned to the
land of Zarahemla (Omni 1:27–28;
Mosiah 9:1–2).

Zeniff's refusal to side with the
bloodthirsty man, who sought an un-
provoked attack upon the Lamanites
then living in the land of Nephi, was
a turning point for the entire
expedition.

The terrible tragedy that had
taken place did not dampen the desire
of Zeniff and many others to make a
second journey to the land of Nephi.
Zeniff admits to being "overzealous"
in his quest to return to the land of
his forefathers (Mosiah 7:21; 9:3). He
was selected as the leader, and later as

the king, of this second expedition
(Mosiah 7:21). The group suffered
much during their journey because
they "were slow to remember the
Lord" (Mosiah 9:3). Nevertheless,
they finally arrived at their desired
destination and entered into a treaty
with the Lamanite king, who allowed
them to possess "the land of Lehi-
Nephi, and the land of Shilom"
(Mosiah 9:4–9).

Whether it was Zeniff's "over-
zealous" desire to possess the land—
or his trusting and naive nature—that
led him to enter into the treaty is not
known. What is clear is that the
Lamanite king was cunning and
crafty in orchestrating a situation
where the new land owners would
improve the land and then be placed
in bondage to the Lamanite king and
his people (Mosiah 7:21–22; 9:10).

Once again, a decision by Zeniff
became a turning point for him and
his followers. Perhaps a lesson to be
learned here is that enthusiasm and
zeal should always be balanced with
good judgment and prayerful fore-
thought. One should be properly cau-
tious when entering into contractual
agreements.

One cannot fault Zeniff's motives, for they always seemed impelled
by righteous desires. He was a good
and respected leader (Mosiah 9:8–9,
17–18; 10:5, 19–21).

ZENOCK

Zenock was among the prophets of the Old Testament whose writings have been lost, but whose existence has been established by the Book of Mormon. He is quoted by Nephi[1] (1 Nephi 19:10), Alma[2] (Alma 33:15–16), Amulek (Alma 34:7), Nephi[3] (Helaman 8:19–20), and Mormon[2] (3 Nephi 10:16).

Zenock was a testifier of Christ, as were all the prophets. He testified of the coming of the Son of God, and he prophesied of the future crucifixion of Christ. He testified that redemption comes only through Christ. It appears that his bold testimony led to his being stoned to death and becoming a martyr (Alma 33:15–17; 3 Nephi 10:15–16). Perhaps in addition to removing his life, Zenock's enemies also have removed his recorded testimony.

ZENOS

Zenos was another of the prophets of the Old Testament whose writings have been lost but whose existence has been established by the Book of Mormon (1 Nephi 19:10, 12, 16; Alma 33:3–13; 34:7; Helaman 8:19; 3 Nephi 10:15–16). Zenos wrote the allegory or parable of the olive tree that Jacob[2] records and then expounds on (Jacob 5; 6:1–10).

Zenos was a powerful testifier of the Messiah. He spoke specifically of Christ's burial in a tomb and of the three days of darkness and the destruction that would come upon ancient America following the crucifixion. He also spoke of the gathering of far-flung Israel. He, like other prophets before him, was slain for his bold testimony and thus earned the martyr's crown. While the devil's henchmen may have succeeded in snuffing out this prophet's life—and destroying some of his recorded testimony, which should have appeared in the Bible—the witness of the prophet Zenos continues in the Book of Mormon.

ZERAHEMNAH

Among the many Lamanite military leaders mentioned in the Book of Mormon, Zerahemnah is perhaps most notable for his treacherous attempt to kill Captain Moroni[1] while under a flag of truce. This, indeed, was a pivotal point in his life.

We are not given any background on Zerahemnah. He appeared on the scene as the chief captain over a Lamanite army, a man who had the capacity to "inspire" his troops in battle (Alma 43:44). However, Captain Moroni[1] and his troops obtained the upper hand in a battle, and he offered to stop the conflict if Zerahemnah and his troops would agree to lay down their weapons and take an oath that they would not come to battle against the Nephites again (Alma 44:1–7).

Recognizing that his army was losing the battle, Zerahemnah approached Captain Moroni[1] and laid down his weapons as a token of surrender. However, he refused to take the oath that he would not again attack the Nephites. Such a condition of surrender was unacceptable to the Nephite commander, who announced that the battle would continue until the Lamanites were either killed or agreed to the terms offered (Alma 44:8–11).

At this critical moment, Zerahemnah grabbed his sword and "rushed forward that he might slay Moroni." Fortunately, an alert soldier ("the soldier who stood by") protected his captain by disarming Zerahemnah and scalping the attacker (Alma 44:12–14).

The fighting resumed, and Zerahemnah, realizing he had lost the battle, finally agreed to Moroni's terms (Alma 44:19).

See also Soldier Who Stood By.

ZERAM

This Nephite military officer was one of four men in about 87 B.C. who are identified as spies sent by Alma[2] to discover the plots of the rebellious Amlicites (Alma 22:1–22). In opposition to the will and voice of the majority of the people, Amlici had been crowned king by his dissident followers and caused a civil war. Zeram and his associates and their men discovered that the Amlicites had joined forces with the Lamanites, had commenced an attack on the Nephites, and were on their way to attack the chief city of Zarahemla. As a result of the spies' report to Alma[2], the Nephites were able to successfully defend their city, Amlici was killed, and the invading army was defeated (Alma 2:23–38).

ZORAM[1]

Zoram[1] was a trusted servant of Laban who had the keys to the treasury where the plates of brass were kept (1 Nephi 4:20). Perhaps Laban's treasury also contained the newly acquired possessions he had stolen from Lehi's sons when they sought to purchase the plates (1 Nephi 3:22–25). After Nephi[1] had obeyed the Spirit and slain Laban, he dressed himself in Laban's clothing. In that disguise, he commanded Zoram[1] to get the brass plates and accompany him to the outskirts of town. Thinking him to be Laban, Zoram[1] willingly took Nephi[1] to the treasury and retrieved the sought-after plates.

Zoram[1] accompanied Nephi[1] to the outskirts of the city, where Nephi's older brothers were waiting for him. Upon discovering Nephi's identity, the servant of Laban "was about to flee . . . and return to the city of Jerusalem," but Nephi physically restrained him from fleeing (1 Nephi 4:24–31).

This became the pivotal point that changed the course of Zoram's life. Holding him fast, Nephi[1] swore with an oath that Zoram[1] would not be harmed if he would join Lehi's family in their sojourn into the wilderness, promising him that he would shed his shackles of servitude and "be a free man like unto us" (1 Nephi 4:31–34). Zoram[1] trusted Nephi's words and promised to join the group, allaying Nephi's fears that the former servant would return to Jerusalem and alert the Jews—who had sought Father Lehi's life—to the family's whereabouts (1 Nephi 4:35–36).

Zoram's joining with the family of Lehi was not coincidental in the divine plan the Lord had outlined for the group. When Ishmael's family joined Lehi's family in the wilderness, there were now an even number of potential marriage partners for Ishmael's daughters. Ishmael[1] had five daughters and, with Zoram[1], Lehi[1] had added a fifth eligible bachelor to his cadre of four sons. Zoram[1] married the eldest daughter of Ishmael[1] (1 Nephi 16:7).

His faithfulness in following the righteous example of Nephi[1] is attested to by the words of Father Lehi[1], who called Zoram[1] "a true friend unto my son, Nephi, forever." Zoram[1] was promised that his posterity would be blessed with the blessings enjoyed by Nephi's posterity (2 Nephi 1:30–32). Zoram[1] continued to follow Nephi[1] in ensuring that this promised blessing became a reality (2 Nephi 5:6).

See also Zoramites[1].

ZORAM[2]

Zoram[2] was "appointed chief captain over the armies of the Nephites" about 81 B.C. (Alma 16:5). At this time an invading army of Lamanites had "destroyed the people who were in the city of Ammonihah" (Alma 16:3), in fulfillment of an earlier prophecy by Alma[2] spoken to the wicked inhabitants of that city (Alma 9:18). Additionally, the Lamanites had attacked others and taken some captive into the wilderness (Alma 16:3).

Zoram[2] was anxious to free the captives and defeat the invading army. His personal righteousness and faith in the Lord and His servants is illustrated by his seeking counsel from the high priest Alma[2] on how to proceed. As a result of Alma's prayerful inquiry, the Lord revealed not only the location of the Lamanite army but promised that Zoram[2] would be successful in freeing the captives (Alma 16:5–6). As promised, Zoram[2] and his two sons Aha and Lehi[2] and their troops were able to defeat the invaders and free those who had been taken captive; "and there was not one soul of them . . . lost that were taken captive" (Alma 16:7–8).

How marvelous it would be if all leaders of armies and governments were so righteous that they could with confidence seek counsel from the Lord's servants!

ZORAM³

This Nephite rebel was the leader of an apostate group known as the Zoramites about 74 B.C. (Alma 30:59). They were responsible for trampling the anti-Christ Korihor to death as he went among them begging for food. Zoram³ "was leading the hearts of the people to bow down to dumb idols" and otherwise "perverting the ways of the Lord" (Alma 31:1). Hearing of such abominations, Alma² was sickened in his heart and determined to take a mission among these apostate people (Alma 31:1–6).

While Zoram³ is not mentioned by name during the course of Alma's mission to the Zoramites², he is referenced later as a "very wicked man." He sought to have those who converted from the falsehoods of the Zoramites² to the truths taught by Alma² and Amulek expelled from the land of Jershon to which they had sought refuge (Alma 35:8–9). When the people of Ammon², who also occupied the land of Jershon, refused to comply with the wicked demand, Zoram³ stirred up the Lamanites to anger against these innocent people and commenced a war that lasted for many years.

See also Zoramites².

ZORAMITES¹

The Zoramites¹ were descendants of Zoram¹, the servant of Laban who swore allegiance to Nephi¹ and became a member of Father Lehi's group, which was brought by the Lord to ancient America around 600 B.C. Jacob² first identified Zoram's descendants as Zoramites¹ (Jacob 1:13). The name next surfaced about A.D. 231 when the Lamanites referred to the "true believers in Christ" as "Jacobites, and Josephites, and Zoramites" (4 Nephi 1:36–37). These Zoramites¹ were among those later called Nephites (Mormon 1:8).

ZORAMITES²

This apostate Nephite group existed about 74 B.C., having been established by a man named Zoram³ (Alma 30:59). They worshiped "dumb idols" and in other ways were "perverting the ways of the Lord" (Alma 31:1). The Nephites were fearful that the Zoramites² would align themselves with the Lamanites. Alma² decided to take some missionaries with him and preach to the

Zoramites[2] in an effort to reclaim them to the true faith (Alma 31:4–7).

The missionaries discovered this apostate group had built synagogues to which they gathered once each week to worship in their perverted manner. They had a high place built called a Rameumptom; one person at a time could stand on this perch and utter a repetitive prayer in which they expounded their false beliefs. Their false doctrines included the nonsense that God was a spirit, that there would be no Christ, and that the Zoramites[2] were "elected" to be saved while all others were "elected" to be cast into hell (Alma 31:13–23).

On the basis of the Zoramites' claim to be God's "chosen and . . . holy people" (Alma 31:18), some critics have found fault with the position of The Church of Jesus Christ of Latter-day Saints to be "the only true and living church upon the face of the whole earth" (D&C 1:30). In response, it should first be noted that this was a declaration of the Lord Himself and not simply an assertion by mortal man. Second, Christ's "only true and living church" is instructed to not hold itself exclusive. The charge to members of Christ's Church is to share the message of the restored gospel with all, inviting them to "come unto Christ, and be perfected in him" (Moroni 10:32). In fact, Latter-day Saints have a *covenant* re-

sponsibility to share the restored gospel with others. While the Zoramites' doors were closed to outsiders, the doors and arms of fellowship of Latter-day Saints are open, beckoning and inviting all to "come and see" (John 1:39, 46).

Speaking of the false worship of the Zoramites[2], Elder Jeffrey R. Holland (1940–) observed: "There is a particularly reprehensible moment in the Book of Mormon in which a group of vain and unchristian Zoramites, after climbing atop their Rameumptom and declaring their special standing before God, immediately proceed to cast the poor from their synagogues, synagogues these needy had labored with their own hands to build. They were cast out, the revelation says, simply because of their poverty [Alma 32:2–3]" (*Ensign,* May 1996, 29–30).

It was among these people, the poor, that the missionaries had success. Because the poor were not focused on position, possessions, and pelf, "they were in a preparation to hear the word" (Alma 32:6). It was to this group of ready listeners that Alma[2] taught his great sermon on faith (Alma 32:21–43). The "more popular part of the Zoramites" expelled those who accepted the teachings of the missionaries "and they were many; and they came over also into the land of Jershon" (Alma 35:3–7).

Zoram[3], "a very wicked man" (Alma 35:8), then demanded that the people of Ammon[2] also expel these new converts from their land. When these peace-loving people refused, a very angry Zoram[3] started a war against them. The Zoramites[2] subsequently gave up their separate identity and "became Lamanites" (Alma 43:4). In this sense, they simply followed the tradition of other Nephite apostates, such as Amalekites and the descendants of the priests of king Noah[3], who had similarly forsaken their heritage (Alma 43:13). Could we say they sold their birthrights for a "mess of pottage"? (see Genesis 25:29–34).

— Bibliography —

Anderson, Richard L. *Investigating the Book of Mormon Witnesses.* Salt Lake City: Deseret Book, 1981.

Benson, Ezra Taft. *Come Unto Christ.* Salt Lake City: Deseret Book, 1983.

Brewster, Hoyt W., Jr. *Behold, I Come Quickly: The Last Days and Beyond.* Salt Lake City: Deseret Book, 1994.

———. *Defining Moments.* Salt Lake City: Deseret Book, 2003.

———. *Doctrine & Covenants Encyclopedia.* Salt Lake City: Bookcraft, 1988.

———. *Isaiah Plain & Simple: The Message of Isaiah in the Book of Mormon.* Salt Lake City: Deseret Book, 1995.

———. *Martyrs of the Kingdom.* Salt Lake City: Bookcraft, 1990.

———. *Prophets, Priesthood Keys, and Succession.* Salt Lake City: Deseret Book, 1991.

Bushman, Richard Lyman. *Joseph Smith: Rough Stone Rolling.* New York: Alfred Knopf, 2005.

Cannon, George Q. *Gospel Truth.* Compiled by Jerreld L. Newquist. Salt Lake City: Deseret Book, 1974.

———. *Life of Joseph Smith.* Salt Lake City: Deseret Book, 1972.

Clark, James R., comp. *Messages of the First Presidency.* 6 vols. Salt Lake City: Bookcraft, 1965–1975.

Corbett, Pearson H. *Hyrum Smith—Patriarch.* Salt Lake City: Deseret Book, 1995.

Dewey, Richard Lloyd. *Joseph Smith: A Biography.* Arlington, VA: Stratford Books, 2005.

Ensign. The Church of Jesus Christ of Latter-day Saints, 1971–.

Garr, Arnold K., et al., eds. *Encyclopedia of Latter-day Saint History.* Salt Lake City: Deseret Book, 2000.

Handbook of the Restoration: A Selection of Gospel Themes Discussed by Various Authors. Independence, Mo.: Zion's Printing and Publishing, 1944.

Holland, Jeffrey R. *Christ and the New Covenant: The Messianic Message of the Book of Mormon.* Salt Lake City: Deseret Book, 1997.

Hymns of The Church of Jesus Christ of Latter-day Saints. Salt Lake City: The Church of Jesus Christ of Latter-day Saints, 1985.

Improvement Era. The Church of

Jesus Christ of Latter-day Saints, 1897–1970.

Jackson, Kent P., ed. *Studies in Scripture, Volume 7: 1 Nephi to Alma 29.* Salt Lake City: Deseret Book, 1987.

Jackson, Kent P., and Robert L. Millet, eds. *Studies in Scripture, Volume 5: The Gospels.* Salt Lake City: Deseret Book, 1986.

Journal History. The Church of Jesus Christ of Latter-day Saints.

Journal of Discourses. 26 vols. Liverpool, England: F.D. and S.W. Richards, 1854–1886.

Largey, Dennis L., ed. *Book of Mormon Reference Companion.* Salt Lake City: Deseret Book, 2003.

Latter-day Saints' Messenger and Advocate. The Church of Jesus Christ of Latter-day Saints, 1834–1837.

Ludlow, Daniel L., ed. *Encyclopedia of Mormonism.* 5 vols. New York: Macmillan, 1992.

Miller, Reuben. Journal, 1848–1849. Archives of The Church of Jesus Christ of Latter-day Saints, Salt Lake City, Utah.

Maxwell, Neal A. *Deposition of a Disciple.* Salt Lake City: Deseret Book, 1976.

———. *If Thou Endure It Well.* Salt Lake City: Bookcraft, 1996.

———. *Men and Women of Christ.* Salt Lake City: Bookcraft, 1991.

McConkie, Bruce R. *Doctrines of the Restoration: Sermons and Writings of Bruce R. McConkie.* Selected and arranged by Mark L. McConkie. Salt Lake City: Bookcraft, 1989.

———. *The Millennial Messiah: The Second Coming of the Son of Man.* Salt Lake City: Deseret Book, 1982.

———. *Mormon Doctrine.* Salt Lake City: Bookcraft, 1958.

———. *A New Witness for the Articles of Faith.* Salt Lake City: Deseret Book, 1985.

Millennial Star. The Church of Jesus Christ of Latter-day Saints, 1840–1970.

New Era. The Church of Jesus Christ of Latter-day Saints, 1971–.

Parry, Donald W., Jay A. Parry, and Tina M. Peterson. *Understanding Isaiah.* Salt Lake City: Deseret Book, 1998.

Reynolds, George C. *A Dictionary of the Book of Mormon.* 3rd ed. Salt Lake City: Deseret Book, 1929.

Reynolds, George C., and Janne M. Sjodahl. *Commentary on the Book of Mormon.* 7 vols. Salt Lake City: Deseret Book, 1955–1961.

Roberts, B. H. *A Comprehensive History of The Church of Jesus Christ of Latter-day Saints.* 6 vols. Salt Lake City: Deseret News Press, 1930.

———. *New Witnesses for God.* 3 vols. Salt Lake City: Deseret Book, 1909–1911.

Sill, Sterling W. *The Upward Reach.* Salt Lake City: Bookcraft, 1962.

Smith, Joseph. *History of The Church of Jesus Christ of Latter-day Saints.* 7 vols. Salt Lake City: Deseret Book, 1932–51.

———. *The Personal Writings of Joseph Smith.* Edited by Dean C. Jessee. Salt Lake City: Deseret Book, 1984.

Smith, Joseph F. *Gospel Doctrine.* 5th ed. Salt Lake City: Deseret Book, 1938.

Smith, Joseph Fielding. *Answers to Gospel Questions.* 5 vols. Salt Lake City: Deseret Book, 1957–1966.

———. *Church History and Modern Revelation.* Salt Lake City: Deseret Book, 1946.

———. *Doctrines of Salvation.* Compiled by Bruce R. McConkie. 3 vols. Salt Lake City: Bookcraft, 1954–1956.

———. *The Restoration of All Things.* Salt Lake City: Deseret News Press, 1944.

Smith, Lucy Mack. *History of Joseph Smith by His Mother.* Salt Lake City: Bookcraft, 1958.

Sperry, Sidney B. *Doctrine and Covenants Compendium.* Salt Lake City: Deseret Book, 1968.

Young, Lucy Cowdery. Letter of March 1887. Archives of The Church of Jesus Christ of Latter-day Saints, Salt Lake City, Utah.

— About the Author —

Hoyt W. Brewster Jr. has written many books, including *Doctrine and Covenants Encyclopedia; Behold, I Come Quickly;* and *Defining Moments.* He holds degrees from the University of Utah, Brigham Young University, and the University of Southern California, and has taught at several universities as well as in the seminary and institute programs of the Church Educational System.

More recently, Brother Brewster has worked for The Church of Jesus Christ of Latter-day Saints in both the Priesthood Department and the Temple Department. He has served on several general Church committees, presided over the Netherlands Amsterdam Mission, and served as a stake president.

He and his wife, Judy, are the parents of five children, and they reside in Cottonwood Heights, Utah.